THE
GREAT
LIVING
SYSTEM

The Religion Emerging from the Sciences

John Ruskin Clark

Skinner House: Boston

Copyright © 1977 by John Ruskin Clark

A Skinner House book published under the auspices of the
Unitarian Universalist Association

Printed in the United States of America

First edition, 1977, Boxwood Press

Second edition, revised, 1984 published by
      Skinner House books

Library of Congress Cataloging in Publication Data:

Clark, John Ruskin, 1911–
   The great living system.

   Bibliography: p.
   Includes index
   1. Religion and science -1946-
   2. Religion-Philosophy
   I. Title.
BL240.2.C548   215   76-53812

ISBN 0-933840-24-1

1M 10/84 2041
1723-000

NOTE

The Unitarian Universalist Association is committed to
using gender-inclusive language in all its publications.
Dr. Clark's text — with his permission — has
been so revised for this edition. However, there is a
great deal of quoted material used in this work. It did not
appear fitting to revise this material so it appears as
originally written. This note is to alert readers to the
presence of such gender-exclusive usage.

Dedicated
to
the Members
of the
First Unitarian Church
of San Diego
whose interest and support
encouraged
the writing and publication
of this book.

Contents

Preface

THIS book is written in response to the hunger in our society for meaningful and viable religion, and is offered to you as reassurance that there are credible answers to the old theological questions—answers that may be implicit in what you already do believe but that you may not realize constitute a profound composition which is religious. If you are disenchanted with traditional religion, you may find it revitalized in the thesis developed here. If you already comfortably accept the wisdom of a religious tradition, you may find reinforcement in a parallel theology. In any case, you will learn that there is an alternative and new interpretation of religion congruent with the sciences.

A "moment of truth" came to me with the reading of Peter F. Drucker's article "The New Philosophy Comes to Life" (*Harper's Magazine,* August 1957). It dawned on me that the old theological questions acquired new answers when asked in the frame of reference of the new philosophy, the new view of the nature of truth, good, the creative process, and the meaning of life. For my own theological satisfaction, I began integrating a conceptual synthesis of the new answers which were correlated with the new philosophy emerging from the sciences.

From what I had learned, I articulated a constructive personal theology during a 1966 summer of independent study at Manchester College, Oxford, which turned out to be a skeletal outline without meat on the bones.

The following year, a sabbatical enabled me to do research at The Center for Advanced Study in Religion and Science at Meadville/Lombard Theological School in Chicago with the guidance and help of Ralph Wendell Burhoe, director and editor of *Zygon, Journal of Religion & Science,* published at The University of Chicago Press. Ralph Burhoe is a prophet in the field of religion and science, both by his writings and by organizing conferences of scientists and religious leaders through the Institute on Religion in an Age of Science. At the Center, I was exposed not only to rich resources in science and religion, but also to seminars Burhoe conducted with distinguished scientists and theologians who are contributing to the dialogue about the emergent theology and ethics. New evidence continually comes to my notice of a raised consciousness emerging in our society which is constituting a new "gospel" or "good news."

This preface, written last, offers me an opportunity to add a postscript from a source which has just come to my attention and which supports a thesis of this book that religion evolves in continuity with empirically validated wisdom of religious traditions. Donald T. Campbell of Northwestern University, in his inaugural address as president of the American Psychological Association, emphasizes his respect for tradition as the repository of the wisdom of biological and cultural evolution, a cultural inheritance which can be regarded as adaptive and contributive to human survival. Campbell (1975, p. 1103) says:

> An argument . . . has to do with the possible sources of validity in recipes for living that have been evolved, tested, and winnowed through hundreds of generations of human social history. On purely scientific grounds, these recipes for living might be regarded as better tested than the best of psychology's and psychiatry's speculations on how lives should be lived. This argument comes from a natural-selectionist theory of social evolution. . . ."

The manuscript of this book has been criticized for "too many quotes." My intention is to integrate what I have learned from many sources, and the quotations are evidence of the contributions of many scientists to theology and ethics and are part of the plan of the book as the "authority" for many of my opinions and as an integral part of the exposition. Nevertheless, the choice, interpretation, and synthesis of the ideas are my own, and this

book from beginning to end is a statement of convictions which, if
not original with me, are my own; at the beginning of each para-
graph stands an implicit qualifier, "I believe . . ."

To Professor James Luther Adams I express my gratitude for
furnishing my mind with information, concepts, and attitudes
during the seven years he was my mentor at the Meadville
Theological School in Chicago.

I thank The University of Chicago Press for permission to
reprint in revised form "The Great Living System: The World as
the Body of God," *Zygon* 9(1) 1974, as chapter 2 of this book. I am
grateful for the early encouragement in this work to Reverend
Lyman V. Rutledge of Kittery Point, Maine; to Dr. Leonard
O'Brien of Elgin, Illinois; and to Leo Bernitz of San Diego. I am
especially grateful to Betsy Stevens, Judith Barney, Elbert J.
Boone, Vicki Siska, Dr. Marston Sargent, Walter Moore, and Dr.
Marc Salkin, all of San Diego, for their critical reading of the
manuscript and for their moral support; and to my wife Alma for
living with my theological obsession, taking care of me, and
reading the proofs.

This edition of *The Great Living System* is underwritten from the
Janet Griswold Bequest by the First unitarian Church of San Diego
with the support of Board Chair Burton Johnson. It has been
degenderized in accord with UUA policy by the director of Skinner
House books Carl Seaburg who enthusiastically encouraged the
republication. For those expressions of confidence in the book I am
very grateful.

John Ruskin Clark
2485 Moonstone Dr.
San Diego, CA 92123

October 1984

Chapter **1**

Questions That Matter Most

IN numerous dialogues between scientists and theologians a new picture of reality is developing as a whole—a new mythos about the creative origins of order and of living beings. *New responses to old religious questions* are emerging in our culture, responses which are coalescing into a new and different theology.

The radical change is in how to know what to believe as true in "epistemology"—the theory of the method and grounds of belief and knowledge. The respective claims of authority for belief distinguish the various religions—the *source* more than the *teachings*, which tend to converge. The general acceptance of the *epistemology of the sciences,* rather than that of "special revelations," is integrating the empirically valid insights and values of the Judeo-Christian tradition with contemporary religious concepts, and is providing moral guidelines for coping with problems of our times.

As a contribution to the dialogue, I report no new revelation inaugurating a new cult; I call attention to the real religion by which many people are living, which, if *raised to consciousness,* alleviates existential anxiety and makes living meaningful. The new image of the human situation is latent on a film exposed to our culture, and I propose to render it more visible. I bring to this developing process the concern of a parish minister to suggest cogent ground for *morale for morality,* a generalist's readiness to go more beyond the data than does the exact scientist, and a

1

theologian's interest in ultimates, infinites, and wholes. I do *not propose a scientific theology;* I do propose that we move into a *new world view* emerging from the sciences and that we use concepts and information which scientists find satisfactory to create a coherent personal faith consistent with what we know about the universe.

In this preliminary attempt to construct what I have no doubt will be one of many approximations to an "organic" or "systems" theology, I am *apologetic* rather than comparative or historical in my discourse. I am trying to put together a jigsaw puzzle with some of the pieces missing, but the pieces already defined by the sciences, when assembled, make a more meaningful picture than the picture made when traditional theological fragments are rearranged. "Religious traditions are dying on their own feet because they have lost their mind—their intellectual coherence and relevance in the modern world," says Ralph Wendell Burhoe, (1966, pp. 5-6), former director of the Center for Advanced Study in Theology and the Sciences in Chicago. He adds:

> I believe that the sciences generally give a much fuller picture of the nature of man and the nature of his dependence upon the forces that molded him. I believe that within this picture many of the insights of the traditional religions will find confirmations, although clearly there is pruning to be done, and new fears and hopes about new evils and new goods are being revealed and will be embodied.

Some of the most insightful theological speculation advanced today is by scientists, prompted by the implications of discoveries in their fields. This is the reason you will find so many quotations from scientists in this book, and they speak with the authority of evidence.

Ultimate Questions

Religion deals with the ultimate questions troubling human beings. Endowed with a capacity for memory and imagination, we are anxious about the future. Since we can imagine a life less

fraught with frustrations and problems than the one *we* experience, we seek to make sense out of what happens to us, we look
for meaning in life. Ward E. Goodenough (1966, pp. 217-18), professor of anthropology at the University of Pennsylvania, comments:

> Whenever we ask, "What is the meaning of life?" what we want to
> know is the meaning of our own individual life. As far as I know,
> this last is something to which all men everywhere feel either that
> they have an answer or that they are in need of one. We rarely
> find men content with no answer; and when we do, they no longer
> care about anything, including life. They are men without a pur-
> pose.... I submit that this concern is natural, that it arises in-
> evitably in any creature, such as man, that has purposes and that
> is also capable of self-awareness.

J. Edward Barrett (1968, p. 171), assistant professor in the Department of Religion at Muskingum College, adds:

> ... the question of the meaning of life is identical with the quest for a
> theological system: a believable, consistent, and comprehensive
> interpretation of the experiences that compose human life, their
> relation to one another, and their ultimate ground and goal. There is
> a definite correlation between the relative dearth of theological sys-
> tems in the twentieth century and the problem of meaninglessness.

You may have already worked out answers to questions about
the meaning of life to your own satisfaction, and you may feel
peculiar and isolated in your departure from traditional or orthodox views, as do so many people in our day. I reassure you that
you are not alone, and that you are traveling in a goodly company
of those who, in our new situation, are moving in the same
direction.

Any enumeration of the questions that matter most is arbitrary,
I suppose, and I propose to respond to five which seem universally to constitute the theological framework of the world religions (Ross and Hills, 1956). These questions may now be responded to with new formulations consistent with contemporary
knowledge:

1. What's the situation? What creates, orders, and sustains the universe? What supports and what limitations does the ordering power impose upon human aspirations? Is the environment we experience fragmentary or is it a unified system? If unified, is there a supreme being, God? And how do we understand this term?

2. What are human beings? Not *who* are *we* as unique individuals, but *what kind* of beings are *we* as members of the species *Homo sapiens?* What kind of creatures are we who ask the questions, and what potentialities and limitations do we have?

3. What is true? Not what is "The Truth" as an absolute, but how do we make up our minds as to what is most probably true? What is the ground for decision?

4. What is good? How do we know what to choose and what to do to be satisfied? What norms can guide us in making decisions that lead to fulfillment? How can we anticipate whether the consequences of our acts will be desirable or undesirable, good or bad? Can we learn anything from the previous experience of others?

5. What is the meaning of living? What makes sense of my experiences? What makes life worthwhile?

We will utilize concepts and information emerging from the sciences to suggest responses which will give a renewed cogency, vitality, and moral imperative to our religious heritage. By explicating the implications of ideas already current among us, we may arrive at a constructive integration of old and new concepts already operative in our culture which provide a theology engendering morale for morality.

A basic change in our perception of ultimate reality is generated by the new epistemology. J. Edward Barrett (1968, pp. 175-76) proposes that ontologically, God can be understood as "the constitutive structure of reality" which "implies an intuition of the unity of things." He says:

Everything we know about the objective world tends to confirm this intuition concerning the structured interrelatedness of the universe.... The sciences seem to provide increasing evidence that all reality is interrelated.... Another way to say this is that every substructure within reality is related directly or (more often) indirectly to every other substructure, so that together they constitute a collective structure which is different from every part, but in which every part lives and moves and has its being—God.

In the next chapter on "The Great Living System" I will summarize the evidences from the sciences which support that intuition of the unity of things.

Religious Decadence

Dinosaurs ranged over much of the planet for about 125 million years before they lumbered off into oblivion. They became extinct when they could not adapt fast enough to a changing environment. Human beings have been striding erect on this planet for only about a million years and already there are ominous portents that we may be making the planet no longer hospitable to our own survival; not because we cannot rapidly adapt to change, but because in Western culture our Judeo-Christian religious tradition does not engender a reverent attitude toward the beautiful blue and white planet which is our life support system. We exploit the finite earth as if it were not sacred. A technological crash program cannot save us because it is the by-products of advanced technology which are doing the damage. Our salvation as a species rests not with increased technology but with a more adequate religion. If we human beings are to survive as long as did the dinosaurs, we need to be saved by a renewing of our minds to produce more adaptive behavior.

The Judeo-Christian tradition has served Western Civilization by helping to achieve personal salvation. Its ethics provided grounds for personal morality. In the past, its cosmic drama of creation, fall, and last judgment—personalized in Christ's birth, crucifixion, resurrection and assurance to believers of personal immortality—provided a meaningful frame of reference in which to endure tragedy and death. Many of its values and moral principles are still valid, for people have always learned something from experience as they do today, and much of what our spiritual ancestors discovered and transmitted is still helpful as a guide to constructive living.

A religion helps form a culture, which people can absorb without figuring out everything for themselves. Daniel Calahan (1972, p.5), director of the Institute of Society, Ethics, and the Life Sciences, Hastings-on-Hudson, New York, comments:

> One function of a culture is to make up for our deficiencies in private wisdom, to take some of the burden off our individual shoulders, to save us from going to the mat on each and every question, to allow us to know things with our feelings which we do not know in our heads. To be sure, every individual will have to seek the truth at some time. But he should not have to do it alone and he should not always have to do it. A culture should assist him.

An example of such cultural assistance was the life of my Grandmother Reed, a prosperous Illinois farmer's wife, whom I came to appreciate as the embodiment of the "Christian virtues" during a summer I lived with her as a college sophomore, even though to my then positivistic and mechanistic state of mind she seemed naive. She simply practiced love and acceptance, compassion and diligence, justice and truth in her daily life without giving much thought to the justification for such behavior—she was too busy raising a family of six. She responded to life in terms of the values she cherished and heard celebrated every Sunday morning at the Wythe Presbyterian Church.

However, the traditional theological foundations for such an implicit faith and values have been eroded by the new concept of truth and by expanding knowledge. It is not so much the practical Christian religion, with its ceremonies and celebrations, its affirmations and moral teachings, which has lost its relevance as it is the theological justification for taking seriously the Judeo-Christian tradition.

We live in a period of religious decadence. The religious institutions with which we are familiar have lost their power to order and justify the human venture. A symptom is the "death-of-God" spokesmen among Christian theologians who announced the end of a world view which had given meaning and direction to life. However, the "death of God" is only the demise of concepts of the supernatural nature of the Supreme Being, not the termination of the inescapable "God," the being that is of ultimate significance.

The inadequacy of religious institutions is a consequence of the *irrelevance of their theology*. Their waning influence, reflected in declining attendance and financial support, stems from their failure to promote a faith which will integrate people with the *whole environment*. Evangelical sects, except for revival crusades, are not suffering the same decline as the major denominations—in fact, some evangelical sects are flourishing, which indicates to me that a positive theology, however incongruous it may be with our state of knowledge, is better than an amorphous theology. Reactionary religions are at least definite. The failure of major denominations is in not responding appropriately to religious concerns.

With the traditional theological reference points obscured, we are in the predicament of an airplane pilot flying blind. Trapped in a cloud without a visible horizon or instruments to provide an artificial horizon, a pilot can lose a sense of direction in every dimension. With no horizon to orient flight, pilots cannot trust to flying blind, for they can inadvertently put the plane in a death-spiral where the artificial gravity induced by the spiraling can disastrously mislead them as to which way is up. They end by flying with open throttle abruptly into the ground.

If you and I, and our posterity, are to survive, we have to know which way is "up." Otherwise, we will be like the woman who fell off a twenty-story building and shouted as she passed the tenth floor, "Everything all right so far!" The intellectual horizon in Western culture has faded as a result of general disenchantment with traditional systems of belief. And the indices of where we are, available in the mass media, are confusing. Lacking a world view, the latest headlines for us assume cosmic significance; each daily event appears to be of eternal significance, each challenge is taken as a threat, and each problem becomes a dilemma. Without relatedness to a meaningful frame of reference, even our own sense of identity becomes indefinite and we tend to become what David Riesman (1961, p. 21) describes as an "other-directed" person, subject to the erratic influence of what the crowd may be doing. Lacking a personal vision of a pattern of meaning and value, personal and family crises become overwhelmingly difficult, and individual effort seems futile.

A contemporary cult of despair, represented by Sartre's play *No Exit*, alleges that life is meaningless and absurd; its devotees see no justification for the struggle to achieve, or hope for the future. To them, nothing is worthwhile or valuable, except the sensations of the moment. Their problem is not that the environment has become any more difficult to live in, but that their view of it is inadequate. They are like the student who returned from an aimless hitch-hiking tour of Europe with nothing to relate; he had no significant experiences because he did not know what was important or what to notice. Too many people are like the young hitch-hikers I picked up one spring day who had only a vague idea of where they were, where they had been, or how they were going to get where they were going—they were not even carrying a map. Many of us are confused, not because the *world is mixed up,* but because we are *not oriented in it.*

You and I are oriented toward experience by assumptions, some of which are unexamined, about the nature of ourselves and of the world we live in, which are acquired by imitation as well as instruction from the culture in which we are nurtured. Our assumptions may be implicit or explicit, but in either case they help determine what we are aware of and how we react to events. The question is, "How adequate are they in guiding us to a rendezvous with our expectations?" If our conceptions of the situation in which we live are not adequate for the coordination of our activities with the actual possibilities, our anticipations will be misled and our satisfaction denied. *It matters what we believe.*

R. K. Richardson, in a course on "Underlying Ideals" during my junior year at Beloit College, penetrated my behavioristic bias to convince me that a society's unexamined assumptions were more important in its development than geography, climate, or natural resources. What is taken for granted about the actualities or the possibilities of existence shapes our plans. Therefore, what we *believe* is critical for what we will *become.*

Our problem is to make explicit, vivid, and valid the assumptions by which we live so they can integrate our fragmentary activities into a meaningful whole. A great deal of personal unhappiness, except for misfortunes and tragedies, does not come from the *circumstances* in which we live, but from the frustration engendered by *inadequate ideas,* either personal or cultural. John R. Platt (1966, p. 38), associate director of the University of Michigan Mental Health Research Institute, comments that "any error in our ideas of being will always lead to psychological and social pathology and dehumanization—whether it is a persecution complex, or the belief that all is predestined, or that all is subconscious," or that one lives for the state.

The peril of erroneous ideas is epitomized in the horror associated with the names of such extermination camps as Auschwitz, Belsen, Treblinka, and Dachau. In 1930, just before the rise of the Nazis to devastating power, physicist Erwin Schrodinger (1964, p. 6) wrote in Germany, warning that as a result of the triumph of the natural sciences and of a loss of a sense of the transcendent, or of the transcendental dimension of the physical, people had lost a sense of moral responsibility:

> The people no longer know anything of these things. Most of them have nothing to hold on to and no one to follow. They believe neither in God nor in the gods; to them the Church is now only a political party, and morality nothing but a burdensome restriction which, without the support of those no longer credible bugbears on which it leant for so long, is now without any basis whatever. A sort of general atavism has set in; western man is in danger of relapsing to an earlier level of development which he has never properly overcome; crass, unfettered egoism is raising its grinning head, and its fist, drawing irresistible strength from primitive habits, is reaching for the abandoned helm of our ship.

It took the terrible expenditure of blood and treasure in World War II to stem the rising tide of Nazism and to shut down the gas chambers in the extermination camps.

Just before the onset of the Great Depression of the 1930's in this country, Walter Lippmann (1960, p. 8) commented on religion: "The acids of modernity have dissolved that order for many of us, and there are some in consequence who think that the needs which religion fulfilled have also been dissolved." With an all-too-familiar ring, Lippmann (1960, p. 3-4) wrote in 1929 of the situation where "whirl is king," created by loss of belief in anything:

> Among those who no longer believe in the religion of their fathers, some are proudly defiant, and many are indifferent. But there are also a few, perhaps an increasing number, who feel that there is a vacancy in their lives and ... who are perplexed by the consequences of their own irreligion.... They have lost the certainty that their lives are significant, and ... they know of no compelling reason which certifies the moral code they adhere to.... They are likely to point to the world about them, and to ask whether the modern man possesses any criterion by which he can measure the value of his own desires, whether there is any standard he really believes in which permits him to put a term upon the pursuit of money, of power, and of excitement which has created so much of the turmoil and the squalor and the explosiveness of modern civilization.
>
> These are, perhaps, merely the rationalizations of the modern man's discontent. At the heart of it there are likely to be moments of blank misgiving in which he finds that the civilization of which he is a part leaves a dusty taste in his mouth. He may be very busy with many things, but he discovers one day that he is no longer sure they are worth doing.

With the traditional frame of reference no longer credible, the human predicament is summarized by Lippmann (1960, p. 9):

> For the modern man who has ceased to believe, without ceasing to be credulous, hangs, as it were, between heaven and

earth, and is at rest nowhere. There is no theory of the meaning and value of events which he is compelled to accept, but he is nonetheless compelled to accept the events.

That is where I came in, since I read Lippmann's *A Preface to Morals* in the early years of the Depression while working as a clerk in the Chicago Loop office of a coal company. I then believed that I could get along perfectly well in a religionless society by accepting Lippmann's scientifically-based "disinterestedness." But the "acid of modernity" continued eating at the foundation of the piety by which my grandmother lived and I began to search for a new formulation of underlying ideals to give form and meaning and significance to the events in which I was inevitably engaged. I report what I have learned.

Secularization

The secularization process which has brought us into a period of religious decadence has its own redeeming qualities. Theologian Harvey Cox has pointed out that secularization is basically a liberating movement. "Secularization," says Cox (1965, p. 20), "implies a historical process, almost certainly irreversible, in which society and culture are delivered from tutelage to religious control and closed metaphysical world view." The word "secular" means "this age" or "this world" of the passing and transient, and traditionally denotes "something vaguely inferior" to the timeless and changeless realm of religion. However, says Cox (1965, p. 21), "Secularization arises in large measure from the formative influence of Biblical faith on the world, an influence mediated first by the Christian church and later by movements deriving partly from it." Borrowing the concept of "disenchantment" from Max Weber, Cox says that the Judeo-Christian tradition first disenchanted nature, providing the grounds for the confident development of science by exorcising the fear of a demon-inhabited nature. It disenchanted the realm of politics, challenging any civil power which claimed divine sanctions, from the Old Testament prophet's protest against the lawlessness of kings to medieval protests against the divine right of kings, thus opening the way for the development of democratic republics. And it disenchanted the human body of evil-spirit possession, preparing the way for medical science. Thus the process of secularization through disenchantment of various sectors of human concern was a liberating benefit to Western culture.

Now the process of secularization, says Cox (1965, pp. 20-21), has moved into the realm of values and meanings. Supernatural sanctions are no longer accepted for what you should believe and what you should do, which not only creates a state of uncertainty but a crisis in values. The process of secularization has ushered in "secularism," which is "the name of an ideology, a new closed world view which functions very much like a new religion." But the religion of secularism provides no grounds for hope or confidence or significant choice. The secularization and relativization of values not only increase personal uncertainty and insecurity, but they dissolve the bonds of social cohesion, and thus threaten the survival of a society. Since hope for the future affects the way we feel in the present, hope releases energy. Without hope, we despair and have little vitality to meet the challenges of today, and have little courage to endure suffering and tragedy.

Neo-orthodoxy, in the works of such writers as Reinhold Niebuhr and Paul Tillich, has striven brilliantly and imaginatively and with some success to relate the *traditional orthodox Christian scheme* of sin and salvation to *contemporary knowledge,* but the stress has been too great for the orthodox system. The old wineskins of orthodoxy have burst when filled with a better understanding of the nature of reality, as Jesus warned that they would: "Neither is new wine put into old wineskins; if it is, the skins burst, and the wine is spilled, and the skins are destroyed; but new wine is put into fresh wineskins, and so both are preserved."(Matthew 9:17). Not that all the insights and empirical values of Judeo-Christian tradition are outmoded and useless, but that the theological scheme in which they were contained has burst. The traditional Christian theology is no longer adequate to integrate old with new;

it is now incredible and does not provide a meaningful frame of reference for our daily lives. Credulity about doctrines in conflict with known truths is called for, instead of faith in doctrines which are beyond testing. Faith in faith is demanded by orthodox leaders, instead of faith in the commanding and transforming nature of reality.

Some religious leaders, to their great credit, have sought to relate religious institutions to the contemporary scene by emphasizing counseling, social service, or social action on the frontiers of race relations, peace, birth control, poverty, and justice. In spite of the significant achievements of religious leaders in these and other fields, the theological framework which justifies and orders such activities remains fragmented. In a different context, but still related, Jesus warned, "... these you ought to have done, without neglecting the others." (Matthew 23:23)

For a period, the Judeo-Christian tradition has conditioned by cultural lag the emotional tone and attitudes of even those who have become disenchanted with the orthodox scheme of sin and salvation. A sense of assurance and of worth has permeated our culture even when the theological premises of orthodox Christianity have ceased to enthrall us. For instance, from the creation myth of the Old Testament Book of Genesis has come a pervasive optimism that the world is good. "And God saw that it was good" is a repeated comment on His creation. Even when Darwin's theory of evolution superseded the Genesis myth of original creation in accounting for the origin of species, the basic confidence lingered that the earth provided a suitable scene for our work and play. The value system of pious generations has been transmitted at an emotional level to the sceptical children of an age of science, but now, without grounding in an hypothesis about the nature of reality and without *reaffirmation in religious institutions, even the posture of faith and hope dissipates.*

The rubble of Christian orthodoxy lies about us, disintegrated by the "acids of modernity" or "secularization," like the beautiful ruins of Tintern Abbey in England, decayed by withdrawal of support when King Henry VIII dissolved the abbeys early in the sixteenth century. Some people stand amidst the rubble of orthodoxy and long to *rebuild* it as it was, while others notice that *a new structure already stands* beside it, as the new cathedral at Coventry stands at right angle to the ruins of the old cathedral gutted by Nazi fire-bombs during World War II. It is symbolic that when the Chapter decided to rebuild Coventry Cathedral, while leaving the old ruins standing as a war memorial, they reoriented the new cathedral with its altar to the north, instead of to the traditional east.

The time is past for mending the fabric of orthodoxy. The time has come to radically reorient our religious ideas, as Jesus did with the wisdom of the Old Testament, and Lao-tse did with the wisdom of the Ancients. If we polarize our ideas, both old and new, around a different axis, a new, more credible, more relevant theological structure emerges. Sanborn C. Brown (1966, pp. 1-2), professor of physics at the Massachusetts Institute of Technology and president of the Institute on Religion in an Age of Science, writes:

> It is my opinion that it is about time we stopped this attempt to compromise the new with the old and start to work toward developing a valid and inspiring theology for the modern world based on our present state of knowledge.... If our current religion is not giving us a sufficient motivation to practice its major tenets (love)—then as a scientific experiment it appears to be a failure and a new set of hypotheses needs to be developed which hopefully can have a more impelling validity.

We do not have to start *inventing new hypotheses* which have a more impelling validity; they are *already in general use*. We have reached a "tipping point" in the development of religion. The accumulation of new ideas in our culture is outweighing the old, and the balance is suddenly shifting.

There are many valid ideas ready to be articulated into a new world view. It is like the process of conversion described by William James (1958, p. 162). Each person works from a group of ideas which form "the habitual centre of his personal energy," says James. "In addition to ideas at the centre, each person has a constellation of ideas at the periphery, and conversion means ... that religious ideas, previously peripheral in his consciousness, now take a central place, and form ... the habitual centre of his energy." He (1958, p. 162) adds, "All we know is that there are dead feelings, dead ideas, and cold beliefs, and there are hot and live ones; and when one grows hot and alive within us, everything has to re-crystallize about it." For example, if old concepts of God be dead, it is a matter of crystallizing new concepts of God about currently hot ideas.

Perhaps the full implications of the new views of the universe are not sufficiently operative in sustaining our morale because we still *identify religion* with a *languishing orthodoxy,* much as do Roman Catholics who rebel against the teachings of their church but who cannot find a religious home in Protestant churches because they still define religion in terms of the Catholicism they reject.

When I listen to the overtones of many of the addresses at meetings of the American Association for the Advancement of Science, I detect implicit assumptions of a *philosophical system* which gives coherence to their various research projects, but which is *not yet explicitly synthesized.* Our problem is to artic-ulate the assumptions by which we really live, and which can integrate our fragmentary activities into a meaningful structure.

Foresight Fails to Overcome Fate

You may feel that the assumptions by which you live are perfectly adequate to orient you successfully to your environ-ment, and they may be. Most of us must be doing something right or there would be more anxiety, frustration, and suffering than there is. Most of the changes of the past few centuries we would prefer to retain: increased longevity, health and comfort, more widely distributed goods and services, and a less capricious economy. We have discovered some processes that extend life and enable us to live more abundantly, and we may not explicitly

realize how they have also changed our assumptions. Most of us
are acting as if we existed in relation to something meaningful and
reliable even when voices proclaim that we are adrift in a
meaningless universe. But there are signs that for many people
the unexamined assumptions by which we live are insufficient.
The more successful we are in gaining control over our environment, the less confident we are that we know what we are doing.
Each solution brings greater problems. Control over disease and
death has produced a population explosion that necessitates
increased use of conception control. Industrial technology pol-
lutes the waters, and automobiles and factories pollute the air.
Our present peril is epitomized in the development of atomic
energy which gives us new sources of power and new resources in
medicine, but which also threatens to destroy life with its radioactive wastes.

The rapidity of change and the increase of knowledge bring a
feeling of insecurity; nothing seems stable, and it is difficult to
anticipate all the contingencies. We need to acquire a sense of
security and personal identity in the midst of change, and of
priorities amidst almost overwhelming available information. As
our society becomes more mobile, with more and more people
able to change their residence and to travel, our sense of identity
is less and less defined by our place of origin. Mobility gives
greater opportunity for personal advancement, but it also begets a
need for identification with a larger frame of reference. If the home
town no longer gives us a sense of who we are and where we be-
long, then we need to find our home in a more inclusive structure.
Perhaps this is the reason that southern California with its high
concentration of rootless people is such fertile soil for all kinds of
reactionary movements, from quasi-religious cults to extremist
political organizations: people are trying to overcome their sense
of anonymity resulting from their mobility by identification with
some authoritative movement.

The irony of our situation is that the more we are able to control
our environment, the more insecure we feel. An affluent society is
not accompanied by a greater sense of well-being. There seems to

be a positive correlation between our creative *achievements,* our power to move about in our environment, and our *anxiety;* the more control we are able to exercise, the more *uneasy* we become. The more we are able to make conscious choice of goals, the more we are exposed to the peril of making choices which do not fit us to survive. It is necessary for us to have some idea of the *ongoing evolutionary process* if we are to *keep in phase with it.*

Viennese psychiatrist Victor E. Frankl (1962, p. 108) reports the feeling of meaninglessness in the lives of contemporary people:

> No instinct tells him what he has to do, and no tradition tells him what he ought to do; soon he will not know what he wants to do. ... This existential vacuum manifests itself mainly in a state of boredom.... In actual fact, boredom is now causing, and certainly bringing to psychiatrists, more problems to solve than distress.

In response to the rising tide of fascism in 1941, Erich Fromm warned that to escape from the anxieties of "moral aloneness" by identification with a totalitarian regime destroys personal identity. He says of human nature:

> The more he gains freedom in the sense of emerging from the original oneness with man and nature and the more he becomes an "individual," the more he has no choice but to unite himself with the world in the spontaneity of love and productive work or else to seek a kind of security by such ties with the world as destroy his freedom and the integrity of his individual self.

The debilitating effects of aloneness are traced by Fromm to the nature of human beings. The dependency of children upon adults makes association with others a matter of life and death. "The possibility of being left alone," says Fromm (1941, p. 21), "is necessarily the most serious threat to the child's whole existence." From such a deep root in our infancy comes our basic need for association with others to survive. Just as compelling is "the need to be related to the world outside oneself, the need to avoid [moral] aloneness." Fromm (1941, p. 19) says:

To feel completely alone and isolated leads to mental disintegration just as physical starvation leads to death. This relatedness to others is not identical with physical contact. An individual may be alone in a physical sense for many years and yet he may be related to ideas, values, or at least social patterns that give him a feeling of communion and "belonging." On the other hand, he may live among people and yet be overcome with an utter feeling of isolation, the outcome of which, if it transcends a certain limit, is the state of insanity which schizophrenic disturbances represent. This lack of relatedness to values, symbols, patterns, we may call moral aloneness and state that moral aloneness is as intolerable as the physical aloneness, or rather that physical aloneness becomes unbearable only if it implies also moral aloneness.

Moral aloneness is an essentially human problem, arising from subjective self-consciousness. The faculty of thinking, which makes a person aware of being distinct from other people and from nature and which makes it possible to anticipate death, sickness, aging, and disasters, also makes one feel alienated and insignificant. With such a capacity for awareness and anticipation, says Fromm (1941, p. 22):

> Unless he belonged somewhere, unless his life had some meaning and direction, [a man] would feel like a particle of dust and be overcome by his individual insignificance. He would not be able to relate himself to any system which would give meaning and direction to his life, he would be filled with doubt, and this doubt eventually would paralyze his ability to act—that is, to live.

There has been a popular notion that religion was born of ignorance and superstition. From this point of view, all you need to do is simply to be more realistic and intelligent and you will be able to handle your world. In the sense that a more intelligent understanding of the nature of the world makes one more adaptable, this is true. But in another sense, the more we know about the world, the more mysterious it becomes. For as we increase the diameter of the known field of knowledge, the boundary of the unknown seems to increase exponentially. As the range of control over our environment increases, our malaise seems to increase disproportionately. With the advance in knowledge, the need for a meaningful frame of reference seems to become greater. Bronislaw Malinowski, the British anthropologist, from his extended study of primitive cultures, has pointed out that religious disciplines do not arise from ignorance and *superstition*, but from the anxieties and forebodings of *intelligent* creatures. Religion, he says, emerges to compensate for the insecurities arising from "the curse of forethought and imagination.... It grows out of *every* culture because knowledge which gives foresight fails to overcome fate." Malinowski (1931, pp. 641-42) explains:

> A whole range of anxieties, forebodings and problems concerning human destinies and man's place in the universe open up once man begins to act in common not only with his fellow citizens but also with past and future generations. Religion is not born out of speculation or reflection, still less out of illusion or misapprehension, but rather out of the real tragedies of human life, out of the conflict between human plans and realities.

You might presume that, since Malinowski's conclusions are based upon studies of primitive cultures, his conclusions do not apply to our more sophisticated culture. Some of our sophisticated contemporaries feel otherwise. The late Clyde Kluckhohn (1966, p. 232), professor of anthropology at Harvard University, said in 1958, "It is an induction from the evidence at the disposal of the anthropologist that religion in the broad sense is essential to the health and survival of any society." And Ward H. H. Goodenough (1966, p. 228), professor of anthropology at the University of Pennsylvania, says:

> As human knowledge has increased through time and as the emotional climate of living has changed, it has become necessary over and over again to find new formulations of the purpose of life that are intellectually and emotionally satisfying. The growth of science is once again forcing us to look for new formulations that we can reconcile with present knowledge, without at the same time destroying everything else we value. This has become for many of us one of the great emotional problems of our time, its resolution one of the great purposes in life.

On the same subject, Theodosius Dobzhansky (1966, p. 319), professor of genetics at Rockefeller University, observed, "A person's individual existence may ... be ephemeral; what really matters is that his existence is believed to be a part of something that endures eternally."

Physicist Sanborn C. Brown (1966a, ch. 5, p. 5) of M.I.T. concludes:

> Man has wrested from nature, that produced him in the evolutionary process, much of the further development of his own species. He has now come face to face with the absolute necessity for developing a meaning, a purpose, and a goal for his social and behavioral evolution so as to properly guide his biological evolution, which means, incidentally, his very existence on earth.

You and I may be doing well in our personal lives, but the ideas in the previous quotations agree that our society needs some comprehensive vision of our situation and direction of movement. When the old answers no longer serve, new answers to the basic questions need to be formulated. There is a correlation between the *answers* we find satisfying and the cultural *context* in which the questions are asked. The answers to questions arising from human perplexities must be relevant to human beings in an existential situation, or they will be useless in orienting us to our living experiences.

The New Situation

The basic questions may remain the same, but the frame of reference in which we ask them has dramatically changed. This is a source of a great deal of our contemporary confusion; we don't see that new answers to the basic questions are available because we are still conditioned by previous frames of reference even when we no longer consciously believe in them. If we ask the basic questions in terms of the frame of reference in which we are really living, we will find the answers as vivid and meaningful as the earlier answers were in the earlier frame of reference. When we realize what we are looking for, we will more readily find it.

John Dewey (quoted in Kluckholm, 1966, p. 223) has warned us that "a culture which permits science to destroy traditional values but which distrusts its power to create new ones is destroying itself." In his lectures at Kings Chapel in Boston in 1926, mathematician-philosopher Alfred North Whitehead (1961, p. 127) proposed "to exhibit the inevitable transformation of religion with the transformation of knowledge." He said, "Progress in truth—truth of science and truth of religion—is mainly a progress in the framing of concepts, in discarding artificial abstractions or partial metaphors, and in evolving notions which strike more deeply at the roots of reality."

Henry Margenau, professor of natural philosophy and physics at Yale University, points out that every new discovery results in movement at three levels. A scientific discovery issues in a technological development, which affects the culture by producing new goods and services. Then he (Margenau, 1957) says:

> But there is another movement, which I shall call Obscure, which also springs into existence when a sufficiently trenchant scientific discovery is made. It proceeds from discovery through new theory, modifications of what is called common sense, changes in our cosmological beliefs, in the theory of knowledge, the nature of the universe, and of man. Ethics, sociology and politics, and ultimately religion, are infected by the germ which is born when a discovery in pure science occurs.

The sciences have been extruding insights, discoveries, information, new concepts and models, useful in their particular disciplines, which have been accumulating in our culture like a tangled pile of jackstraws. We may not fully understand them, but we increasingly take them for granted. Peter F. Drucker (1957, p. 9) comments, "Within the past twenty or thirty years these new concepts have become the reality of our work and world. They are 'obvious' to us." Our new situation is characterized, says Drucker (1957, p. 40) by such concepts as unity, purpose, and process. "Today," he says, "our task is to understand patterns of biological, social, or physical order in which mind and matter become meaningful precisely because they are reflections of a greater unity." We need to integrate and synthesize such concepts into a new theology—a "system" or "wholistic" theology.

The increased prevalence of the concept of *unity* is manifest in the more frequent use of such terms as patterns, configurations, systems, syndromes, gestalts, and ecology. In short, the concept of unity is a renewed interest in how elements behave when *integrated in a structure.* An implication of the concept of unity is the displacement of the concept of a two-story universe. The dualism of matter versus mind, or physical versus spiritual, or body versus soul, and natural versus supernatural, is obviated. The qualities indicated by these dichotomies are seen to be inherent in reality as a continuum integrated in various ways; mind, for instance, is the way matter functions when unified in a certain configuration.

The second concept of *purpose* is a recognition of the direction-ality of behavior of elements when coordinated in a unified order, and of how elements arrange themselves to serve the purpose of the whole. Since the word "purpose" implies a mind which projects symbolic goals and then works toward them, an intel-ligent capacity not possessed by all beings, I will be speaking instead of the intentions or directionalities exhibited by all self-organized living systems. To designate this bent, I will later use the word "entelechy," which is in disrepute among biologists because of its vitalistic association. In my usage of "entelechy," I mean the *natural impulse* of any organism to fulfill the grave *demands of its own being,* a non-intellectual drive emerging from the pattern of its internal interaction, which is uniquely supplemented in human beings by conceptual goals.

The meaning of words is being continuously modified to reflect new understandings. We do not refrain from using the word "atom," though we have learned that atoms are splitable, or the word "psyche" as in "psychology," though we have learned that the psyche is not distinguished from the body. The word "god" has historically gone through a series of permutations. "Entel-echy" is too valuable a concept not to be rehabilitated, as will be many other words used in this theological dialogue.

The third concept of process has issued from the theory of evolution. It emphasizes growth, development, change, and continuity. Creativity is seen as an inner process rather than as a pattern imposed by an outer force. It emphasizes a *dynamic* rather than a *static* universe. Since the evolutionary process can be traced in the development of atoms, biological organisms, social organizations, and constellations, *all* being is conceived as intimately related, as existing in a continuum. The evolutionary process has opened up conceptions of space and time; space is now measured by light-years used by astronomers; and time is measured by epochs of millions of years used by geologists. We no longer live in a closed little cosmos.

The sciences which undermined the certainties of the earlier world views have also provided the concepts from which a new world view may be synthesized. It is the function of theology to *synthesize generalizations* in order to arrive at conceptions of the *nature of comprehensive reality*. Concepts which helped us resolve *particular* questions may now help us to resolve more *general* ones. Circumstances now seem to be ripe to use concepts from the sciences as clues to the resolution of otherwise insoluble perplexities. To overcome the uneasiness caused by the "malady of multitude and immensity, says Teilhard de Chardin (1961, p. 227), "... I believe that the modern world has no choice but to follow its intuitive imagination unhesitatingly and right to the end."

We will see how new responses to the generic religious questions emerge from the new situation to provide a radically different wholistic systems theology, if not a new religion.

Chapter **2**

The Great Living System

WHAT is the human situation? We experience the universe from a limited perspective and therefore piecemeal. If we are to make sense out of our fragmentary experience, we have to ask what the *universe is like as a whole.* Does the total environment establish conditions for human fulfillment and aspiration, or are we engaged in a meaningless dance, hopping around to avoid being crushed in a turmoil of random events? Is there anything going for us, or are we on our own in an indifferent world? How did we and our environment get here? Is there any creative power beyond ourselves?

Religions in different cultures have developed myths in response to these basic questions. In our Western culture, informed by the Judeo-Christian tradition, such questions are answered by affirming the existence of a supernatural creator. In the beginning "the earth was without form and void," and God created the earth and all its creatures "originally," according to the myths in the first two chapters of the Biblical book of Genesis. Human beings, made in the image of God, could achieve the good life by obeying the will of God. Suffering, death, and injustice were compensated for by assurance that history was moving toward a Judgment Day when the Kingdom of God would be established on earth, with peace and justice for the believers. When time passed with no such divine intervention, the compensation for the righteous was

24

projected into a Kingdom of Heaven, with hell for the unrighteous, to be experienced in another realm after death—with personal immortality. This myth gave each believer a sense of participating in a significant drama and made the ambiguities and tragedies of life meaningful. Within its limitations, and when taken seriously, this ethical monotheism produced morally responsible people.

Theism is Dead

The Judeo-Christian myth has been broken and transformed many times. In order to make the creating and sustaining power conceivable, it has been described by analogies. In the Bible, we can trace the development of concepts of God from a tribal deity to a universal sovereign power; from a local deity assisting a band of nomads in war to a supreme god of love and justice who controls the destinies of all nations; from a deity who inhabits the nearest high place and may be transported in an ark or housed in a temple to a deity whose domicile is in the heavens; and from a divine being known by analogy with an autocratic tribal leader and called a Judge or a King to the metaphor used by Jesus of Yahweh as a loving, disciplining, and redeeming Father. Then, among the early Christians, Jesus himself was transmuted into the image of God. (Fosdick, 1938, ch. I, Passim.) God was conceived in the human image, with human attributes — anthropomorphism. Because human beings are the most creative beings we experience, it is difficult to avoid using anthropomorphic terms to describe the creative process which transcends us.

Another way to conceive of the creative source of being is by the development of *philosophical concepts*. Early Christian theologians, influenced by Neo-Platonic philosophy, described God in terms of Platonic Ideals (absolute ideas) which were the creative principles emanating from the divine or cosmic reason—the Logos, first cause or unmoved mover.

The philosophical concept most satisfactory to Christian theologians is "theism." *Theism* conceives of God as both *immanent* (in the world of nature) and *transcendent* (above and distinct from the world of nature); immanent as a *personal* God who enters into relationships with the worshipers and continuously controls the course of events in the universe; and transcendent as the supernatural being who originally created the universe. The theistic concept assumes that the natural world is dependent upon a static reality beyond itself and is not self-explanatory.

Eighteenth century *deists* described the creator as a wholly transcendent, impersonal deity who created the world and then left it alone to work according to immutable natural laws, like a watchmaker and the watch. Rationalist proofs were advanced to support deism, though it was not institutionalized in a worshiping community.

Pantheism, with a root meaning of "theism-in-all," identifies the creative source, which is entirely immanent in the world, with the manifestations and forces of nature.

Monism, a modification of pantheism, sees an identification between God and the totality of beings taken together as one fully unified and all-embracing system for which the theory of evolution offers a natural explanation requiring no external designing intelligence or power; the world is self-explanatory — my concept.

Theism is dead as a philosophical description of God, as is deism. Since the theory of *evolution* has disclosed the continuous process of creativity, we can now see the *creation and the creator as one.* A supernatural creator is redundant and, taking the word "redundant" in the British sense, God is unemployed, which partly accounts for God's demise. Unitarian Universalists have acknowledged for some time that such theological concepts are dead, and recently radical Christian theologians have led a god-is-dead movement which obviates not only theism but any concept of a transcendent creative process.

Has the reality denoted by the name of god changed, or just the concepts and analogies? Since the total environment is as creating and sustaining as it ever was, modern human beings with a better understanding of its structure and dynamics than had earlier people may be better able to adapt to it. Christians, and people of other religions, use the name of god as a talisman with magical powers if properly invoked; it is not the name but the operative reality which is effective. Martin Buber asks (1958, pp. 75-76), "What does all mistaken talk about God's being and works ... matter in comparison with the one truth that all men who have addressed God had God himself in mind?" The question is whether the creativity that brought humans into being has vanished.

In responding to the question about the nature of the environment as a whole, we will see whether "the commanding, transforming reality," of which James Luther Adams speaks, or "the ground of our being," of which Paul Tillich speaks, can be made concrete. In an attempt to fill the *credibility gap* in religion left by the death of god, I invite you to share a flight of fancy with me and then, having heard my exposition out, see whether you find from your experience that the model I propose describes something real.

I propose the concept of a *living system* as a model for the universe. The premise of my speculation is that the process of evolution issues in a continuity of being and implies a unity of all being which, when certain dynamic relations are observed, can be visualized as a "great living system" rather than as a mere congeries of events. My hypothesis that the continuity of all being concresces in an emergent, unified being with a character and self-directedness, which affects us as participant beings, is difficult to conceive. Therefore, I will proceed by using the relatively well-understood concept of a *biological cell* as an analog for the newer concept of a living system which, through systems analysis of a wide variety of configurations in our environment, is becoming increasingly useful in helping us understand aggregates as wholes. Then we will see whether the concept of a living system can be a satisfactory *model* to help us know reality as a whole.

The image of the universe as a living system has already been proposed in the philosophy of *organism*, or process philosophy, of Alfred North Whitehead and Charles Hartshorne. Some thirty years ago Hartshorne first gave me a glimpse of this way of looking at things when I heard him say, "The world is the body of

God. When man rejoices, God rejoices; when man suffers, God suffers." Then a course with Hartshorne at The University of Chicago introduced me to the *organic philosophy* of Alfred North Whitehead, particularly through an assigned study of his book *Process and Reality* (1929). The organic philosophy of Whitehead and Hartshorne, now becoming more concrete in "general systems theory," is providing common ground for the current exciting dialogue between scientists and theologians.

General systems theory, says Ludwig von Bertalanffy (1968, p. 37) of the University of Alberta, is "a general science of wholeness," a study of system "of various orders not understandable by investigation of their respective parts in isolation." And (1968, p. 31), "It is necessary to study not only parts and processes in isolation, but also to solve the decisive problems found in the organization and order unifying them, resulting from dynamic interaction of parts, and making the behavior of parts different when studied in isolation or within the whole." A *system* may be defined as a set of elements *organized* by interactions, absorbing high *energy* matter and achieving a *steady state* of centralized *order*.

General systems theory is valuable in understanding such diverse systems as biological individuals, biomes, industries, governments, and computers. Von Bertalanffy (1950, p. 142) suggests the correlating benefit of general systems theory when he says, "The existence of laws of similar structure in different fields enables the use of systems which are simpler, or better known, as models for more complicated and less manageable ones."

An elemental example of a living system is a biological cell whose structure and dynamics may help us understand more general systems. All *organisms* are by definition *living systems,* while all systems are not necessarily living in the ordinary sense of the word. Later in this essay, we will have to confront the question of the definition of "living" to see how generally it may be applied to systems. First, we will look at an indubitably living system, a cell.

We will not take the human being as an example of an organism for two reasons. First, humans are such an extraordinary emergent in the process of evolution due to the development of their minds and hands that they are misleading as a model for other systems. They are so *unique* an event in the universe, with such unusual capacities for imaginative creativity and for autonomy, that they would be confusing as an analog for living systems. Secondly, we already have too much of a tendency to read ourselves into the universe. Our anthropomorphisms have already made traditional concepts of God incredible as the creative power in the universe. A cell is less complex than a human, so we will not inadvertently carry over peculiarly human traits to living systems in general.

Why Is There Not Nothing?

The German philosopher Friedrich von Schelling early in the nineteenth century asked, "Why is there not nothing?" Or, at least, why is there not nothing more than an inchoate glob of primeval stuff? What we call the "natural order" is not natural; it is *improbable*. For, according to the principle of *entropy* which, following the Second Law of Thermodynamics, says that *closed systems* tend to run down and arrive at a state where the available energy is so evenly distributed within the system that the system becomes inert, the natural state should be placid chaos. Entropy is also a measure of disorder. Erwin Schrodinger (1956, p. 72), German physicist, said: "We now recognize this fundamental law of physics to be just the natural tendency of things to approach the chaotic state (the same tendency that the books of a library or the piles of papers and manuscripts on a desk display) unless we obviate it." What is amazing is that form and order have emerged in spite of entropy, that creation has produced such *open systems* as organisms which can *utilize energy*. As Hartshorne (1941, p. 201) suggests:

> A creative side of nature there must be, and its local manifestation in planetary life cannot exhaust its reality, or there would have been no cosmos to "run down" toward the "heat death." The presupposed "running up" or creation cannot be *less* fundamental as a cosmic function, however hidden from us its larger operation may be.

In the presence of entropy we are trying to account for the natural process of creativity.

Mere *chance* is not an adequate explanation for the occurrence of creativity, for the emergence of new forms of order. Dutch biologist C. A. van Peursen feels strongly that an infinite number of monkeys pecking randomly at an infinite number of typewriters could not produce in an infinite number of years a Shakespearean sonnet. In the first place, we don't have infinity for the occurrence of such a miracle; we have only about five billion years, and yet from a condition "without form and void" such sonnets have been produced. Moreover, as van Peursen pointed out, such an event does not occur all at once; it takes *cumulative* development of increasingly complex forms to produce such an artistic creation as a sonnet. Some structures must have sufficient *stability* in order to record each minute gain in capacity; for random biological variations to occur, there first must be genes to mutate.

In addition, all that chance explains is that in the restless moving of particles there are many random meetings; chance does not explain why some meetings are an *event* in which new relations are established, and thus a new form of order originates, while in other random encounters nothing occurs.

For instance, if I take a glass jar and fill it half way with white sand and top it off with red sand and stir it for a while, the sand will intermingle and become pink. No amount of stirring it in the opposite direction will, with any reasonable probability, sort out the sand again into its pure red and white constituents (Mendelsohn, 1961, pp. 37-39). Although energy is being added to the jar of sand, no *selective* principle is at work. Some organizing power is needed to restore the original order. Something more than chance must be operative for anti-entropic forms of order to occur. Some capacity for establishing selective relations seems to be necessary to creativity.

Life Is Organization

Given a planet such as ours with a source of energy in the sun, under favorable conditions, systems have organized themselves

which are capable of utilizing energy. At a point in their development, we identify more *complex* systems as living. It is open living
systems which have succeeded in organizing structures able to
use energy in a more efficient way. "Everyone is aware of the fact
that life is an antientropic struggle against the dissipative forces of
nature," writes A. Katchalsky (1971, p. 111), Director of the Poly-
mer Research Laboratory, Weizmann Institute in Israel. "Since all
real processes require, however, a positive production of entropy,
life has chosen the least evil—it produces entropy at the lowest
rate."

To produce entropy at the lowest rate, living systems have been
spontaneously organized by components into bounded structures
capable of cooperation within and of selective interaction with the
undifferentiated environment. *Selectivity*, says Katchalsky (1971,
pp. 120-21), "is one of the foremost requirements of living organization...." For a selective response to the environment to occur,
some stable form of ordered relations has to be integrated into a
system. J. Bronowski (1970, p. 33), late Resident Fellow at the
Salk Institute for Biological Studies at La Jolla, California, suggests the concept of "stratified stability" for such organizations,
and says the natural world "has turned out to be full of preferred
configurations and hidden stabilities, even at the most basic and
inanimate level of atomic structure." Such biochemicals as amino
acid products and nucleic acid bases that appear by natural processes can, under conditions of drying and wetting, form cell-like
structures (coacervates), which demonstrate the inherent tendency of matter to organize itself into living systems capable of
metabolism.

Life is a *process* by which order is created out of disorder in the
universe. Biologist Edmund W. Sinnott (1966, p. 96) defines life as
*"the organized process by which matter is brought together in
organized and integrated systems capable of self-perpetuation
and of change."* Non-living aggregates, such as substantial-looking
mountains, slowly *degenerate;* erosion through time, provided
other variables remain constant, will reduce all elevations in the
landscape to an inert level. But where there is *life* there is *persis-*

tence of form and order. The cells are the smallest units of living matter which are capable of maintaining order through metabolism, growth, and reproduction.

Many *single cells,* such as protozoans, various simple algae, and bacteria, are individuals able to live independently and to reproduce their kind. They are large enough to be seen through a microscope. I recall the time at college I saw amoebas and paramecia, both one-celled animals, moving around in a drop of water under a microscope. I was amazed to see such tiny creatures quietly and adequately going about their business. They seemed to know what they were doing, and had been at it for a long time, too, I was told.

Other cells have organized themselves into *multicellular* organisms, a plant or animal, in which various cells develop specialized functions more efficiently to serve each other's needs in a cooperative division of labor, and achieve a new level of *stability.* Biological cells, with the same fundamental structure, can assume an enormous variety of forms and functions.

Organization Of A Cell

A normal cell is composed of a nucleus, containing the genetic information that specifies the general structure and function, surrounded by cytoplasm laced with microsomes containing ribonucleic acid, which carry on protein synthesis, and mitochondria, which with the aid of catalytic enzymes metabolizes nutrients into usable *energy.* This schematic description of what is really a very intricate little system is meant only to indicate that a cell is an amazing organism with a highly ordered behavior pattern and ability to selectively utilize elements from its environment.

The ability to exploit energy from its environment is a function not only of the cell's internal structure but also of its *boundary.* A membrane encloses the unified diversity of entities and operations. The membrane is selectively permeable, admitting some chemicals from the environment and not others, which makes possible creative processes within the cell that could not take place in the undifferentiated environment. Since the skin of the cell permits selective transactions with the environment, the cell is an *open system*—which is one of the characteristics of a living system (von Bertalanffy, 1950, p. 155).

The significance of the cell's organization of entities within a boundary is emphasized by A. I. Oparin (1953, pp. 160, 163), associate director of the Biochemical Institute, USSR Academy of Science, in his suggestion as to the possible mode of the precellular organization of matter. He assumes that organic substances in the primordial chemical "soup" coalesced into "coacervates." He says:

> The formation of coacervates was a most important event in the evolution of the primary organic substances and in the process of autogeneration of life. Before the event organic matter was indissolubly fused with its medium, being diffused throughout the mass of the solvent. But with the formation of coacervates organic matter became concentrated at different points of the aqueous medium and, at the same time, sharp division occurred between the medium and the coacervate.
>
> So long as there was no delimitation between the organic substance and its aqueous environment; in other words, so long as it was still dissolved in the waters of the original hydrosphere of the Earth, the evolution of organic substance could be considered only in its entirety. But as soon as organic substance became spatially concentrated into coacervate droplets or bits of semiliquid colloidal gels; as soon as these droplets became separated from the surrounding medium by a more or less definite border, they at once acquired a certain degree of individuality. The future history of coacervate droplets could now follow different courses. Their fate was now dependent not only on external conditions of the medium but also on their own specific physico-chemical structure or organization.

It is the organization into a definite unit which makes it possible for a cell to be creative. Edmund Sinnott is convinced (1966, p. 21):

> that the presence of this biological organization is the most distinctive feature of life. Form itself is the visible expression of it.

The recent great advances in biochemical genetics have tended to obscure this fact and to focus attention primarily upon the individual genes and their composition. But the organism is more than a collection of genes. It is bound together as a unit. In every cell of an individual there seems to be something that represents the organized system as a whole, for every cell has the potentiality of reproducing the individual if conditions are favorable. This "something" is apparently an inherent norm or pattern to which development, from fertilized egg to adult, tends to move.

The Coalescent Dynamic

In the description of a cell as a bounded organization, we have left an implicit mystery which we now must consider: what dynamics bring the constituent elements together to form a cell? The crucial question is whether there are coalescing powers inherent in some types of matter which impel them toward combination. What starts the process going? Why are some chance meetings the beginning of a beautiful friendship? Is the *power* of organization primordial in *matter* itself?

In looking for the forces of *cohesion*, we need not posit some power *external* to reality, some supernatural agency imposing order according to some preconceived plan of its own, or some vitalistic phenomenon which adds life to inert matter. The success of the sciences in tracing the continuities of evolution precludes the concept of any extraneous power. Instead, we find the dynamics for creating elementary forms in the special capacity of some atoms to establish covalent bonds. Therefore, in accounting for the emergence of elementary organisms, such as cells, we look to the nature of the components for the rudimentary forces which got them together.

Before organic chemists had synthesized practically all known organic substances in their test tubes, it was inconceivable, says Oparin, that organic substances could have been generated in the long process of natural evolution. But, since we now know the conditions for synthesizing organic substances, we need only to prove the possibility of such primary syntheses during remote periods of our planet's existence. Spectroscopic analysis of the light from stars reveals that among the elements of the cooler stars, carbon compounds are found. On our planet, carbon dioxide, vital to living organisms, is originally formed in the high temperatures and pressures of the interior of the earth and thrown out in volcanic eruptions. Willard F. Libby (1965, p. 3) describes how Dr. Stanley Miller, then a graduate student, with Dr. Harold C. Urey, then professor in the Department of Chemistry at The University of Chicago,

> . . . showed that simple inorganic gases, when mixed and subjected to electric discharges, can produce amino acids, and that these amino acids, which are the building blocks for proteins, can therefore be understood as being present—even in such simple systems—and ready for the magic wand or magic act, the life-giving touch which makes the beginning of life.

Carbon has a remarkable quality of forming complex compounds because of the ability of its atoms to unite into chains or rings. Some coagulation of the helter-skelter of randomly moving particles is achieved because some of the "particles are already to a certain extent oriented with regard to each other," says Oparin. (1953, p. 162) We also find that proteins, essential constituents of all living cells, have a special proclivity for combination. Oparin states that: "Meyer and Mark have shown that owing to their high content of the fat absorbing 'lipophil groups' (phenyl, methyl, etc.), proteins manifest a very strong tendency to form molecular associations (Oparin, 1953, p. 147). In summary, Oparin says (1953, p. 136):

> The carbon atom in the sun's atmosphere does not represent organic matter, but the exceptional capacity of this element to form long atomic chains and to unite with other elements, such as hydrogen, oxygen, and nitrogen, is the hidden spring which under proper conditions of existence has furnished the impetus for the formation of organic compounds. Similarly, protein is by no means living matter, but hidden in its chemical structure is the capacity for further organic evolution which, under certain conditions, may lead to the origin of living things.

Such mutual attractions can account for the formation of organizations. Protein molecules bring us, says Harvard biologist George Wald (1965, pp. 22-23):

> . . . to the borders of biological structure, for such giant molecules as the phospholipids, have enormous tendencies to spin higher orders of structure, highly organized aggregates that at times are hardly to be told apart from the structures of living cells.
>
> A notable example is collagen, the principal protein of cartilage. . . . In collagen fibrils we are dealing not with single molecules but with great aggregates of molecules, regularly oriented with regard to one another and regularly spaced as in a crystal. The extraordinary thing is that one can dissolve collagen, so completely randomizing this structure, and then by very simple means precipitate it out of solution, when it reaggregates in this specific, quasi-crystalline condition, hardly to be told apart under the electron microscope from what one finds in the connective tissues of living organisms.

The *forces* causing the atoms in carbon and protein molecules to combine in their particular patterns are some among the several natural forces (electromagnetic fields, gravity) known to shape behaviors and structures ranging in size from subatomic particles to galaxies. Kirtley Mather is quoted (by Sinnott, 1966, pp. 74-75) as saying that such forces "come as near to being ultimate causes as the mind can grasp. They cannot be directly experienced by sense perception, but their reality is now beyond challenge."

These observations about the dynamics of coalescence, while not exhaustive nor conclusive, seem to me to indicate that the cohesive forces which form organisms are functions of qualities of attraction *inherent* in the constituents, and make it unnecessary to posit additional and extraneous force.

Once elements cluster, what process organizes them into forms? What is the origin of their structure? Morphogenesis, suggests A. Katchalsky (1971, p. 113), may be a consequence of the ability of chemical processes to structure matter in patterns. Referring to a number of experiments which support this hypothesis, he concludes, "... the interaction of diffusional and chemical flows leads to a distribution of substances which might play an important role in the processes of differentiation and morphogenesis." This is a way of envisioning how order emerges from disorder, but still does not account for life.

The Alchemy

The alchemy, or what Libby previously called "the life-giving touch," in an organism is the *interaction* of its parts. If, when entities were brought together, there were no interactions, there would be no life. The process of creativity begins when the entities which have formed an organization enter into *cooperative* relations through which the activities of each supplies the needs of others.

The entities behave differently when interacting in a cell than when swimming freely, and new capacities emerge. Von Bertalanffy (1950, p. 148) comments:

> If you take any realm of biological phenomena, whether embryonic development, metabolism, growth, activity of the nervous system, biocoenosis, etc., you will always find that the behavior of an element is different within the system from what it is in isolation.

And Oparin (1953, p. 148) points out that

> Rubinstein has shown that such properties as heat coagulation, surface precipitation, permeability, electrical properties, etc., cannot be explained on the basis of the properties of some one protoplasmic component, like the proteins, lipids, etc., but are the resultant of correlation and reciprocal action of different colloidal systems, which make up the protoplasm.

Sinnott (1966, p. 255) concludes, "There appear to be no specific living *substances* at all; but life inheres, rather, in the way these various things are related and built into a precise system." Thus, it seems to me, the living quality of a cell is a function of the interaction of its parts within an organization, from which new powers emerge. Such new creative powers are the alchemy of life.

Living processes could not occur within a system without the input of *energy*. Thus, cells or any organisms are what Katchalsky (1971, p. 107) calls "dissipative flow structures . . . they survive only on energy input which is dissipated in the maintenance of structure." The requirement of input and conversion of energy distinguishes open living systems from "equilibrium structures," such as a chair, which do not require energy investment but maintain their closed structures by strong bonds.

Metabolism, which transforms energy within a cell, is a breakdown of chemicals from the environment into forms usable for the vital processes, a conversion facilitated by enzymes, which are powerful catalytic agents, when their reactions are properly and mutually coordinated.

Mutuality

Who *directs* the operations within the cell? The answer seems to be that no one does; the constituents mutually influence each other. Who does what seems to be a function of both relative *position* and the *sequence* of operations of the constituents. Jacques Monod (1971, p. 63), Director of the Pasteur Institute in Paris, says the operations within a cell form a coherent system through "microscopic cybernetics." As the coordination of cells in a whole body is provided by the nervous and endocrine system, "... we now know that within each cell a cybernetic network hardly less (if not still more) complex guarantees the functional coherence of the intracellular chemical machinery...." Control operations are handled by specialized proteins acting as detectors and transducers of chemical information. The regulatory patterns by which functions are coordinated are: "feedback inhibition," when the product of an enzyme catalysis inhibits further production and thus governs its own rate of synthesis; "feedback activation," when the product of degradation of a compound activates an enzyme to produce more of the compound, thus maintaining the necessary compound at an optimum level; "parallel activation," when parallel sequences of metabolism activate each other to produce balanced amounts of metabolites for assembly into larger molecules, and activation of an enzyme by the material on which it acts. Thus, there is no higher authority which directs the operations according to a preconceived plan.

The type of products of an interaction within a cell are dependent upon both the structure of the relationships and the sequence of operations. Oparin (1953, p. 201) says,

> Alteration of the inner physico-chemical structure also changes the sequence in which one reaction follows the other and, therefore, changes the character of the entire biochemical process. It is in this manner that organization determines the course of vital phenomena.

For instance, in the process of fermentation, the products of one reaction are immediately subjected to the next reaction and if the sequence of reactions is somewhat altered, an altogether different end product is formed. (Oparin, 1953, p. 120)

Sinnott (1957, p. 41) makes it clear that the pattern of relations in a cell affects the nature of their interaction when he says, "The fate of every particle is the result of its position in the whole."

The interactions within a cell are *coordinated* by the exchange of chemical and electrical messages, a *communications system* with feedback which makes it possible for one constituent to alter its messages when another entity begins to behave differently. Activities going on within a cell seem to be a dynamic system of checks and balances.

Edmund Sinnott (1957, pp. 95-96) provides a good summary of what we have been discovering about the organization of cells so far:

> A living thing is not a collection of parts and traits but an *organized system,* well called an organism. In this no part or process is an independent event but each is related to the others. . . . They are not aggregates but *integrates.* This process of *biological* organization is the unique feature of living things. If anything

distinguishes them from purely physical mechanisms, this, I believe, is it. Life is more than a series of lifeless chemical processes. These are part of it, but it transcends them and pulls
them all together. I can best define life as *the process by which
matter is brought together in organized and integrated systems
capable of self-perpetuation and of change.*

The New Being

The cell as an integrated system is a new being; it exists as an
island of self-organized order using energy from the environment
to maintain itself. The evolutionary process has produced a *novelty,* the emergence of a new form, a new gestalt. Michael Polanyi
(1967) says the process is ". . . a self transformation that achieves
a higher existence, and its structure is akin to that of a creative act
by which man can achieve a higher existence."

The new form comes into being when an integrated system
manifests qualities not found in the components. Oparin (1953,
p. 147) points out that even a mixture of chemicals takes on the
nature of new chemical compounds because electrostatic and
electromagnetic fields of force of the separate components may act
upon each other, whereby new means of attraction are produced.
"Thus," he says, "on mixing different substances new properties
appear which were absent in the component parts of the mixture."

When the elements mixed are not chemicals but complex
chemical entities, and when the mixed entities assume patterned
relationships, significant order arises from disorder. This *emergent* novelty, says Alfred E. Emerson (1966, pp. 55-56), The University of Chicago Professor of Zoology Emeritus, answers the
very important question of how new beings are created, or how
life comes from the non-living, or even how mind evolves from pre-
mental life. "The hierarchy of organization," he says, "... illustrates
the process by which simpler units or entities become parts of
larger whole systems, and these larger wholes have new characteristics emerging from the synthesis of the new system."

C. Lloyd Morgan in his 1922 Gifford Lectures on *Emergent
Evolution* advanced the concept that life is an emergent from life-

less matter in the process of evolution. Traits and properties emerge which are radically different from anything which has gone before. We may infer that the specifically human traits of intelligence and spirit have emerged through the same process of physical-chemical interactions in a complex order. Alfred Stiernotte (1954, p. 36) comments: "Life is not some factor which intervenes *ab extra,* but something which supervenes at a certain degree of complexity of physico-chemical motions and is born of these motions."

"Synergism," the action of two or more substances, organs, or organisms to achieve an effect of which each individually is incapable, is the word we might use today to describe this creative process. To account for the mystery of new beings, we need not look beyond the synergistic process which spawns new beings at each level of complexity. We need posit no *dualism* of forces extraneous to nature to account for the creativity in nature; the creative dynamics inhere in nature.

Self Direction

Here we come to another critical point in this line of reasoning. We have noted that the entities which constitute a cell determine their relationships to each other in forming an organization. The question is whether a cell, or any living system, actively determines its relation to other entities in its external environment. Does a cell have an *attitude* which causes it to respond selectively to events around it?

We have already noted that cells are not preformed or preordained; they constitute themselves. It is the same process as that described by George Wald (1965, pp. 21-22), when he raises the question of who winds the helices:

Deoxyribonucleic acid, DNA, which forms the stuff of genes, characteristically forms a right-handed double helix, in which two nucleic acid chains form a spiral ladder, the rungs of which are made of complementary pairs of nucleotides. . . . Proteins again take characteristically the form of a spiral of helix, this time single and very tightly wound.

There was a time when all this was first becoming plain, when I asked myself—and I hope you will forgive the wording, which was just shorthand for what I really meant—Who winds the helices? The answer was not long in coming: The helices wind themselves. The most stable and hence the most probable condition for a nucleic acid or a protein molecule, or an artificial analogue of either, is to collapse into this characteristic geometry.

The question is whether the "characteristic geometry" of a helix or of a cell then has its own sense of *direction* in forming larger associations or in communicating with elements in the environment? Jerome Letvin (1965) suggests that neurons have a "point of view," selecting more of this and less of that kind of stimuli to transmit. Whitehead (1929, p. 35) calls the act of selecting "prehension," which is an exercise of preference, accepting from the environment what is consistent with an entity's form, rejecting what is not, according to its inherent appetites.

That a cell manifests a sense of self-direction is generally recognized. But there seems to be a problem in the use of words to describe it, a hang-up which obscures the significance of the self-orientation of living systems. The confusion seems to come from the implications of words we normally use for a sense of direction; traditionally we speak of *purpose* or *goal*, which implies an objective which has been preformed or preordained by some other authority. In our reaction to externally posited goals, we obscure the fact that cells have *subjective* intentions.

Some people who speak of a "regulatory system" generally mean self-direction, even when they also use the words "purpose" or "goal." For instance, Sinnott (1957, p. 68) says:

> Protoplasm is not a *substance* but a *system*. We must regard protoplasm, I think, as possessing a pattern which so regulates the course of changes that go on within it that a specific form or activity tends to result. This pattern is the "purpose" which leads to the achievement of the "goal"—the form of activity produced.

By making "pattern" and "purpose" synonymous, Sinnott has opened the way to getting past the hang-up caused by implicit notions of predetermination in such words as "purpose" and "goal." But in order to avoid the mental block to recognizing the factor of subjective intention or inner-directedness in non-human beings, we had better eschew the use of such anthropomorphic terms as "purpose" and "goal," as well as "teleology."

Instead, I suggest that we redeem the old word "entelechy," used by Aristotle for that which realizes or makes actual the otherwise merely potential. In my usage, it means the drive of an organism to fulfill the requirements of its own form, an inherent orientation. The word has been corrupted for many scientists, especially biologists, by Leibniz's identification of his category of "monads" or spiritual substances as entelechies by virtue of their inner self-determined activity, and especially by Driesch, in connection with his vitalistic biology, who used the term "entelechy" to denote an external perfecting principle. But the root meaning of "entelechy" is the compulsion of a being to perfect or complete or make real its own form. It is the pre-symbolic drive of an organism to counter the tendency toward entropy and maintain or perfect its own nature. For an organism, a state of maximum entropy is death and disintegration. The entelechy is a basic and powerful selective principle, which in human beings is more determinative of behavior than ideas or goals.

Consciously to hold a *purpose* or *goal* is a peculiarly *human* capability which is misapplied to other forms of beings without highly developed brains. "True purposiveness is characteristic of human behavior, and it is connected with the evolution of the symbolism of language and concepts," says von Bertalanffy (1950, p. 160). A being's inner intentions can be oriented toward an externalized goal only when the sense of direction can be objectified in symbols or words. Therefore, by definition, only language-using human beings can speak of purpose. Ralph S. Lillie (1945, pp. 196 and 201) has said:

> Conscious purpose, as it exists in ourselves, is to be regarded as a highly evolved derivative of a more widely diffused natural condition or property, which we may call "directiveness." . . . In the characteristic unification of the organism an integrative principle or property is acting which is similar in its essential nature to that of which we are conscious in mental life. . . . Conscious purpose is to

be regarded as only one form of biological integration; the integration shown in embryonic development is apparently unconscious, and the same appears to be true of most physiological relations. Such biological facts point to the existence of a more general integrative property or activity of a fundamental kind which is universally present in living organisms, from amoeba to man.

Non-human living systems without conscious purpose thus have a capability for *orienting* themselves in, and organizing elements from, their environment. "When dead matter, random and fortuitous in its distribution, enters a living organism," says Sinnott (1957, p. 41), "it comes under the control of a regulatory system which molds this hitherto disorganized system into a complex organic pattern of a very precise sort." This self-regulatory system is clearly manifest in the way an injured organism restores itself. He (1957, p. 33) points out:

> The precise form an organism assumes is a visible expression of its organization, and the orderly development march is the means by which this comes to being. . . . If normal development is disturbed, there at once begins a series of processes which tend to restore it. Injuries are healed. Missing parts are regenerated. Altered patterns are reconstituted so that a whole and typical individual tends to be produced. The *self-regulating* capacity of organisms is often shown more dramatically in these modifications of their development progress than in the normal development itself. . . . Organization is a regulatory process.

The self-regulatory process in non-human organisms is apparently different in degree from that in human beings, but not in kind. When an organism builds itself according to a plan of its own, this "plan is experienced subjectively as a purpose, the beginning of mind," says Sinnott (1957, p. 212). This self-designing, he continues, "is the vital difference between a lifeless mechanism and a living one." Bergson points out that when a chick pecks its way out of its shell, a new instinct has not taken over, but the behavior is the continuance of the pattern which has brought its embryonic life thus far. In the same way mind has emerged as an extension of the self-regulatory pattern. In support of this view, Sinnott (1957, p. 48) quotes from J. C. Smuts, "Mind is a continuation, on a much higher plane, of the system of organic regulation and coordination which characterizes Holism in organisms." Sinnott (1957, p. 48) concludes, "Mind is thus the direct descendent of organic regulation and carries forward the same task." Mind is thus, if you accept these suggestions, also an emergent from the continuous evolutionary process, operating at a significantly higher level of complexity but nonetheless part and parcel with the process.

I belabor this point about mind being an extension of self-regulation and intention because it will be important to remember when we come to consider living systems of greater magnitude which do not have a brain, but do have subjective orientation.

Self-regulated cells coordinated in a larger system exercise a mutual influence. W. H. Goodenough points out (1962, p. 111): ". . . the processes going on at one level of organization affect the patterns which emerge at a higher level of organization. This is as true of cultural as of biological evolution. A community takes its shape, and its institutions are established, as a result of the actions of individual people." Conversely, N. Botnariuc (1966, p. 97) says, "The functioning *direction* of the system of laws of a certain level is determined by the more general laws of the higher level systems." The influence of the pattern of self-regulation of a higher-level system upon the development of its constituents is what is really happening in natural selection. The direction of natural selection is determined by the laws of the ecological system within which a species lives. It is species, not individuals, which are selected because biological adaptation through random mutation of genes occurs at the species level; individuals strive for *adequacy* through varying "counteractive responses to changes in the environment," says Botnariuc (1966, pp. 95, 97). Natural selection is a link in the control mechanism of an ecological system, he says:

The modification of the relations within the biocoenosis [a community of diverse organisms living in a circumscribed environment] will inevitably lead to the change of place occupied by the species in the economy of the ecosystem, to a change of direction in natural selection.

Or, as Fuller and Putnam (1966, p. 110) put it:

> In a sense the theory of evolution does not so much explain the origin of the diversity of the forms of life as pass the buck to the diversity in the environment. It is the highly specialized and varied ecological niches that produce patterned diversity of plant and animal life on the basis of adaptive radiation into the available niches.

Thus, living systems exercise determinative *influences* on other systems quite aside from the use of intelligence or symbolic communications. Smaller systems communicate with larger just by what they produce, and larger systems determine the direction of growth of smaller systems by "natural selection"—a mutant perishes which does not fit into its ecological niche.

An Autonomous Individual

When a cell consistently acts according to its own self-direction, it becomes a *centralized* system and therefore an individual, as von Bertalanffy (1950, pp. 150-151) points out:

> The principle of centralization is especially important in the biological realm. Progressive segregation is often connected with progressive centralization, the expression of which is the time-dependent evolution of a leading part. . . . At the same time, the principle of progressive centralization is that of progressive individualization. An "individual" can be defined as a centralized system.

The focusing of the tendencies within a cell, the channeling of all the preferences of the constituents of a cell through a central point, gives a *unity* to the cell that makes it an *individual.*

Now, the question is whether a cell in a larger system has *freedom* to initiate action, or simply reacts to its environment. Except for one-celled organisms, cells are integrated into larger organisms whose collective tendencies condition the action of the cells, which raises the question of whether cells are in any sense autonomous. We have already seen that the cell as a bounded unit responds selectively to its environment; as an open system it chooses what other entities it will relate to. Moreover, by definition a cell is free or it could not enter into relations to form a larger whole, according to Hartshorne (1962, p. 202):

> The social view of organic unity is that individuals form organs for other individuals. This proposition is convertible: namely, if individuals are organs, organs are individuals, singly or in groups. Now an individual is self-active; if there are many individuals in the ultimate organism there are many self-active agents in that organism. Being is action, what is really many must act as many. The higher is compounded of the lower, not by suppression but by preservation of the dynamic integrity of the lower. The cosmos could not guarantee that the many individuals within it will act always in concord; for to carry out such a guarantee the cosmos must completely coerce the lesser individuals, that is, must deprive them of all individuality. Existence is essentially social, plural, free, and exposed to risk, and this is required for our conception of organism. For if the action of the parts had no freedom with respect to the whole, there would be no dynamic distinction between whole and parts and the very idea of a whole would lose its meaning.

The degree of *autonomy* or freedom depends upon the degree of *interdependence* of the parts within the living system. The constituents of a cell may be so tightly structured and so interdependent that they have little autonomy, although the malignancy of cells when they become cancerous and destroy the organism within which they live, and hence themselves with it, illustrates that even with high interdependency there is final local autonomy. Alvin W. Gouldner defines the correlation between autonomy and interdependence when he says that there are varying degrees of interdependence, depending upon whether an individual exists in mutual interchange with all other parts of the system, or with only one other part, and the autonomy varies accordingly. Gouldner (1959, p. 254) adds:

Still another way of viewing interdependence is from the standpoint of the parts' dependence upon the system. The parts may have varying amounts of their needs satisfied by, and thus varying degrees of dependence upon, other system elements. A number of parts which are engaged in mutual interchanges may, at one extreme, all be totally dependent on each other for the satisfaction of their needs. In this case the *system* they comprise can be said to be "highly" interdependent, while these *parts* can be said to possess "low" functional autonomy. Conversely, a system may be composed of parts all of which derive but little satisfaction of their needs from each other; here the system may be minimally interdependent and the parts would be high on functional autonomy. Operationally speaking, we might say that the functional autonomy of a system part is the probability that it can survive separation from the system.

The *functional autonomy* of parts of a system is necessary to its survival, says Gouldner; otherwise there would be no possibility of the system's increasing its *adequacy* by changing to respond to tensions produced by changes in the environment. When new challenges emerge in the environment, the system would either collapse under the impact of powerful disruptions, or it would have to undergo radical structural reorganization. (Gouldner, 1959, p. 261) *Internal rigidity unfits a system for survival.*

With such functional autonomy, how can there be relative stability to maintain the integrity of an organism? If entities within the system are *free* to do as they choose, how can the system become and remain *organized?* Some of the entities in the system will be disorderly, but overall stability is maintained if a sufficient number of constituents respond cooperatively to the messages circulating in the system. We are here confronted with a situation where the *laws of probability* or statistical mechanics apply. By which I mean that the integrity of the system is maintained by the correlated functioning of a *majority of the constituents; the pattern of operations is a statistical* one. Organisms have back-up mechanisms so that when one channel of operations breaks down, another takes over. The indeterminacy of action of particular parts becomes determinate, probabilistically, when a sufficient number of constituents are involved. Thus a relatively stable configuration of activities is manifested in a living system with autonomous parts.

Duration

A cell is not eternal, but its form does endure. To counter disorganization, it is not necessary that a particular structure be permanent. It is necessary only that the *form persists.* How does a living system achieve duration of its own order? Duration of order is achieved by maintaining *continuity of order* through *change in substance.* This is done in two ways. First, the persistence of the pattern is achieved by constantly and rapidly replacing the constituents of the cells. "It is the basic characteristic of every organic system that it maintains itself in a state of perpetual change of its components," says von Bertalanffy (1950, p. 155):

> In the cell there is a perpetual destruction of its building materials through which it endures as a whole. . . . In the multicellular organism, cells are dying and are replaced by new ones, but it maintains itself as a whole. . . . Thus every organic system appears stationary if considered from a certain point of view. But what seems to be a persistent entity on a certain level, is maintained, in fact, by a perpetual change, building up and breaking down of systems of the next lower order; of chemical compounds in the cell, of cells in the multicellular organisms, of individuals in the ecological system.

Duration through the constant restoration of substance underlines the fact that it is the *pattern* and not the *substance* which endures, as J. Z. Young points out (1966, p. 242):

> Individual chemical atoms remain in the cells for only a short time; what is preserved must be the pattern in which all these interchanging atoms are involved. . . . Biology, like physics, has ceased to be materialist. Its basic unit is a non-material entity, namely an organization. . . .

The organization maintains the dynamic and exquisitely complex physical and chemical components of its system in a state of delicate balance or homeostasis. Without some connecting *unity* of organization, the components would *fragment.* The steady-state is the consequence of the system's capacity "to maintain multiple variables within a stability range. This steady state is maintained despite wide environmental fluctuations by negative feedback processes," says James Miller (1965, p. 108). Oparin (1953, p. 186-87) points out that the decomposition of organic compounds within a system releases energy necessary for the synthesis of new substances, but duration is achieved by the preponderance of the synthesizing process:

> In the protoplasm, owing to the existence of a definite physico-chemical organization, the chemical processes are so reciprocally coordinated that a decomposed substance is at once replaced by a newly synthesized one, and a structure which had been destroyed is immediately restored. Thus, there is a constant exchange of substances, but synthesis always predominates over destruction, and this creates the dynamic stability of the system.

However, in the process of self-renewal "copy errors" accumulate and gradually undermine the capacity of the organism to maintain its organization. Microscopic entities "undergo quantum perturbations, whose accumulation within a macroscopic system will slowly but surely alter its structure," says Monod (1971, p. 111):

> Aging and death in pluricellular organisms is accounted for, at least in part, by the piling up of accidental errors of translation. These, in particular affecting certain components responsible for the accuracy of translation, tend to precipitate further errors which, ever more frequent, gradually and inexorably undermine the structure of those organisms.

Since the replacement of the constituents of an organism gradually *degenerates* an organism, cells and organisms have evolved a second strategy for duration, that of *duplicating* themselves. Cells or one-celled animals accomplish reproduction by dividing in two, following which each half grows to a normal cell, an exact copy of the parent cell. In more complex organisms of structured cells, reproduction is mostly *sexual,* in which case half of the genes randomly selected form each parent produce a new offspring, with novel characteristics, thus introducing variety into the species. In any case, order issues from order through reproduction. Or, as Whitehead (1948, p. 127) has put it, "Endurance requires a succession of durations, each exhibiting the pattern."

In summary, I think we can say that a cell is a very successful little living system in its self-organization to produce order from chaos. The *primordial dynamics of attraction* in the chemical or electromagnetic bonds of the elements amalgamated the basic elements in ever increasingly complex forms of organization which comprised an open system with a boundary within which selective interactions could achieve new functions, including the conversion of energy, in order to maintain the form through change. Once established, the cell becomes determinative of its parts, and *self-directs* its further development, thus becoming an autonomous individual in control of its own destiny, and achieves *duration*. In short, the cell has become an organism, a highly complex structure of parts so integrated that the relation of the parts to one another is governed by their mutual relation to the whole.

By what stretch of the imagination can we assume that the anatomy of a cell can teach us something about the nature of reality as a whole? Two concepts from the sciences can justify our tracing "hidden likenesses" between cells and larger orders of being: the concept of the *continuity* of all being, and the concept of the *hierarchy* of levels of organization. I have already used the words "continuity" and "levels," but let us see what the implications of these words are as generalized concepts.

Continuity of Being

The continuity of all being has become evident to us in the continuing process of evolution. The conclusion of Darwin that each existent species evolved from a pre-existent type, rather than having been created as an original type, leads to the recognition that all being exists in a continuum, a spectrum of entities including the inorganic and the organic, the inanimate and the animate. This conception of continuity has been reinforced, as Ralph Burhoe (1966), has pointed out:

> The scientists in this century particularly have built a web of relationships and interdependence among entities and their histories located along a dimension of increasing inclusion of subsystems, such as the interdependence ranging from the system of human civilization down through subcultures to individual men, to their organic parts, to the hundred billion cells that constitute these, to the chemical compounds that constitute these, to the subatomic particles that constitute these. Nowhere are there encountered any disruptive discontinuities, although in the realm of the more infinitesimal entities one must now be satisfied with laws which are valid only for large numbers of the hypothecated events.

In this continuity of being, the boundary between the living and the non-living is wavering and vague. If we look down the scale of organization of organisms, we come to a system which under varying conditions exhibits the properties of life and of non-life: a virus. The tobacco virus, for instance, in crystalline form seems to be a dead system which can be heated, frozen, and dissolved and recrystallized, but it cannot reproduce itself. Then put the tobacco virus into a nutrient cell at a proper temperature and it becomes a living system, growing and reproducing itself. (Brown, 1966, ch. IV, p. 3.)

It becomes increasingly clear that the evolutionary process shapes the development of matter in all its forms. Harlow Shapley (1966, pp. 280-81), Harvard astronomer, is of the opinion that:

> *All* the chemical elements, all matter, we now believe, has evolved, and is currently evolving, from the simplest and lightest of atoms—from hydrogen.
>   Thus we have evidence of a truly wide Cosmic Evolution from hydrogen to *Homo,* and probably somewhere an evolution beyond the *Homo* level of sentiency. We have in Cosmic

Evolution a fundamental principle of growth that affects the chemical atoms as well as plants and animals, the stars and nebulae, space-time and mass-energy. In brief, everything that we can name, everything material and non-material, is involved. It is around this Cosmic Evolution that we might build revised philosophies of religion.

If all matter has evolved from hydrogen, it obviously follows that we would expect to find the same elements throughout the universe, which is confirmed by MIT physicist Sanborn C. Brown (1966, ch. III, p. 4), "There is ... no indication that what we observe as the structure of matter in the farthest reaches of space is different in any detail than those we see in our laboratories or find on the surface of the earth."

Not only are the same structures of matter observable throughout the universe, but the same chemical and physical laws operate throughout. The law of gravity works just as specifically to hold me to my seat as it does to hold the planets in their orbits, or the laws of physics and chemistry work just as precisely to produce the energy in the sun by fusion of hydrogen nuclei as they do in producing the explosion of a hydrogen bomb.

Theodosius Dobzhansky, late Professor Emeritus of Genetics at Rockefeller University, said in a lecture at The University of Chicago (May 1, 1967) that evolution is a differing process at inorganic, organic, and human levels, but however disparate the processes, they are part of a single story: "The whole show is a single undertaking."

Hierarchy of Levels of Organization

The second concept from the sciences which justifies our use of analogies in order to understand the nature of reality as a whole is the concept of levels, or hierarchy. The evolutionary continuum has differentiated the organization of matter and entities in organizations on a scale of magnitude and on a scale of complexity. In its evolution, the stuff of reality has burgeoned in distinctive forms that emerge as an hierarchy of integrated beings. Charles Hartshorne (1941, p. 207) is of the opinion that:

... we shall never understand the world, or the problem of God, until we learn to see reality as a system of individuals on many levels and of many kinds, and that individual in the primary sense of *dynamic one* is to be contrasted with mere segments of reality carved out more or less arbitrarily by the beholding mind.

And von Bertalanffy says (1950, p. 164):

Reality, in the modern conception, appears as a tremendous hierarchial order of organized entities, leading in a superposition of many levels, from physical and chemical to biological and sociological systems. Unity of Science is granted, not by a utopian reduction of all sciences to physics and chemistry, but by the structural uniformities of the different levels of reality.

The concept of levels refers primarily to the emergence of new definite forms with an order of their own and with qualities hitherto non-existent, such as life, mind, and culture, and which, while novel, exist in continuity and interaction with entities at other levels. Each level of being has its own style of being according to its own laws. "Methodologically," says Abraham Edel (1966, p. 93), "a new level requires new descriptive concepts and, many believe, new empirical laws, independent of those on the old level." Hence, when we speak of levels, we are speaking not only of the emergence of integrated organizations but also of laws which describe their predictable operations.

Botnariuc (1966, p. 93) says that the features of open systems, from the atomic level to ecological systems, of wholeness, self-control feedback circuits, and steady state

... are shared in common with all the representative units of the various levels of organization, but they are differently realized in the units belonging to different levels, owing to the fact that each organization level has its specific organization and functional features, as well as its own laws.

A significant implication of the levels of systems is stated by Botnariuc (1966, p. 95):

Due to their simultaneous existence, the open systems are in relations of successive subordinations, so that the individual

level systems may be considered as subsystems of the population (species) system, the latter being in its turn a subsystem of
the biocoenosis system, etc.

The successive subordination of biological systems of various
levels is also reflected in the relations between the specific laws
of different levels. *The direction of the law's action at a certain
level is determined in the last analysis by the more general laws
of the next level.*

Thus the line of development of a particular system is circumscribed by its participation in the next higher level of organization,
unless the particular system decides that messages from other
sources, perhaps still higher levels, are more pressing and risks
"insubordination."

Since many configurations of reality can be conceived as a
hierarchy of systems organized in ever more comprehensive
levels, why should we presume that the self-organizing activity no
longer prevails beyond the level of organisms, especially of human
beings? Why should we presume that all existence more inclusive
than an organism is composed only of aggregates of autonomous
entities? It may be a conceit of ours that, since we are so successful
in adapting the environment to our needs, we are the ultimate
living system.

James G. Miller suggests (1965, p. 110) that each system is a
subsystem of a suprasystem:

Thus, *cells* form the *tissues* and *organs* of an organism. ...
Organisms usually live together in different sorts of groups—
herds, families, tribes, working teams, and many other face-to-
face groups. *Groups* are subsystems of *organizations*, which in
turn make up *societies*. There are limited supranational systems, like alliances or economic communities, and in recent
years early precursors of world-wide supranational systems may
be beginning to appear. Finally, there is the largest living
organization of all—the biota of the world, all the life on the
planet. This forms a system [biosphere] with the planet itself.

Living Systems

Now we can see whether what we learned about a living system
from an analysis of an organic cell can give us insights into the

nature of living systems as a generalized concept. We have seen that living systems emerge as a voluntary association of interacting parts which form a self-directed organization, and that the most stable elements in reality are not aggregates of matter but patterns of relationships of integrated particles of matter. The question is whether the categories characteristic of cells are analogous to categories in all living systems. We will not expect to find a one-to-one correlation, nor do we require it, as each level of order acquires its own style and laws corresponding to its structure and functions.

The concept of reality as an hierarchy of wholes is difficult to visualize, since we are inside the larger wholes. But the conception of wholes is becoming much more general. The concept of "wholeness" is becoming more central in biology, psychology, sociology, and in other sciences, as indicated by the more frequent use of such expressions as "system," "gestalt," "organism," "interaction," and "the whole is greater than the sum of its parts." Botnariuc comments (1966, p. 93), "Wholeness is the most striking feature of the systems at all levels of living matter. It arises and develops as a result of structural differentiation and functional specialization within the given system."

In considering levels of wholes, we have to distinguish between magnitude and complexity. Complexity is not a function of magnitude; in fact, some larger wholes are less complex. Teilhard de Chardin (1966, pp. 23-24) points out that there are not only the infinitely small and the infinitely large, but also the infinitely complicated. Cosmic evolution, he says, moves in two main directions: expanding from the infinitesimal to the immense and, folding in upon itself and centering on itself, from the extremely simple to the immensely complex. Therefore, we will not expect to find a correlation between magnitude and complexity. The greater system will not through the whole scale of magnitude always be the more complex and efficient. In short, *suprasystems will not necessarily have all the attributes of human beings.*

Another confusion can be cleared up by making a distinction between living and non-living systems. A living system, we have seen, emerges from non-living matter as order from disorder or chaos. Dead matter is not the opposite of living matter, for it is the system that lives, not the material. "Dead" as an adjective describes an *organic form* which has once lived but has lost its power to maintain its organization. There is a difference in kinds of organization of matter. All living systems are organized matter, but not every organization of matter is a living system. A *living system* is distinguished by self-organization, interaction, a communication network with feedback, self-direction, autonomy, and duration achieved by self-replacement and replication. A cell or a person has these qualities.

We also speak of systems which have none of those qualities and are *not living,* such as sewer systems or mechanical systems. My typewriter, for instance, is a beautiful *mechanical system,* but it is not living: it is not self-organizing, it is made by people; it is not interacting in its parts but is a one-way mechanical linkage; it has no internal signal system or feedback circuits; it is not self-motivated but is activated by the force of my fingers; it has no autonomy; and though I expect it to last a few years, it has no duration either by self-replacement of worn-out parts or by duplicating itself. Incidentally, we might avoid confusion if we did not use mechanical analogies for living systems (speaking of "cell mechanisms," for instance) since living and non-living systems function differently. The exertion of force to induce a reaction is appropriate only for non-living systems with mechanical linkages, not for living systems where interaction is coordinated by a communications network.

We have no difficulty recognizing that in animals cells are organized into organs which perform various functions, and the organs are integrated in an organism, a being about whose quality of living we have no doubt. But when we consider more *inclusive if less complex systems,* we are only coming to realize that they have *qualities of life.* Why assume that the self-organizing, self-directing, energy-using activities cease at the level of human beings? I propose that we conceive of our immediate environment, at least to the level of the whole planet *Earth,* as *a living system* with the characteristics of a cell if not of a person. I have already quoted James G. Miller's remark that systems exist at various levels and that "Finally, there is the largest living organization of all—the biota of the world, all the life on the planet. This forms a system with the planet itself."

The relatively new science of *ecology*, the study of the inter-relations between organisms and the environment as a series of interlocking systems, is opening new vistas into the nature of the total environment. Paul Bigelow Sears (1967, v. 7, p. 922), Emeritus Professor of Conservation, Yale University, comments that "it should be kept in mind that earth, atmosphere, individual organisms, and communities of organisms all represent dynamic systems, or processes, whose mutual interplay is the concern of the ecologist." Plants and animals are interrelated in highly complex ecological communities which, with their non-living environment form ecosystems on land and in the sea. Ecosystems perform "community metabolism" and use energy more efficiently.

Ecosystems evolve from simple to more complex forms, tending to converge in a climax community suitable to the climate of the region. An example of such succession is when a lake fills in and becomes a grassy prairie or a beech-maple forest. Such climax communities endure unchanged, unless new factors are introduced, such as climatic changes, fire, pests, or bulldozers. Thus, ecosystems organize themselves for the more efficient use of energy under given conditions. Sears says (1966, vol. 7, p. 922):

> Succession represents a process of increasing integration between life and environment. It apparently tends to follow the principle of Le Chatelier as developed by Bancroft, i.e.: heterogeneous systems tend progressively toward a condition of minimum disturbance by external forces and internal stresses. So far as the somewhat limited evidence goes, succession also tends towards a progressively more efficient use of energy. The climax community is a close-knit and delicately balanced system which stores and uses solar energy. So intimately adjusted are the nutrient and reproductive cycles of its constituent organ-

isms that the minimum of useful energy is wasted in the chain of metabolic relationships. Thus the climax community represents the maximum in organic economy, as contrasted with the extreme of energy waste in a bare area which receives solar energy only to dissipate it into space without benefit to living organisms.

The oceans provide habitats for numerous plant and animal communities which merge in a vast ecosystem with overlapping borders at the beaches with other ecological systems.

The thin layer of atmosphere forms a global weather system, and pollution of the air in sufficient quantity anywhere affects the quality of the air everywhere.

Human beings, wherever they live, are parts of these ecosystems, often modifying or destroying natural communities as a consequence of density of human population or the advanced development of technology, which so far has flourished at the expense of the exploitation of energy stored in fossil fuels, or the ruthless harvesting of plant and animal life. We have also learned to husband plant and animal life to the benefit of our own food chain.

With our distinctive capacity for intentional behavior, we also have organized our own form of living systems, human communities from families to nations. You can trace the succession of human communities toward more complex and efficient organization just as you can that of certain natural ecosystems toward a climax forest. But to make a long story short, let's look at the (so far in human history) climax social system—a nation, specifically the United States of America, as a living system.

The constituents of the nation are its citizens who are voluntarily associated to increase survival ability (a dynamic obscured by birthright citizenship) by mutually serving each other's needs through specialized activities. Within the nation are subsystems (organs) to serve particular needs, such as families, businesses, industries, schools, hospitals, churches, clubs, city and state governments, et al. The system converts energy by raising and distributing food and by manufacturing power with water, fossil fuel, and atomic energy electrical generating plants. The nation has a boundary which it defends against invasion, but which is open to a selective exchange of people, goods, and services with other nations. It has a complex web of communications which integrates its activities. The nation is self-forming, self-directing, and autonomous. All of its tendencies are centered in a national administration which expresses the sense of direction of the whole, thus achieving individuality epitomized in such phrases as "national policy," "the American way of life," or "Uncle Sam." The nation achieves duration by constantly replacing its population and renewing its subsystems, though it is still an open question whether it has achieved the stability of a climax forest, since it has not yet developed an efficient use of energy.

It seems to me that a nation as a living system has most of the attributes of a cell. And there are compulsions toward forming the nations into a global human community, such as increasing economic interdependence and satellite communication systems. Human intentional communities as well as biological communities tend toward forming planetary living systems.

Teilhard de Chardin (1966, pp. 40-41), the French priest and paleontologist, suggested that the earth's being round brings the biological systems around to meet themselves and form a global system, the biosphere, which he proposes is "a truly structural layer of the planet, a sensitive film on the heavenly body that bears us." He also thought that the sphericity of the earth is forcing culture to become "totalized" into a "noosphere (or thinking sphere) superimposed upon, and coextensive with (but in so many ways more close-knit and homogeneous) the biosphere." The very shape of the globe sets a boundary within which all of life and all of culture are bound to interact. If the earth were flat, these phenomena would simply dissipate continuously away from themselves, forming no systems. But the oceans, the atmosphere, the biosphere, and the noosphere do form interdependent global systems, which indicates to me that the *earth itself is a great living system*. The whole earth may be seen as a vast dissipative energy-flow structure using energy from the sun to create and sustain order from disorder, with the same self-organizing characteristics as a cell.

Since the earth is part of larger orders of the solar system and of the Milky Way galaxy, why not carry the living-systems analogy further up the scale of levels of being? Simply because at some point, it seems to me, we cross the indeterminate boundary of the living. The dimension of magnitude loses something on the scale of complexity which is so essential to life.

Our solar system is certainly an order held together by gravity balanced by centrifugal force, but it seems to be a simple system in which there is not much interaction. Only the earth seems to be in a position to capitalize on the energy flow from the sun and provide conditions for the emergence of living forms. Certainly the solar system is self-created, but it has not achieved the capacity of self-renewal or reproduction in order to achieve duration on its own scale. Astronomers predict the eventual "heat-death" of the sun by exhaustion of the sun's energy-producing mass through radiation, although not for billions of years. The planets in their orbits around our sun seem to be ordered more by its mass than its energy flow, and as the mass is dissipated, so will the order be disrupted. But on the human time scale, *billions of years are a practical eternity.*

The Milky Way galaxy in which our solar system floats seems to be a relatively stable gravitational order which is more of an aggregation than a system. Though it is self-ordered and contains millions of energy-radiating suns, the amount of energy reaching our solar system is of such small consequence that interaction is negligible. In our galaxy we can not trace the characteristics of a living system. Although Harlow Shapley predicts that there are probably billions of other planets where conditions are as favorable for the evolution of living systems as they are on our planet, there is so far no interaction of any significance. The distance to the nearest star is about four light years, while the distance to our own sun is only about eight light minutes. Since light travels at the rate of 300,000 kilometers per second, we are speaking of "astronomical" distances. In our experience, a distance measured in light years is a *practical infinity.*

Beyond our galaxy, we don't seem to know what shape space is in. We are presented by astronomers with a number of cosmological models. Our galaxy may be an island universe among other island universes. Indeed, our "cosmos" conceived as an orderly system may be no more inclusive than the Milky Way, so that the "universe" does not comprise all constellations of matter in one system; beyond the galaxies is chaos.

We ask about the nature of *our environment* only insofar as it is relevant to our needs and interests in the *middle range* of time and space where we live. Reality is significant to us only to the extent that we interact with it. Selective interaction, as we have seen, takes place within a boundary. The levels of organization of matter seem to diffuse from indubitably living systems to nonliving cosmological orders and ultimate chaos where there is no boundary or interaction. At the macroscopic as well as the microscopic level, the borderline between living and non-living is indistinct.

However, the unclarity of ultimate boundaries is not critical. If we begin with the concrete organizations of the environment we experience, as we move out the scale of magnitude toward more remote organizations with which interaction is inconsequential, they also become less significant. I suggest a hypothesis that for us the *boundary of the cosmos as a living system* is to be found where *forces of attraction cease to operate to form communities within which important interaction takes place.*

One of Newton's laws specifies that every particle in the universe attracts every other particle with a force inversely proportional to the square of the distance between them. At some point, for all practical purposes the degree of separation makes the attraction inconsequential, and the distant entities are of little consequence to us.

In any case, for us it is not a critical question how far away the boundary of the great living system is, for the system is determinative not because of its *infinity,* but because of the conditions set by the *immediate continuities* of its organization. We are an intimate part of the interacting system in its *concrete immediacy,* and the question of how far beyond us the hierarchy of living systems ranges before they are finally bounded is not significant. What is critical for us is that we are involved in a hierarchy of living systems, a concrete continuum of related structures. The *middle range* of structures of the great living system affects us in positive correlation with its immediacy. The great living system is composed of all its subsystems and manifests itself in its dense inner structures, not just at the periphery—in its *immanence* as well as its *transcendence.*

So let us return to the level of order which makes some difference to us, planet Earth. How the earth fares in its solar system does ultimately make a difference to us, but only insofar as any changes affect the earth as a great living system.

The Earth as the Body of God

From our human observation point inside the larger systems, we find it difficult to realize that *our being is conditioned by our participation in larger systems,* including the great living system of the earth. We have the myopic vision of a cell in a human body, as suggested in the theological parable about the liver cell who said to a neighbor, "What's this I hear about there being a man?" To which the second cell responded, "Pay no attention to such superstitions; that's just the figment of some brain cell's imagination."

In constructing cosmologies, Howard Percy Robertson (1967, vol. 6, p. 582), Professor of Mathematical Physics at the California Institute of Technology, points out that humans "in attempting to bring order into the universe as a whole ... must hew to those lines of thought by which he has already brought order into that portion with which he is most familiar." It is at least reasonable that the concept of a living system, which is so useful in helping to understand formations as wholes, from cells through organisms to ecosystems and human communities, can help us to understand the environment as a planetary whole.

Besides, if our environment were not bonded in a unity, its constituents would disperse over the horizon like the galaxies in space. There is a logical necessity for a comprehensive unifying order to hold the subsystems in relations or they would repel each other. Oparin writes that it is characteristic of bounded organizations to be somewhat antagonistic to their environment, as persons are to other persons. Selective interactions also imply rejections, and negations would tend to drive systems apart were they not structured in a larger organization. For the interactions to take place which we observe on a global scale, it is necessary that the parts be organized in a comprehensive system.

British philosopher Samuel Alexander suggests a way of thinking about our relation to the great living system (Stiernotte, 1954, p. 57):

For any level of existence, deity is the next higher empirical quality. It is therefore a variable quality, and as the world grows in time, deity changes with it. On each level a new quality looms ahead, awfully, which plays to it the part of deity.

The great living system is most vividly known to us in the next higher order, and becomes less vivid, the more comprehensive the order is.

To me, the concept of a living system as a model for the environment conceived as a whole seems *real*. From this point of view, I feel as Copernicus did when he imagined himself standing on the sun and observing the solar system—everything falls into place and makes sense. However, also like Copernicus who could not fully account for the movement of the planets because he assumed their orbits had to be a perfect circle (a difficulty removed when Kepler showed that planetary orbits were elliptical), my own mind-set has no doubt left contradictions in this conceptual system. Still, the living-system analogy is satisfactory to me in making the environment coherent, and in describing how there comes to be meaningful order in reality.

Moreover, the living system model for the structure of being, culminating in a great living system of the earth, obviates some old theological problems of the Judeo-Christian tradition. The source of creativity in that tradition has been ascribed to a supernatural creator who is eternal and immutable. This model leaves a problem, "Who made God?" The assertion that God is uncreated, or the "unmoved mover" of Platonic thought, *assumes* as true the very assertion that is being questioned; it dismisses the question without responding to it. In this usage, "god" is the name given to the mystery of creation, not a contribution to understanding it.

The living-system model, on the other hand, helps us understand how the hierarchical order of living systems was self-created in an evolutionary process. We have not accounted for the origin of atoms and molecules, but we have seen how order emerges from disorder, and how the process culminates in an emergent great living system which is determinative for the behavior patterns of its constituents. Instead of a supernatural power, we see that order is produced by a "democracy of influences" which function through a communications system rather than by the exercise of force. As self-created by the dynamics of its own constituents, the living system is self-explanatory.

The living-system model also obviates the anthropomorphism characteristic of Christian theology, making God the human image. Now we can see that the ground of our being has less the attributes of human beings and more the attributes of a biological cell. For instance, Christian theology often speaks of the "mind of God," as if the supreme being had a brain capable of thinking in symbols, communicating in language, and for projecting conceptual purposes. The great living system is immense in magnitude, but not in complexity, so there is no evidence of the emergence of a brain with those qualities at that level, or of sense organs for hearing and seeing. The great living system functions more like a cell, manifesting self-direction or subjective intention at such a comprehensive level that it is determinative in setting the conditions for self-fulfillment of all its participant beings. This is the equivalent of the "will of God"; it is not a self-conscious projection of a conceptual goal, but is the realization of the form in the pattern of internal relations of the great living system. We have long intuited the operation of such a *regulating power* and, from the systems point of view, I think we can more clearly apprehend its working as simply the process of *natural selection* requiring that every being adapt to the conditions set by participation in the next higher order or more inclusive system. The unique presence of mind in humans does not negate the transcendent control of the great living system; it only emphasizes our responsibility to exercise our intelligence to understand the conditions of our successful existence and not to project our fantasies as "live options."

The living-system model for the supreme being also obviates the dualistic view of the environment: the natural and the supernatural, the immanent and the transcendent, with the attendant problem of how one realm communicates with the other. Christian orthodoxy has allegedly bridged this gap by postulating "special revelation" (the divine word recorded in the holy scripture). The concept of the hierarchical levels of being makes the supreme being *both immanent and transcendent,* just as I experience the United States as both immanent in the political order in which I participate, and transcendent in the coalescent character of the nation as a whole. Hartshorne (1941, p. 208) points out that the perception that immanence and transcendence exist in a continuum "is in fact the only way to achieve a just synthesis of immanence and transcendence, the only way to avoid the twin errors of mere naturalism and mere supernaturalism."

When dualism is rejected in favor of the continuum of the immanent and the transcendent in the living-system model, two other consequences immediately follow: first, the old distinction between the sacred and the secular is abandoned, and *all existents are seen as sacred* since they are constituents of the supreme being. This has implications for the way we value and treat not only human beings but all beings in our environment.

Second, the old epistemological distinction between revelation and reason is obviated in favor of the recognition that knowledge about all levels of being is acquired through insight and intuition confirmed by observation and experience. *All truth is knowledge of God.* The *scientific method* has regularized the process for confirming an hypothesis by controlled experimentation, which systematically increases knowledge and our ability to cope with all levels of reality. This mode of knowing can provide common ground for dialogue between the various religions of the world, which is impossible on the grounds of special revelations.

A popular assumption in our culture is that if you don't believe in God, God need not be reckoned with. If the word "god" is loaded with false connotations for you, abandon it; there is no magic in using the right word. But the referent, an *ultimate ordering and controlling reality, cannot be successfully ignored.* The living-system model for the environment as a whole is an inclusive order of interactions that are inescapable and determinative of the viable behavior of its parts. As an ancient Chinese sage said of the Tao ("the way of nature"), "The Tao that can be departed from is not the real Tao." The Old Testament poet referred to the same inescapable God when he sang:

> Whither shall I go from thy Spirit?
>   Or whither shall I flee from thy presence?
> If I ascend to heaven, thou art there!
>   If I make by bed in Sheol, thou art there!
> If I take the wings of the morning
>   and dwell in the uttermost parts of the sea,
> Even there thy hand shall lead me,
>   and thy right hand shall hold me.
>   (Psalm 139:7-10, R.S.V.)

This way of perceiving reality as a living unity is no recent innovation; it has been intuited by many for some time. The Apostle Paul seems to have the same kind of supreme being in mind when he wrote of the "unknown god" whom the Greeks in Athens were seeking: "Yet he is not far from each one of us, for 'In him we live and move and have our being'; as even some of your poets have said." (Acts 17-28.)

Alexander Pope (1901, pp. 23-24) the British poet, wrote in 1732:

> All are parts of one stupendous whole
> Whose body Nature is, and God the soul:
>
> . . . .
>
> To him no high, no low, no great, no small;
> He fills, he bounds, connects, and equals all.

The contemporary physicist Sanborn C. Brown (1966) finds contemplating the whole complex of the "almost incredible laws of nature" a "truly satisfying religious experience," and says, "The scientific cosmos is more like the God of inescapable Law in the Old Testament. It is a single integrated system of reality, and the law of its operation creates and sustains all that is from everlasting to everlasting."

And the contemporary process philosopher Charles Hartshorne (1941, p. 192) summarizes his view: "Thus on every ground we may well consider seriously the doctrine that the world is God's body, to whose members he has immediate social relations, and which are related to each other, directly or indirectly, exclusively by social relations."

If you accept this monistic model of a great living system as the nature of the creating and transforming reality as a whole, your experience in the world makes sense; your sense of the meaning of life, your values, your ethics, and your strategy for survival are reliable. We live in such a web of interconnections and dependencies that no action is without moral consequences for good or evil. This paradigm changes the Biblical notion that human beings are intended to have "dominion over the earth"; instead of dominating and exploiting our environment, we will use our intelligence to understand and live in harmony with it. We see ourselves as subordinate parts of the total environment, conscious participants in the creative process, and we accept our responsibility for living interactively and constructively with the great living system.

Chapter **3**

The Unfinished Animal

WHAT are we, not as unique individuals, but what kind of creatures are we as members of the species *Homo sapiens?* How did
we get here? In spite of the inexhaustible variety of human
personalities, we are still more like each other than we are like
other creatures. Archaeologists may have difficulty discriminating
between the fossil remains of pre-humans and humans, but in the
evolutionary process we have emerged as a distinctive species.
Although we human beings have evolved great differentiation
among ourselves, we still have no difficulty distinguishing between
human beings and any other primate. It is this species we are trying
to understand when we ask, "What are we?"

What we believe about ourselves affects our expectations
regarding personal fulfillment, social relations, and our interaction
with our environment. "A society holds together by the respect
which man gives to man; it fails, in fact it falls apart into groups of
fear and power, when the concept of man is false. We find the
drive which makes society stable at least in the search for what
makes us men." (Bronowski, 1965, pp. 44-45.) The future of the
human species depends upon what we believe about ourselves

and the resultant behavior. Inadequate beliefs about human nature have misguided us not only in relation to our fellow human beings, but in relation to our environment. If we are to be a successful emergent from the evolutionary process, it is important that we more correctly understand our place in the great living system—our limitations as well as our potentialities. Otherwise, we have the capability of making our planetary life-support system humanly uninhabitable, not only by releasing atomic warfare or toxic wastes from atomic generating plants, but also by making excessive demands upon the ecosystem to support overpopulation, by wastefully exploiting its natural resources, and by polluting its air and water.

Many of us, especially those of us living in technologically advanced countries with a high standard of living, have been like the prodigal son in Jesus' parable, wasting our substance by riotous living. The day may soon come when we will realize that we have squandered our inheritance.

It is simply not true that the more idealistic opinion we have about ourselves the greater our achievement will be. It is as frustrating to misjudge the capacity of a person as of a truck — an over-loaded truck is apt to break a spring. Some people burden humanity with too high expectations and, when they do not measure up, become cynical about human nature. A cynic has been aptly defined as a disillusioned idealist. Some form of authoritarianism tends to become the social and political theory of those who have lost faith in people.

Therefore, it is very important that we correctly assess ourselves in order to be able to live peacefully and constructively with ourselves as individual persons, with our fellow human beings, and with our environment.

Humanism Is Dead

"Man is dead," proposed Dr. C. A. van Peursen, Dutch scientist, at the Congress of the International Association for Religious Freedom in London, August, 1966. We are dead in the sense that the classical image of the human has become as out-moded as the classical image of God. The classical image of people as having a dualistic nature is no more tenable than the concept of a supernatural God. The dualistic image of humans was inherited by Western culture from the philosophy of Plato and of Descartes. It assumes that we have two natures: material and spiritual, body and mind, flesh and soul. Such a split-level view is being displaced by an organic view of our species as a holistic entity, a unified being with various properties but only one nature. Such concepts as soul and body are useful, says van Peursen, to orient ourselves to various aspects of our being. The concept of the soul emphasizes that we are more than a biological organism. But if we assume that such concepts refer to distinct levels of being, a body and a disembodied substance called a soul, then such concepts of people are dead. Of such a dualistic nature, van Peursen (1966, p. 173) writes that various dilemmas arise, such as that:

> . . . shut off inside its own private castle, the soul's substance must wonder whether the strongholds all around it are inhabited too. In other words, all inter-relationships are negated and the open structure of man, which points outward beyond itself, is sealed off.

A number of recent developments in the sciences have contrib-uted to the "death" of the species. New understandings of human nature have simply undercut some of our traditional assumptions about human nature. Our image of ourselves has been changed by recent discoveries in biology and in genetics which can account for the observed phenomena of human behavior without resort to the incursion of an extraneous vitality, such as a soul. Although all the answers are not yet in, enough of them are in to indicate that the human organism can be accounted for without resort to supernatural causes. The biological sciences conceive of people as a unified organic being.

Neurophysiology, says van Peursen, shows that we are not only biochemically programmed but are also in continuous interaction with our environment. The mind is not a receptacle for receiving pure ideas from some supernal realm, but is a system for selecting and using information from the environment. The central nervous system, including the brain, receives information from experience (including communication) and selectively stores it as symbols, feelings, and attitudes. Whatever valid ideas we have have been garnered by interaction with the world, rather than infiltrating from another level of reality or being inborn.

Contemporary social sciences visualize us as a system integrated with the world, not as isolated beings estranged from the world. The social sciences define us largely in terms of our spontaneous inter-actions with our social and cultural environment. In short, says van Peursen, we are how we respond. We are open systems fed by significant events, which then shape our further orientation toward life. Our abstract concepts and scientific theories are like index cards in our mental files by which we systematize events, and which reflect the history of our interaction with the world. "Mind" and "spirit" are names for the ways we order and regulate the phenomena of human history. Thus, we build our own identity on the foundations of our biological inheritance, accumulating it as a pattern from the exper-iences of our own life history. Personality is acquired as a store of personal knowledge, which in turn conditions what further exper-ience will be chosen, and thus how the personality will develop further.

Psychologist Abraham Maslow (1962, p. 177) comments about the impact of such changing concepts:

> When the philosophy of man (his nature, his goals, his potentialities, his fulfillment) changes, then everything changes. . . . We are now in the middle of such a change in the conception of man's capacities, potentialities, and goals. A new vision is emerging of the possibilities of man and of his destiny, and its implications are many, not only for our conceptions of education, but also for science, politics, literature, economics, religion, and even our conceptions of the non-human world.

"We are dead," or at least the classical assumption in Western culture that we have a dual nature is dead, because it has been replaced by a unified view of the species. The wholistic concept of people gives us a new vision of our potentialities and limitations. Instead of viewing ourselves as beings alienated from our environment by a disembodied soul or by pre-existent ideas, we see ourselves as an integral part of the whole environment. With both feet planted in the world, we are in a position to influence the future course of the evolutionary process which produced us, so long as we are mindful that the creative forces of the great living system were at work before we arrived on the scene and that they set the limits and conditions for our fulfillment.

Not only is the classical doctrine of the species with a dualistic nature dead, as van Peursen says, but so is one definition of 20th century humanism. I do not mean the current usage of "humanistic" to affirm an interest in the whole person, in contradistinction to the behavioristic psychology focus on human behavior and its conditioning; nor the humanistic concern for human values in contradistinction to materialistic values; nor the Renaissance humanism interest in the humanities, in contradistinction to medieval scholastic studies.

I do mean that "religious humanism" which, while ascribing primary importance to human powers, interests, aspirations, and well-being, in reaction to theism defined the human as alone in an indifferent if not hostile universe. Curiously, religious humanism retained the Judeo-Christian belief that we are sovereign over the earth, but are now untrammelled by recognition of any higher power. Human beings are seen as alienated from the rest of life, finding only such satisfaction as can be created by their own will and ability. For instance, I recall religious humanist A. Eustace Haydon at The University of Chicago about 1947 poetically describe the evolution of life from the primeval waters to humans standing erect and surveying the earth, and then we seemed to have taken over and be the only influence in history. And Julian Huxley (1959, p. 252) writes, "Man's destiny is to be the sole agent for the future evolution of this planet." Whatever became of the evolutionary process which did very well for billions of years before we emerged? Huxley (1959, p. 253) goes on to say of the species, ". . . thanks to Darwin, he now knows that he is not an isolated phenomenon, cut off from the rest of nature by his unique-ness. Not only is he made of the same matter and operated by the same energy as all the rest of the cosmos, but, for all his distinc-tiveness, he is linked by genetic continuity with all other inhabi-tants of this planet. Animals, plants, and microorganisms, they are all his cousins or remoter kin, all parts of one single evolving metabolizing protoplasm." But Huxley seems not to recog-nize that the evolutionary process is just as active, creative and controlling as it ever was; he seems to share Bertrand Russell's view that there is no cosmic support for human aspirations. He seems to assume that since we have added a psychosocial layer to our biological evolution, we have escaped involvement in the process which produced us. Religious humanism seems to view human beings as against the universe. This is like what anthro-pologist Loren Eiseley (1958, p. 124) calls "the war of parts," commenting that "if continued, it forecasts the death of all we claim as human."

The Newcomer

As a species, we only relatively recently made the scene. We are a newcomer on this planet (Dobzhansky, 1967, p. 1). Our late arrival means that, as the Biblical creation myth rightly emphasizes, we come into a world we never made, and that we should honor and respect the great creative system we belatedly have become aware of. The world had a head start on us and got along very well without us for a long time. We are not coexistent with creation, and as a latecomer to the game, we did not establish the rules. This means that if we are going to play the game successfully, we have to *learn the rules of creation and obey them.*

The rules of creation, which in the Christian tradition have been called "the laws of God," are the principles describing the probable operation of evolution through natural selection. Given the emergence of life as outlined in the previous chapter, organ-isms evolved by a process of cumulative change—generally, but not always, toward increased complexity and efficiency of bio-logical organization. Charles Darwin won general acceptance for the theory of evolution by presenting copious evidence in support of it in his book published in 1859, *The Origin of Species,* which inspired a revolution in thought. The concept of evolution plausibly organized a great deal of already existing data and concepts. Darwin also proposed a simple and reasonable explanation of how it worked through random variation and natural selection of the best adapted to survive in a specific environment. Random variation can occur in a species by chance mutation of the genes, or by mixing the genes in sexual reproduction, producing a modified characteristic which is inheritable. Fitness for survival is determined by the conditions in the environment.

The process of natural selection is pragmatic: if some evolutionary form is capable of coping with its environment, it endures; and if not, it fails and may become extinct. The term "natural selection" does not designate a purposeful power selecting forms according to some predetermined standard, like the mechanical gadget in TV ads for a pea soup which kicks aside undesirable peas, but refers to the fact that some beings are successful in finding a survival niche in their environment, while others fail and do not reproduce themselves in sufficient numbers to survive as a species.

The fossil record shows that evolution is not a smooth and steady process but moves by zigs and zags, by pauses and spurts. Some morphological changes have negative adaptive value.

Human beings have emerged from primate mammals, and are most closely related to apes. "All evidence agrees and the conclusion is unequivocal," says George Gaylord Simpson (1966, p. 473), professor of vertebrate paleontology at Harvard, "that man is clearly related to the apes, particularly chimpanzees and gorillas, though he is not identical with them." Apes and humans apparently shared a common ancestor, with the separation in lines of evolution probably occurring between 10 and 25 million years ago. The prehuman beings became less specialized, evolved more acute bifocal vision and less efficient sense of smell, an erect posture with bipedal locomotion, prehensile hands, and an enlarged brain. It became the only animal who uses tools to make refined tools. Human beings are an interbreeding group, regularly exchanging genes, though races of humanity have evolved under the selective pressure of local conditions as sub-species which grade into each other. *Homo sapiens,* or human beings, did not appear until 99.9% of present geological history had passed.

The newcomer status of homo sapiens was not obvious to our ancestors who first began thinking about the human situation. They were not aware of the long history of the earth written in rock formations. From their limited perspective, early Greek philosophers could propose a cyclic view of history, a repetitive cycle of occurrence without novelty, since they were not aware of the record of change inscribed on the earth. As late as the 17th century, Archbishop Usher could propose, on the basis of time-spans suggested in the Bible, that the earth was created in 4004 B.C. The science of geology has relatively recently expanded our concept of time by tracing the history of rock formations over 4 billions of years. Any amateur can realize something of the time spans the geologists deal with by standing on the rim of the Grand Canyon and with the guidance of a ranger see geological formations which have been eroding for more than a million years in strata of rock whose ages have been dated up to 2 billion years. From the dating of the oldest rocks on earth at around 3 billion years, and of the main group of meteorites falling in from space at around 5 billion years, says chemist Willard F. Libby (1965, p. 2), "it seems to be a reasonable assumption that the earth itself was formed about 5 billion years ago." Of that 5 billion years of earth history, about the first 2½ billion years was a period of chemical evolution, at the end of which we begin to find traces of organic life—algae. Most plants and animals began to emerge before the Cambrian period more than 500 million years ago, and we emerged only about 1 million years ago, though others speak of us emerging about 2 million years ago.

In fact, the theory of evolution was inconceivable until the geologists had expanded our time consciousness. The original and special creation of fixed species was the only conceivable origin of the variety of living forms in the context of time defined by millennia. Until the limits of conceivable time had been pushed way back, Charles Darwin could not have had time at his disposal to make the theory of evolution plausible.

Although the concept of evolution and data to support it had been available for some time, general acceptance of the concept was retarded by the power of religious assumptions. "Creationism," the Biblical notion of an "original creation" with a consequent static world, was entrenched so thoroughly that the possibility of a steadily evolving world and species emerging at different times was unthinkable (Mayr, 1972, pp. 982-983). Darwin was from a Unitarian background which liberated him to seriously explore the possibilities of evolution, a concept already adopted by his grandfather Erasmus Darwin.

With the expanded time background and liberation from orthodoxy, new possibilities could occur to Darwin as he saw so much evidence of change and of continuity in species on his long voyage on the Beagle, eventuating in the publication of *The Origin of Species* in 1859. With the modifications and refinements of his theory of evolution by natural selection, we now see that all forms evolve from previous forms and that creativity is a process rather than a single feat. A consequence, of course, is that the older theory of original creation is dead. A further consequence should be that as we fully accept the fact that the world was not created by divine decree, we will also learn that the world cannot be successfully changed by arbitrary human actions.

We human beings are so impressed by our own history that we lose sight of the scale of evolutionary history. This struck me when visiting Westminster Abbey in London during the celebration of its 900th anniversary. As a midwestern American impressed by any house built before 1890, I was duly awed by the nine centuries of English history embodied in Westminster Abbey. Then it occurred to me that I was looking at the epitome of most of significant British history. True, the legends of King Arthur come from the 5th century, and the first stones were placed in the Stonehenge about 2000 B.C.; still, a mere millennium encompasses most of English history significant to an understanding of our own social and political antecedents, including the Magna Carta.

About the most ancient and most beautiful person I am aware of is Queen Nefertiti, wife of King Ikhnaton of Egypt about 1375 B.C., a copy of whose small bust I have often visited at the Oriental Institute in Chicago. She seems remote until I am reminded how relatively few generations separate her from me. George Wald (1965, p. 32), Harvard University professor of biology, comments that if we count thirty years to a generation,

> It is rather astonishing to realize that only one hundred ancestors in line carry one back to 1000 B.C. [while] . . . one thousand generations would bring us back to about thirty thousand years ago, when Cro-Magnon man was painting those interesting pictures on the walls of caves in the Dordogne.

On a geological time line, the dawn of human history is relatively recent. This gives us a whole new perspective on humanity.

As a consequence of our expanded concept of time, Willard F. Libby (1965, pp. 6-7), comments that *homo sapiens:*

> . . . is only now becoming fully acquainted with his environment. He has been here such a relatively short time—as far as we can tell, only a few million years at the outside. . . . It is by no means clear at this moment just how long man has been on the earth, but it seems very likely that our total span is minuscule compared with that of the dinosaur, which lasted for some one hundred twenty-five million years. We have arrived fairly recently. This is pointed up by the fact that, as a result of the population explosion, today's world population represents about 5 per cent of all the men who have ever lived.

Not only are we newcomers, but with dizzying speed we have been discovering what we can accomplish. Since my mother's birth (1882), we have accomplished many of our proudest achievements: we practically eradicated some of the killing diseases such as smallpox, tuberculosis, malaria, and polio; we developed new forms of transportation in the automobile, airplane, and spaceship; we invented new forms of communication in the telephone, radio, and television; we developed new forms of power by atomic fission; and we increased our visual acuity with electron microscopes and our brain power with computers. Ten thousand years probably cover the discovery of the use of the lever and wheel, and of the working of metals, as well as the domestication of some animals and plants — which made it possible for people to cluster in villages and towns and develop the cultural and technological attributes of civilization.

The trouble is that we are now discovering to our dismay that this is a *finite* planet and that many of our achievements have been made by exploitation and pollution of limited natural resources. At the rate we are using up the resources of our planet, we cannot survive much longer at such a high level of civilization, if at all.

We have been warned that those who do not learn from the history of past mistakes are bound to repeat them. We look to history for clues to the solution of our problems. The trouble is that we take into account too short a span of history, the 4 thousand years or so of recorded human history. Human history can teach us something about the trials and errors of human society, but to learn significant lessons about how this great living system was formed, and so how it can be kept in order, we need to study and adapt ourselves to the creative processes going on beneath and beyond human cultures. Instead of *devising schemes* for manipulating the world, we need to be *studying the order* of the world and cooperating with it.

Still, considering the newness of human beings, there is no precedent for what we may become. Not our limited past, but our potential extensive future is the context in which our human significance can be seen. Though much of our progress has been heedless, we are after all only beginning to understand our environment. Today is not forever, and whatever our present ecological perils, the future need not be like the present or the past. For the process of evolution is now going on at an accelerated pace at the level of culture change. We can achieve a steady-state in relation to the environment by a more efficient use of energy, recycling our wastes, and modifying our requirements.

More Like Yeast

A century ago, many people were upset by Darwin's hypothesis that we shared a common ancestor with apes. What seemed to be at stake was their notion of the ground for our supremacy over all other creatures because we were uniquely created so. They thought it was demeaning to be told that they were descended from monkeys. Imagine how they would feel if they were told, as biologists now believe, that we have a common ancestor with yeast. What is significant is not that our species had such humble beginnings, but that we are so intimate a part of the total life process.

George Wald points out that in spite of the tremendous variety of biological forms which have developed through the process of evolution, the basic biological entities are amazingly limited and universal. The biological cells which constitute a maple leaf, a caterpillar, and a human brain are basically the same in structure and components; the organisms have achieved different forms by organizing the cells in different patterns and calling upon them to perform different functions. The code for organizing a particular organism is laid out in the genes, or more specifically in the complex molecules of deoxyribonucleic acid of the genes on the chromosomes. This delicate arrangement is subject to continuous reordering, causing random variations or mutations in the genetic message. With the constant mutations going on in the genes, it is amazing that there is not more variety in biological cells. Continuity of form in the cells has been preserved, says Wald, because of a paradox in which the disorder in the genes is matched by stability in the organism. It seems to me that this implies that some changes in the microworld of the cell are overruled in the macroworld of the organism, a case of the laws of the more inclusive order supervening by internal natural selection over the laws of its parts, even though unusual messages from the microworld may also change the order of the macroworld. In any case, Wald (1965, p. 29) comments:

It appears that, plentiful and common as are individual mutations, it takes about ten million years to establish in a species a single change in the amino acid sequence of the protein, or a single change in the nucleotide sequence of the corresponding gene.

None of us had ever dreamed before that such intimate relationships hold together the entire world of the living organisms—that with such vast stretches of evolution coming between, we still retain so close a genetic relationship with yeast. . . . We are more like yeast than we are unlike it.

Acceptance of this evidence of our continuity and intimate relationships with all other forms of life has implications for what we believe about human nature. We are a product of the same internal organizing principles and selective forces as are all other creatures. We were not singled out for special treatment by the Creator, and our destiny is shaped by the same operation of natural selection as is the destiny of all life forms. Such a natural process operates as inescapably as it ever did, at every level testing adaptations to a changing environment. Thus, human beings stand under a more unavoidable judgment than was conceived by the Old Testament prophets.

Natural selection is not an infallible process for arriving at perfect forms. For instance, the pain experienced by the human female during childbirth has no evolutionary advantage, but it is connected with a survival advantage: the possession of hands, driven by a relatively huge brain, hence a large head. The pangs of childbirth are correlated with erect body posture, and without standing on their hind legs people could not have evolved the manipulative use of their hands, nor developed tools. "Women suffer childbirth pains because they (and also men) are bipeds instead of quadrupeds," says Dobzhansky (1966, pp. 322-323). This account of the origin of birth pangs updates the Genesis explanation that "in sorrow thou shalt bring forth children" because Eve had committed the original sin of taking the forbidden fruit from the tree of the knowledge of good and evil. "Original sin" does not account for birth pangs, nor does it account for the children of Adam working to secure food: "In the sweat of thy face shalt thou eat bread." All creatures labor to secure nourishment. The history of evolution shows many imperfections and failures, but not original sin or punishment for exercising curiosity. We do sin, but birth pangs and the sweat of one's brow are functions of survival. Biological forms do not necessarily turn out to be perfect — just to be adequate enough to survive.

Another consequence of our close affinity with all living beings is that we can see that our fate is bound up with the fate of the other creatures we dominate. When ornithologists discovered that the brown pelican population on the coast of southern California was declining because of DDT pollution of its food chain, they were alarmed not only for the birds but for people. DDT had so disordered the pelican's hormone system that its eggs were laid soft-shelled and broke before they could hatch. We don't yet know what DDT concentrated in our food supply would do to our hormone system, but we are not all that different. Since we have minimized DDT pollution off the California coast, the pelicans are increasing—but the incident was a warning.

If all the instruction-bearing codes contained in the chromosomes of human egg and sperm cells were disarranged, *Homo sapiens* would become extinct. The DNA molecules of our germ plasm—there is about a thimbleful in the whole world—are, says Hudson Hoagland (1966, p. 144), "... certainly the most precious material that exists anywhere so far as the human species is concerned." The egg and sperm cells carry the key to the duration of the human species. The eternal life of human beings is not found in individuals as such, but in "the continuity of the germ plasm," according to August Weismann who in 1876 in Germany first proposed the theory that the germ plasm was the basis of heredity.

The significance of human participation in pervasive life forms is well summarized by George Wald (1966, pp. 46-47):

> The past few years have made us aware as we have never been before of the depth of kinship among all living organisms. For one thing, every organism alive today can boast a genealogy that goes

back in an unbroken line to the first living organism on the planet.
. . . Beyond that general thought, however, it has recently become
apparent that over a great reach of this development we have been
working on the same genes. It turns out that surprisingly few
changes have occurred in the structures of the proteins, and a still
smaller proportion of changes in the genes that determine them.
. . . Yeast is a contemporary organism, with which in the remote
past we shared a common ancestor. From that remote ancestor,
yeast went its way, and we went ours. The journey has been made
twice, yet has resulted in such minor differences.

So all life is akin; and our kinship is much closer than we had ever
imagined before. Yet within that family of living things, man is also
unique and adds new dimensions.

The Mysterious Black Box

We are unique and add new capabilities to the evolutionary
process as a consequence of the size and complexity of our brain,
giving us powers of visualization and abstraction. More specifically,
the development of the forebrain is what distinguishes us from our
nearest kin in the animal kingdom. Our brain is our chief hope of
survival. With the development of our brain, pre-humans took a
quantum jump beyond other creatures in the ability to adapt to the
environment, or to adapt parts of the environment to our needs. But if
we are not to precipitate new crises in our environment to which we,
especially, are not fitted to adapt, we had better understand the
limitations as well as the powers of our brain.

Human intelligence is a product of environmental stress. The
most rapid development of the forebrain occurred during the
extremely difficult living conditions of the ice age. The enlarge-
ment of the brain is a relatively recent event. R. W. Gerard (1962,
p. 57) says, ". . . when Australopithecus lived, hominid brain size
was still around 650 cc., while some three or four hundred
thousand years later, brain size had increased to 1500 cc. This is
an extraordinarily rapid rate of evolution." Brain growth seems to
have been unaccompanied by any noticeable increase in body
size. But the artifacts the paleontologists discover associated with
larger craniums show a generally progressive increase in perfection and adaptability, which in turn indicates an increase in

intelligence and skill among the people who made them. The forebrain evolved in the humanoids and helped them to adapt to the rigors of the environment during the waves of ice sheets which crept over the northern continents. The humanoids could take appropriate measures to adapt to the changes. We can do so again in the environmental crisis which we are inducing.

As distinctive as the human brain is, it is still in continuity with organic evolution. It is not a unique structure found in no other creature, but a complexification of organic matter. The difference in the cerebral cortex of humans, in contrast to that of other primates such as apes, is not in quality but in quantity. There is little difference in neurons and fibers, receptor and effector cells between us and more primitive vertebrates. "What is different," says R. W. Gerard (1962, p. 109), "is the kind and effectiveness of neuron interactions, if you will, and, still more, the sheer number available. Clearly, neurons collectively constitute a new entity." And he adds:

> More units of the same kind, even interacting in the same way, can do things that fewer units cannot do, things that are actually quantitatively different, so, as man's mind is more than the sum of neuron minds, so the collective mind of mankind is clearly a very different thing from man's individual mind.

The difference between the brain structure of human beings and other primates is of about the same order as the difference between their respective learning capacities. Other animals can to varying degrees learn and communicate with each other, at least to the extent of uttering warning signals. The difference is in degree, not in kind. There is continuity in the development of the brain, so the work of the human mind may be brilliant, but it is not separated in the evolutionary process which produced the capacity in other animals to engage in a degree of intelligent activity.

Edmund Sinnott (1955, p. 17) suggests that the same kind of directive activity goes on at all levels of organic being:

> This integrating and directive control that guides bodily growth and development resembles in so many ways the equally unexplained

directiveness of man's behavior which we call mental or psychic activity as to suggest the exciting possibility that those two may be expressions of the same underlying biological process.

The continuity between the ordering processes of the body and of the mind may be further supported by an exciting new finding reported by Hoagland. It may be that the same chemical process which fixes the genetic code with directions for growing a body may also operate in the brain cells to fix messages for directing the body as a whole. Hoagland describes recent findings about "how the brain records new information from the environment and stores it in the form of chemical traces in brain cells," and explains (1966, p. 152):

As you know, the substance deoxyribonucleic acid (DNA) comprises the genes and carries a code of chemical information that is the basis for the phylogenetic memory of the species. It is the material basis of our evolutionary memory. Now research indicates that ribonucleic acid (RNA) appears to be the substance involved in storing memory traces in our own brains. Thus the learning process involves passage of nerve impulses over extensive patterns of nerve pathways, and with repetition of the experience there appears to be a cumulative synthesis of RNA in the nerve tracts involved. The RNA synthesizes new protein structures within the nerve cells. Evidence has been presented that these new protein structures then delineate the pathways which have been used in the particular learning process. If true, this is a very exciting thing, because it indicates that both personal and phylogenetic memory are determined by the same chemical systems.

The chemical basis of thought is confirmed by other discoveries reported by Hoagland. Chemical substances have been discovered which can wash out learned experiences from the brain, and other chemicals which facilitate learning.

In thinking, we humans do not tap some extraneous source of wisdom, we carry on the same process at a more complex level as goes on in the ordering and direction of the organs of our body, or the body of any other animal. The point that I am trying to make is that in pure intellectualism, whether of the variety of Platonic idealism or of modern idealism, the mere conception of an abstract idea does not necessarily mean that the world will conform. *Ideas* are at best only hypotheses and have no validity until they have been tried and found helpful. Neither the physical nor social world can be refashioned arbitrarily according to the projections of our imagination, but only by using our imagination to understand the pattern of relationships in the system and modify them accordingly to enhance the order on its own terms. Ideas are creative only if they *correctly identify* the creative forces in the living system and orient us to cooperate with them, much as a physician first learns the structure and dynamics of the human body in order to heal it or help it grow. "... reality not only *does,* but *should* determine the ideas and not the ideas the reality," says James Luther Adams (1976, p. 37), distinguished lecturer on ethics at Meadville/Lombard Theological School in Chicago.

Mind cannot be reduced to matter. *Mind* is inherent in the particular pattern of *organization* and *interactions* in the brain. Roger W. Sperry, professor of psychobiology at the California Institute of Technology, suggests how the mental processes may operate as a consequence of the pattern of interaction of the cells and neurons in the brain. He points out that the various atomic elements are "molecule bound" in the sense that their activities are controlled by the *configurational forces* of their encompassing molecule, and then relates this configurational force, by analogy, to the operations of the brain. He says (1965, pp. 79-80):

> . . . the flow and the timing of impulse traffic through any brain cell, or even a nucleus of cells in the brain, are governed largely by the over-all encompassing properties of the whole cerebral circuit system, within which the given cells and fibers are incorporated, and also by the relationship of this circuit system to other circuit systems.

All the elemental chemical and electrical forces of the atoms, molecules, and cells in the brain retain their characteristic operations when encompassed in the brain, but their organization in patterned interactions gives the brain its functioning property.

This organic interpretation of the brain as a living system resolves the classical dualism of matter and mind by making *mind* the *function of an organization of matter.* Identifying the operation of the mind with the pattern of interactions also obviates the materialistic "nothing but" fallacy, notes Sperry (1965, pp. 84-85), which reduces the mind to nothing but the flow of chemical and electrical impulses. The phenomena we identify as operations of the mind are, says Sperry, "what the physicists might class as 'higher-order effects' or 'co-operative effects.' "

The "higher-order effects" in the brain, as in any organization, are like the binocular vision gained when the two eyes moved from the side to the front of the head; what was gained was not simply two overlapping fields of vision, but a new faculty of depth perception. The brain is not only more highly organized centralization but also an integration of nerve structures to react concurrently, providing better coordination of responses to a complex environment.

Loren Eiseley (1958, p. 124) calls the human brain "unnatural," explaining:

> . . . unnatural, that is, in the sense that there is nothing else like it on the planet. Even Darwin confessed that his principle of limited perfection—that is, the conception that life would evolve only sufficiently to maintain itself in competition with other life or to adjust to changes in its environment—had been upset in the case of man. A part, such as a tooth or an eye, could reach perfection only for a given purpose in a particular environment. With man, however, Darwin professed to observe no foreseeable limit to the development of the mental faculties.

In spite of some of our advances in understanding this most characteristic organ of human beings, the brain is still mysterious. Roger W. Sperry (1965, p. 77) comments:

> Our explanatory picture for brain functions is reasonably satisfactory for the sensory input pathways and the distal portion of the motor outflow. But that great in-between realm, starting at the stage where the incoming excitatory messages first reach the

cortical surface of the brain, still today is very aptly referred to as
the "mysterious black box."

At least we know where thought generates, if not precisely how.
This gives us an advantage over our ancestors, such as Plato, who
could account for the emergence of ideas only as universals
incurring from another realm. Without such understanding as we
now have, ideas were thought to have almost magical potency.
The phenomenon of the brain was not yet even recognized when
some of the classical concepts of philosophy and theology were
being worked out in Western culture. For instance, Harry Emerson Fosdick, minister and Bible scholar, points out that some 80
different portions of the body were named in the Hebrew books of
the Old Testament, and adds (1938, p. 83):

> The brain, strangely enough, is not mentioned and there are no
> terms for nerves, for lungs, or for the diaphragm. Thinking is
> associated with the heart, not with the brain. In the ancient world in
> general, such ideas held sway and even Aristotle conceived no
> function for the brain except to cool blood.

Certainly we can now employ our brains more effectively for
problem solving than could our ancestors who misunderstood not
only the process of thought but even its organ.

The enlarged and more complex brain confers a number of
benefits upon us. The elaboration of the general circuit properties
of the cerebral system in us prepared us for a quantum jump in the
evolutionary process: the development of symbols, languages,
ideas, concepts, and culture. But it did not happen all by itself. The
development of the brain was more like the elevation of a building
crane invented by a Swedish contractor which raises itself on the
building it is constructing. The "sequential view" that first the brain
evolved followed by the development of language, ideas, and
thought is false, says Clifford Geertz, professor of anthropology at
The University of Chicago, because there are evidences of cultural
overlap between pre-humans and humans of a million years ago
during the Ice Age. He says (1965, p. 94):

What this means is that culture, rather than being added on, so to speak, to a finished or virtually finished animal, was ingredient, and centrally ingredient, in the production of that animal itself. The slow, steady, almost glacial growth of culture through the Ice Age altered the balance of selection pressures for the evolving *Homo* in such a way as to play a major directive role in his evolution.

The physical evolution of the brain and the development of human culture, in short, went on hand-in-hand by interaction. They emerged concurrently.

How language developed among early humanoids is lost in prehistory, but we have some idea how infants recapitulate the experience of learning to communicate by advancing from the use of signs, a cry to indicate discomfort or fright, to the use of symbols to convey abstract ideas. Gardner Murphy describes how an infant learns to use symbols or words. Using the vocal system with which they are genetically endowed, infants make random noises in imitation of what they hear, some of which they are delighted to find elicit responses from the adults around them. A basic and universal sound which infants have discovered produces attention is "ma." Different sounds bring different results under different conditions, and the infant by what Murphy (1947, p. 249) calls "trial and error" learns to reproduce them when desiring an associated effect. The same process is followed in putting words into combinations or sentences.

It seems to me that, since culture is part of the human environment, the identification of sounds with responses might equally well be called a process of natural selection. Children do not so much select the appropriate word to get what they want as repeat the particular word which from experience they have learned their environment will respond to. The selection is made by the environment, in this case the attending adults, which rewards the infant by gratifying its expressed need — an inadvertent Skinnerian reinforcement.

The biological capacity for speech is genetically given, but the particular language that the child learns depends, of course, on the culture into which it is born. At this stage in our cultural evolution, many languages have been developed. Part of the process of becoming human is learning the language of the particular culture in which an infant is born. Thus, a human being does not mature in isolation; some society has to complete it by exposing it to a language.

The Word

Language is "man's monopoly," says von Bertalanffy (1968, p. 258). Other animals communicate information by audible signals, odors, patterns of movement, color displays, etc., as do human beings. "Yet human language is absolutely distinct from any other system of communication in other animals," says George Gaylord Simpson (1966, p. 476):

> Nonhuman vocables are, in effect, interjections. They reflect the individual's physical or, more frequently, emotional state. They do not, as true language does, name, discuss, abstract, or symbolize. They are what the psychologists call affective; such purely affective so-called languages are systems of emotional signals and not discourse. The difference between animal interjection and human language is the difference between saying "Ouch!" and saying "Fire is hot."

Though speech is associated with the left temporal lobe, and all mammals have left temporal lobes of varying sizes, says Simpson, "Those with smaller lobes do not speak just a little and those with larger lobes more. There is no graded sequence: normal men speak completely; other animals, whatever the relative size of their temporal lobes, do not speak at all." He adds (1966, p. 477),

> The essential anatomical and physiological basis of speech is nevertheless in the structure and function of the brain. That basis is not fully known, but it evidently involves not just a language center, such as might be localized in the temporal lobe, but an intricate and widespread system of associative connections throughout much of the brain. . . . Thus sensations of any kind derived from an external object or event can be generalized according to similarities with others. Each kind can then be associated with a distinctive symbol,

which does not resemble the object or event at all but which arbitrarily stands for it. That symbol, a supreme element in the nature of man, is the word, and it is not surprising that words . . . have acquired such mystical and philosophical overtones.

Human beings, with the identical genetic capacity, have developed many languages, with different sounds and scripts meaning the same thing in different cultures and subspecies.

With the development of language, a whole new range of possibilities opened up for us. By associating experiences with symbols, and storing the symbols in our memory, we are able to expand our environment. That is to say, we may respond to what is symbolically present in our mind as well as to what is actually impinging upon us at the moment. We can determine our activity in terms of possibilities which are not immediately present, even in terms of possibilities imaginatively rearranged in our mind. Other animals have a memory; a rat can learn a maze, a salmon can return to its spawning ground, and a dog can find its home. But only humans can use a map to guide themselves to a place they have never been before, thus benefiting by the experience of other people and presented to them in symbols. We direct our activities not only with reference to our present circumstances, but also with reference to a spectrum of concepts, including those written by people far away or long dead. We transcend our immediate environment by reacting to it at a distance inserted between stimuli affecting us and our responses to them by a range of alternate possibilities present symbolically in our minds. This capability is what makes us a creative participant in the great living system.

Physical evolution is slow and intelligent human beings can speed up the process; in natural evolution, change comes through trial and error, but in the realm of ideas experimentation can be a mental process, a rearrangement of symbols—like measuring to see if a refrigerator will fit into a kitchen nook, rather than the physical labor of moving the refrigerator before knowing whether it will fit. When confronted by a problem, we can symbolically try rearranging the situation in various ways and evaluate the foreseeable consequences, and then act only on that possibility which seems most likely to succeed. Thus we can minimize false starts and reduce the lead-time necessary for developing new ways of coping with the environment. We have learned enough about how elements in the environment serve a purpose so we can design a project, say a bridge, before we start building it. After rehearsing simulation procedures, we can even put humans on the moon the first time we try.

Language not only gives human beings superior powers of communication, but also the capacity to *think,* to carry on an interior dialogue, to solve problems mentally, or to live for the future. It enables us to be goal directed or purposive. "True purposiveness, however, implies that actions are carried out with knowledge of their goal, of their future final results; the conception of the future goal does already exist and influences present actions." (von Bertalanffy, 1968, p. 258.) Our purposes help shape the future. *Foresight,* the human capacity to predict the outcome of our own actions, makes us responsible for them. Ethical judgments are for us not only possible but necessary.

However, thought and foresight do not make human beings omniscient or omnipotent. Simpson (1966, p. 478) warns that a person "bends the qualities of nature to his own ends, but he is as fully subject to nature's laws as is any other animal and is no more capable of changing them." Moreover, human behavior is not always determined by rational considerations. Thought is a conscious activity but a great deal of what we do is determined subconsciously. Much human experience is recorded non-symbolically at an emotional level and is not easily retrievable, but nonetheless is motivating. An experience is associated with positive or negative feelings which conditions the response to a subsequent similar experience. And we share instinctive reactions to experience with other animals. "The vestigial organs that are concealed here and there in our bodies and which tell tales of the long past—of trees and waters in our lost ancestral world—have their corollary in the mind of man." (Eiseley, 1958, p. 125.) We often act irrationally, justifying our behavior by rationalizations.

"Except for the immediate satisfaction of biological needs, man lives in a world not of things but of symbols," says von Bertalanffy (1968, p. 215). A conceptual environment makes human beings more vulnerable to aberrations than other animals. An animal or a person can be made neurotic, emotionally unstable without demonstrable physical basis, by subjecting it to continued frustration or arbitrary insecurity. Only human beings can become psychotic, a fundamental mental derangement, apart from disease, characterized by defective contact with reality. Von Bertalanffy (1968, p. 217) suggests that, though the definition is not generally accepted, "mental illness is a specifically human phenomenon. . . . Animals cannot have the disturbances of symbolic functions that are essential ingredients of mental disease. In animals there cannot be disturbance of ideas, delusions of grandeur or of persecution, etc., for the simple reason that there are no ideas to start with."

Relating to the environment through symbols and concepts has its own built-in limitation. We never capture the whole of reality in words; any concept we have is an abstraction, a simplification. "Any description in our present formalisms must be incomplete, not because of the obduracy of nature, but because of the limitation of language as we use it." says Bronowski (1966, p. 5). Moreover, the language we think in delimits what we become aware of. Benjamin Worf's view is that the linguistic patterns themselves determine what individuals perceive in their environment and how they think about it. People who think in different languages actually perceive the world differently. Even objective scientists tend to pay attention to data that fit the categories of their language. Words can blind us to reality.

Since words are abstract symbols, even the concept of the "self" in "self-consciousness" does not reflect the full complexity of the existential self. What we are conscious of is a partial representation of our own identity. It is an act of imagination to project an image of the self; it is not the real me. The validity of what we learn about ourselves through self-conscious analysis is correlated with the adequacy of our self concept. We can through

introspection learn much about our identities, but we remain at
least partial strangers to ourselves as wholes.

The capacity of imagination to project an image of one's self is
the source of the peculiarly human quality of *self-transcendence*.
We can stand outside ourselves and not only recognize our own
objective existence—know we are alive—and our identity with
other people, but also we can imagine ourselves at another point
in space or time and appreciate what it is like there. We can
identify with the past and the future. This is part of what Loren
Eiseley (1958, p. 125) calls our "strange heritage." "It is a heritage
which must be preserved in our schools and churches, for in a
society without a deep historical memory, the future ceases to
exist and the present becomes a meaningless cacophony."

Laughter also seems to be correlated with the capacity for self-
transcendence. A sense of humor arises from self-detachment. If
we are the only animal who laughs, it may be we are the only one who
needs to, not only because we are capable of seeing that the situation
we are in is absurd, but also because we are peculiarly able to get
ourselves into incongruous situations by responding to our own
fancies rather than events. Incited by our own imagination, we can do
things inappropriate to our environment, and when the incongruity
strikes us, we can break out into convulsive laughter to relieve the
tension. A humorous response to our own absurd predicaments
keeps us from being preposterous.

The impulse to social organization derives from the "black
box." The process of symbolic thinking which makes it possible
for us to be self-conscious also makes it possible for us to identify
with other human beings. Many animals form rudimentary organizations for mutual benefit — a herd for protection against predators, or a pack to be more successful in hunting. The social organization of ants seems to be directed by behavior coded in their genes,
and hence is predetermined. Our outstanding success in surviving
springs largely from our capacity to form voluntary, cooperative
social relations. Our social organization stems from our sense of
mutuality engendered when we contemplate others by the same
symbol with which we identify ourselves. For instance, we are the

only creature who knows that we are going to die as a consequence
of identifying ourselves with the death of another human being.
"The hypothesis to be considered is that the death-awareness is a
sequel to self-awareness," says Theodosius Dobzhansky (1966, p.
322), and explains:

> Only after having developed the ability to see himself as an object
> among other objects, did man gain a perspective in which he could
> begin to understand the relations between process and events.
> Some understanding of these relations is obviously indispensable
> for survival in human environments at even the most primitive
> levels. A concomitant of self-awareness is, however, death-aware-
> ness.

Only humans bury their dead, points out Dobzhansky, which is a sign
that we recognize a common mortality. There are some hints of
a concern with death in human beings as early as Peking Man, a
representative of *Homo erectus* who is presumed to be ancestral
to *Homo sapiens*. With the Neanderthal tribes of *Homo sapiens*,
the evidence of a reverent care for the dead is unmistakable. This
ultimate expression of human identification with other human
beings points to the motive for our concern for supplying the needs
of not only our own children, but for feeding starving children
who are more or less remote from us. Compassion is a distinctly
human trait which prompts us to extend our caring for others
to wider circles than other animals are capable of. It also inspires
us to form associations for mutual benefit through cooperation.

The quest for meaning is another derivative from human
intelligence which has survival value. All animals are more or less
curious, exploring their environment. A dog in a strange place will
crisscross the area, just learning what is there. But only humans are
inquisitive in the sense of not only wanting to know what is there,
but *how* it got there. We want to understand our environment,
to identify new events with familiar ones whose outcome we
already know. We want to know what an occasion means. "The
more highly developed the brain among animals, the more
pronounced [is] the animal's curiosity," says Hoagland(1966, p.)

154). Curiosity leads human beings to climb the highest mountain "because it is there," or conceive of the formula E=MC² in an attempt to unify knowledge, or fly people to the moon in the quest for information. Curiosity has prompted some of our most significant achievements.

Human beings who can anticipate the future are the only creatures who are anxious. Anxiety prompts us to formulate religions to sustain our morale in spite of frustration, suffering, and tragedy. Human intelligence gives us among all creatures an unparalleled ability to foresee consequences, to make predictions, and to exercise control over parts of our environment, and thus to play a creative role in the evolutionary process. But the ability to capture experience in symbols makes it possible for us to recall undesirable past experiences and to anticipate that they will probably happen again. We can't control all the contingencies we can imagine. It is this corollary to intelligence which makes us the only creature who is religious, who proposes hypotheses about the nature of reality as a whole that provide a context within which undesirable events become meaningful, and who celebrates ceremonies to allay our anxieties. Belief in a transcendent order makes bearable the immediate disorders we experience, and gives us grounds for making moral choices which serve a higher order than would be served by gratifying pressing desires.

The Unfinished Animal

The most significant thing about us is not so much that we can learn, but that we have to learn to become human. Geertz (1965, p. 109) says that ". . . what sets him off most graphically from non-men is less his sheer ability to learn (great as that is) than how much and what particular sorts of things he *has* to learn before he is able to function at all." We are born with practically no built-in survival processes, no natural endowments for coping with our environment. The "peculiar larval nakedness," as Loren Eiseley describes our condition at birth, really characterizes the destitution with which we all of our life face the world. We have very little going for us except our prehensile hands and our enlarged brain. We have no natural protection against heat and cold. We cannot run away, skip up a tree, or burrow into the ground to escape our predators. We have no biological offensive or defensive attributes and practically no "instincts" (inherited, complex behavior patterns). We have a prolonged helpless infancy during which we have to learn almost everything we need not only to survive but to become a fully human being. It looks as if we were a natural born loser — except that our defenselessness and helplessness are correlated with our genius: unspecialization.

The implications of human inadequacy and incompleteness are well summarized by Geertz (1965, p. 108):

> The behavior patterns of lower animals are, at least to a much greater extent, given to them with their physical structure; genetic sources of information order their actions within much narrower ranges of variation, the narrower and more thoroughgoing the lower the animals. For man, what are innately given are extremely general response capacities, which, although they make possible far greater plasticity, complexity, and on the scattered occasions when everything works as it should, effectiveness of behavior, leave it much less precisely regulated.

We are so remarkable just because we are *unspecialized* and are not "precisely regulated." Most other species have adapted for survival by biological specialization, which makes them unfit when the environment radically changes. But we have remained unspecialized, *learning* what was necessary to survive under widely varying and changing conditions.

Unless we learn a lesson from biology, we can lose the advantage of unspecialization. We have adapted to various environments through culture—the techniques for survival embodied in thought, speech, behavior patterns, forms of social organization, and artifacts or technology engendered by our capacity for learning and transmitting knowledge to succeeding generations by demonstration, language, and systems of abstract thought. Culture patterns, too, can become specialized, rigid, and maladaptive. The poetic naturalist and anthropologist Loren Eiseley

(1961, p. 92) comments:

> We are now in a position to see the wonder and terror of the
> human predicament: man is totally dependent on society. Creature
> of dreams, he has created an invisible world of ideas, beliefs, habits,
> and customs which buttress him about and replace for him the
> precise instincts of the lower creatures. In this invisible universe he
> takes refuge, but just as instinct may fail an animal under some shift
> of environmental conditions, so man's cultural beliefs may prove to
> be inadequate to meet a new situation.

In our history we have repeatedly demonstrated the perils of
specializing culture as fixedly as behavior patterns are coded in
the genes of other creatures. Robert S. Morrison (1966, p. 351),
director of the division of biological sciences at Cornell University,
observes that totalitarian societies, which rigidly specify individual
functions and behavior within the state, enjoy a short-run
advantage in dominating a specific historical situation but find that
they have atrophied individual abilities and limited the capability of
their social structure to cope with changed world conditions, and
so become deselected.

Part of the revolt of youth all over the world has been directed
against specialized cultures which are unable to cope with
emerging problems, such as warfare with weapons of annihilation,
racial injustice, and the ecological crisis. But part of the revolt
seems also to be based upon a sort of immaculate conception of
ideas, as if youth, without benefit of wisdom, perceived a priori
that the problems stemmed from the existence of culture—"the
system." Without some sort of culture, we have no place to stand
to improve our relation to our environment, including our human
environment. Ralph Waldo Emerson said, "When me you fly, I am
the wings." It is culture that informs protests against the
inadequacy of certain culture patterns. Without culture, we are
entirely helpless. Geertz (1965, p. 108) comments:

> Undirected by culture patterns—organized systems of significant
> symbols—man's behavior would be virtually ungovernable, a mere
> chaos of pointless acts and exploding emotions, his experience
> virtually shapeless. Culture, the accumulated totality of such

patterns, is not just an ornament of human existence but—the principal basis of its speciality—an essential condition for it.

Geertz (1965, pp. 112–113) summarizes our inadequacy without culture as follows:

> We are, in sum, incomplete or unfinished animals who complete or finish ourselves through culture—and not through culture in a general but through highly particular forms of it: Dobuan and Javanese, Hopi and Italian, upper-class and lower-class, academic and commercial. Man's great capacity for learning, his plasticity, has often been remarked, but what is even more critical is his extreme dependence upon a certain sort of learning: the attainment of concepts, the apprehension and application of specific systems of symbolic meaning. Beavers build dams, birds build nests, bees locate food, baboons organize social groups, and mice mate on the basis of forms of learning that rest predominantly on the instructions encoded in their genes and evoked by appropriate patterns of external stimuli: physical keys inserted into organic locks. But men build dams or shelters, locate food, organize their social groups, or find sexual partners under the guidance of instructions encoded in flow charts and blueprints, hunting lore, moral systems, and aesthetic judgments: conceptual structures molding formless talents.

We are thus an unfinished animal because we have to absorb our culture in order to become fully human. Without the rounding out of our being by learning the significant symbols and skills of a culture, we would be helplessly inadequate to survive. "Man owes his place in nature," says Robert S. Morison (1966, p. 350), "to the fact that he is much better than all other animals at learning from experience and, above all, at sharing his experience with other members of his species." Michael Polyani (1965, pp. 59-60), British mathematician and philosopher, emphasizes:

> The distinctive qualities of man are developed by education. Our native gift of speech enables us to enter on the mental life of man by assimilating our cultural heritage. We come into existence mentally, by adding to our bodily equipment an articulate framework and using it for understanding experience. Human thought grows

only with language and since language can exist only in a society, all thought is rooted in society.

We cannot treat education in our society as a luxury with a low priority in spending our dollars. Nothing is more important to the survival of the human race, especially as our culture becomes more complex, than providing ample opportunities for education of our children. And not entirely formal or academic education, but opportunities in relations with their peers and adults to learn to act like human beings.

We have to learn not only abstract ideas, but also emotions and values. The need even to develop emotions is illustrated by the Harry Harlow experiments with young monkeys which reveal that our primate relatives need to learn to love and make love. Infant monkeys raised alone in cages with substitute or surrogate mothers—chicken wire constructions with nursing nipples, and sometimes terry cloth covers to make them more cuddly—so the infants had no body contact or affection, on reaching adulthood were incapable of affectionate play or sexual mating with other monkeys. We already know how dependent human infants are upon tender, loving care so that they as adults have the capacity to enter warm, affectionate human relationships. Infants can be deprived of opportunities not only to understand their environment, but also to experience how to establish intimate interactions with their fellows. The results of the Harlow experiments suggest that for primates, monkeys and human beings, even sexual intercourse is not instinctual but is a learned response. We seem to have been born more incomplete than we realized.

Society is not the enemy; it is the bearer of the culture so necessary to our completion as human beings. Our dependency upon culture has implications for our attitude toward culture, points out Abraham Maslow (1962, p. 150):

> The main social parallel to this change in our philosophy of human nature is the rapidly growing tendency to perceive the culture as an instrument of need-gratification as well as of frustration and control. We can now reject, as a localism, the almost universal

mistake that the interests of the individual and of society are of *necessity* mutually exclusive and antagonistic, or that civilization is primarily a mechanism for controlling and policing human instinctoid impulses. All these age-old maxims are swept away by the new possibility of divining the main function of a healthy culture as the fostering of universal self-actualization.

This view of the interdependence of culture and personality is shared by sociologists Clyde Kluckhohn and Henry A. Murray (1948, Introd., p. xi) in their "field" approach to personality. They explain:

> . . . we regard the conventional separation of the "organism and his environment," the drama of "the individual versus his society," the bi-polarity between "personality and culture" as false or at least misleading in some important senses. Knowledge of a society or a culture must rest upon knowledge of the individuals who are in that society or share that culture. But the converse is equally true. Personal figures get their definition only when seen against the social and cultural background in which they have their being.

Setting the development of humanness firmly in a particular culture has radically altered our image of ourselves. Thus anthropologist Geertz (1965, p. 99) comments:

> For the eighteenth-century image of man as the naked reasoner that appeared when he took his cultural costumes off, the anthropology of the late nineteenth and early twentieth century substituted the image of man as the transfigured animal that appeared when he put them on.

Our culture dependency may throw some light on the reason that we, of all creatures, are most destructive of our own kind. With our capacity for identification with others, it seems incongruous that we should have such a reputation for mass slaughter in war within our own species. The degree to which culture shapes human personality indicates that we may not be so much the same species as the biological indices, including interbreeding, indicate. We may not have taken enough into account the fact that cultural differences nurture radically different beings who do not identify with each other. Cultural conditioning has introduced what Stephen C. Pepper (1969, pp. 9-10), professor of philosophy at the University of California at Berkeley, says is an entirely novel form of competition in evolutionary history, "the competition between diverse social groups within the same species." He adds that:

> A cultural pattern of social organization is just another biological species emerging on a high plane [and concludes that they] constitute a biological species on the cultural level—"an interthinking population" George Simpson calls them in distinction from "an interbreeding population," which would be the whole human species. But note that a cultural species also interbreeds, propagating its specific cultural pattern.

Thus, when we human beings in one society feel ourselves threatened by those in another society, we deeply feel that it is more than our life that may be attacked; it is the culture that makes our particular kind of human beings which might be destroyed. It is not just *homo sapiens* killing each other; it is human embodiments of differing and competitive cultures in ideological conflict. We can free ourselves of such destructive competition, not by trying to institute a universal culture with its own dangers of rigidity, but by recognizing cultural pluralism. Then perhaps we can be as accepting of cultural differences as we are of biological differences.

A corollary of our incompleteness and need for a prolonged period of acculturation is the uniqueness of human sexuality; not just biological sex as a process for getting sperm and egg together, as occurs periodically in most other animals, but the whole gamut of emotions which makes sexuality a constant and major dynamic among human beings. Loren Eiseley (1961, p. 92) notes that as pre-humans began to develop their unspecialized characteristics, with their native helplessness and need for extended nurture, it ". . . involved the growth of prolonged bonds of affection in the subhuman family because otherwise its naked helpless offspring would have perished." And Lawrence K. Frank (1966, p. 177) points out that human sexuality has evolved into a different activity from the basic mammalian pattern. Among most mammals, copulation takes place only when the female is ovulating and ready for conception. Hence, infrahuman sex is primarily for procreation, while human sexuality serves an additional and significantly creative function. Human sexuality is an almost year-round activity in which man and woman enjoy repeated mutual satisfaction. It serves to form prolonged bonds of affection, instead of just serving for procreation, as the Catholic Church has too long presumed. Among human beings, *sex is a nexus,* a bonding agent stabilizing an elementary social unity, the family, in which human infants have a chance to learn what they need to know to survive on their own. To promote such a stable relationship, the human female makes herself attractive with all the arts at her disposal, while among most other species it is the male who is attractively arrayed and who struts and preens when he seeks the favor of a receptive female.

Sexuality among human beings is more a function of the mind than the body. The pleasure of sex can be constantly present in the mind so that interest is stimulated by the thought of sexual activity without direct stimuli from a potential partner. The brain which requires so much care in maturing its potentialities also provides the constancy of sexual attraction that establishes a monogamous relationship to nurture the mind of the next generation. Like all biological promptings, the unifying urge of sexuality is not inevitable; it can lead to various forms of relationships, or to sheer exploitation for its own sake, but heightened sexuality to provide care during the prolonged infancy of unfinished human beings confers survival value. (Chase, 1965, p. 152.)

From the point of view of humans as an unfinished animal, the old axiom is obviated that "you can't change human nature." Human nature is not unalterably defined biologically, but is a dynamic configuration constantly changing with evolving culture. There is not only a wide variety of cultures, but each culture can and does evolve, some more and some less. Human nature was not established from the beginning, and it can be reshaped, as it constantly has been, by transformed culture patterns. As our technology reshapes the environment, we can modify our culture to adapt our progeny, at least, to the new values and techniques required for survival of the species. Assuming that we have not already gone past the point of no return in our disruption of the ecosystem earth, we can anticipate that people, a million years from now, will be as well or better prepared to cope with their environment than were our ancestors a million years ago, unless our culture is so specialized for exploitation that we cannot adopt a symbiotic relation with the environment.

A Free Spirit

We are an integral part of the continuity of being, but we are under no duress. We are free, as all organisms are free, but we are *more* free than the rest because our intelligence has made us less dependent upon biological adaptation for survival. We are creative. But ultimately we and all our works stand under the same judgment as all other creatures — natural selection, which tests our fitness to survive as part of the great living system.

So far, I have been speaking of us as a category, as species *homo sapiens,* as we are shaped by our biological and cultural inheritance. But we are concrete only as individual men and women. Individuals are not locked into biological or cultural systems; they are free beings. Individuals do not simply react, they act on their own initiative to fulfill their own wishes and desires. They are self-directing in pursuing their own intentions and purposes, even to the point of personal or social self-destruction.

Freedom means self-determination, doing what you want, not the absence of effective causes; it is the freedom to act without duress, not without motive. Gardner Williams (1968, p. 74), professor emeritus of philosophy at the University of Toledo, says, "A free will is a successful participation in the causal processes of nature, not an escape from them. The only relevant unfreedom in this connection is produced by obstacles that cannot be overcome and that compulsively defeat the will." Freedom does not mean pure randomness, or that activities take place in a vacuum. Roger W. Sperry (1965, p. 87) comments:

To a very real and large extent, a person does determine with his own mind what he is going to do from among a number of possibilities. This does not mean, however, that he is free from the forces of his own decision-making machinery. . . from the combined effects of his own thoughts, his own reasoning, his own feeling, his own beliefs, ideals, and hopes, nor does it free him from his inherited makeup or his lifetime memories.

Freedom is being not subject to restraint or compulsion; even though a decision results from a combination of influences, the decision is personal and free.

An understanding of the individual decision-making process has implications for the way we should order decision-making processes in our societies. For convenience, we speak of the "central decider" in our organism. But there seems to be no central core in the individual where the decisions are made for the whole individual. Instead, decisions seem to emerge from a knot of potencies whose interactions make a pattern which coordinates the individual's voluntary activities. Mechanical cybernetic systems reflect some light on how the brain functions, particularly in the operation of feedback. Control is exercised by a signal that a certain need is filled, and the source shuts down the supply, or vice versa, much as a thermostat calls for more or less heat from a boiler. The thermostat does not decide; it senses and reports, and the boiler responds. Computers are cybernetic mechanisms involving says Hoagland (1966, pp. 146-47) "a remarkable complex feedback process including the utilization of information storage and its retrieval, which corresponds in us to memory and recall," and he adds:

> While feedback devices of control have developed rapidly in engineering in the past twenty years as a product of special evolution, biological evolution by natural selection brought these mechanisms to a high order of perfection some hundreds of millions of years ago, and the engineers have been copying in principle some of these processes. Cybernetic mechanisms are dominantly ones of nerve nets and central nerve ganglia or brains. Regulation, for example, of patterned contractions of muscles enabling us to breathe in and out involves alternate excitation and

inhibition playing back and forth in a feedback process from the actions of these muscles and central nervous mechanisms.

The involuntary operation of the diaphragm muscles by the autonomic nervous system is an example of a simple two-way communications system like a temperature control, but the behavior of the whole person is determined by a much more complicated communications system more like a computer, the brain. However, the brain is not linear in operation like a computer. A brain has multiple circuits which function simultaneously and can process many bits of information concurrently, making choices among variables according to perceived values and personal preferences. A computer is faster than a brain and is a marvelous tool for processing quantities of information, but a computer must be programmed while a brain programs itself by self-instruction and by what it chooses to pay attention to. A maxim about computers applies also to the brain—"garbage in, garbage out." The quality of human decisions depends upon the quality of information input—what we experience, hear, read, or watch on TV.

A computer makes no decisions; it follows instructions. A brain is a decision-making process, but there is no "central decider," no entity with power to impose decisions upon the rest of the system. In the brain, decisions are made by the integrated interactions of the whole communications system; a decision emerges as a pattern of sub-decisions. The process of cooperative decision-making in the brain is a model for the decision-making process in any living system, including human voluntary associations—the democratic process.

The phenomenal success of some Japanese corporations seems to be an exemplification of the cybernetic principle in business management. Japanese executives, guided by their traditional sense of courtesy and reluctance to put oneself forward, refrain from claiming credit for their own ideas and from domination. Since company policies are a consensus of the opinions of all the executives, no one person is responsible for success or failure, which is reported to make such companies innovative and risk-taking. Willingness to let public policy be shaped by the interplay of social communications benefits any society; the successful administrator is then the central person who is assigned authority to announce decisions, rather than who autocratically makes them.

A person is a *free spirit*. The "spirit" is not an incorporeal vital or animating principle, it is the product of the intellectual processes, it is the work of the mind. A person is a free spirit in the sense of being unconfined by biological or cultural conditioning since he or she may be motivated by symbols as goals projected into the future. In the phrase of Thoreau, a person "marches to a different drummer." Commitment to a vision of an alternate or better possibility moves a person to transcend the culture's norms. A new conception of how things might be arranged becomes a more powerful motive than the patterns sanctioned by society. Maslow (1962, p. 14) says of that dynamic role of the future in an individual that "self-actualization is meaningless without reference to a currently active future . . . man has his future within him, dynamically active at this present moment."

The capacity to think, to explore, to satisfy curiosity, is one of the basic human drives. Maslow (1962, p. 144) says that "Capacities clamor to be used, and cease their clamor only when they *are* used sufficiently. That is to say, capacities are needs, and therefore are intrinsic values as well." From his study of animals confined in zoos, Desmond Morris (1968, p. 78) discovered the same need for what he called "behavioral outlets." Some well-fed animals in zoos may still be neurotic because they have no outlets for their instinctive behavior. People living in "human zoos" (slums) are likewise deprived of outlets for their natural behavior drives, including what Morris finds to be characteristic of us, namely the need to explore our environment. An individual's sense of well-being is frustrated if denied behavioral outlets, spiritual as well as physical.

Future-oriented conceptual goals, or *hope*, can also be a source of frustration. Our aspirations can exceed our capacity to perform, leaving us with a false sense of inadequacy or cynicism. To reverse an old adage, our failure lies not in ourselves but in our stars — our presumptuous goals.

However, the pursuit of conceptual goals is a primary source of *human creativity*. Our aspirations are a force for more successful adaptation to the environment. Sinnott (1955, p. 81) points out that, "Human history has been molded by the aspirations of that minority of individuals who had the capacity to want something very much." Not only to want something, but to believe in something not yet realized. Belief in a conception of a different possible order creates martyrs. A martyr challenges the finality of an established way of doing things because he or she serves a vision of some "higher" truth or good. A society may be doomed which martyrs creative individuals who call for change. It is salutary for individuals to challenge a culture, often in terms of concepts and values current in their culture but not yet implemented. A society which arbitrarily restricts the freedom of its citizens to modify their culture in view of new possibilities destroys one of the advantages of culture, its rapid adaptability to changing conditions. Freedom is a necessary condition of creative response to the changing requirements of a dynamic environment, and restrictions upon the freedom of individuals, groups, or subcultures within a culture limit the capacity of the whole culture to survive.

The processes encapsulated in the flesh and bones of an individual acquire a personality or character from the persistent pattern of interactions in the communications system. To each of us subjectively, the personality is known as the "self." George Wald (1965, p. 33) says, "That private self that is you or I is the unique composition and structure that come to us via metabolism and inheritance, coupled with a unique personal history that is forever growing." Edmund Sinnott (1955, p. 157) speaks of how remarkable and mysterious the self is:

> This self, this psychological pattern of goals, developing from the simpler biological pattern of the self-regulating organism, is the basis of human personality. It is a most remarkable thing. It maintains its integrity in space and time. It persists. It has a history.

However long its history may be, however varied its surroundings and its activities, it remains the same individual. Matter enters and leaves it, and its material constitution may be replaced many times, but its fundamental organization is unaltered. It is unique; not just one of a long series of similar units, but unlike—or so it seems—any other individual that ever lived.

An unchanging genetic constitution is doubtless of basic importance here, but characteristics acquired during the individual's history—bodily skills, memories, tastes, and prejudices—are also built into the persisting self. For any living machine to maintain the delicate physiological balance necessary for life is remarkable enough, but to preserve its specific character as well, unaltered by the flux of chemical and physical change, is indeed past understanding now. Human personality, tenuous as it may sometimes seem to be, is of surprisingly tough fiber. The knot of norms, goals, steady states, potencies, and purposes of which it is composed is almost impossible to loosen. To kill it is easy, and to direct the course of its development not difficult; but to break it down and make it into something different as a sculptor does with his clay; to shake it free from its past, to destroy its identity—this the organized pattern of personality most successfully resists.

The identity of a person receives part of its stability by identification with the traditions of the culture, as Erik H. Erikson (1950, p. 232), psychoanalyst, emphasizes. Of the identity of a person he says:

It is a comradeship with the ordering ways of distant times and different pursuits, as expressed in the simple products and sayings of such times and pursuits. Although aware of the relativity of all the various life-styles which have given meaning to human striving, the possessor of integrity is ready to defend the dignity of his own life-style against all physical and economic threats. For he knows that an individual life is the accidental coincidence of but one life cycle with but one segment of history; and that for him all human integrity stands or falls with the one style of integrity of which he partakes. The style of integrity developed by his own culture or civilization thus becomes the "patrimony of his soul," the seal of his moral paternity of himself.

In view of the "culte de moi" which is recurring in this age, it is important to note that there can be no personality, no character

with integrity, without identification with something more enduring than self by relating to meaningful processes that transcend
the contingencies of individual life. Teilhard de Chardin (1961, p.
263), the paleontologist, warns against the errors of egoism:

> Its only mistake, but a fatal one, is to confuse individuality with
> personality. . . . To be fully ourselves it is in the opposite direction,
> in the direction of convergence with all the rest, that we must
> advance—toward the "other." The goal of ourselves, the acme of
> our originality, is not our individuality but our person; and accord-
> ing to the evolutionary structure of the world, we can only find our
> person by uniting together. There is no mind without a synthesis.

Thus we can see that a person is born with a potential identity and
achieves character and personal integrity by identifying with the
values of the culture or subculture.

Long before we had a better idea of the structure and dynamics
of selfhood, we were aware of the unique significance of the
individual; we called the mysterious essence of the individual the
soul. This is still a useful word to indicate that the processes which
go on within the body coalesce in a unique identity of character.
You don't *have* a soul; you *are* a soul. The identity of the
individual was so unique that earlier people thought it was an
essence or soul which pre-existed and entered the body at birth to
give it life and which, for that matter, had a post-existence when it
left the body at death. Now that we have a better understanding of
the nature of the soul as an emergent property of the organized
interaction of the individual living system with the environment,
we also understand that the soul does not exist apart from the
organism of which it is the characteristic manifestation, any more
than does personality or character. Individuals are not immortal
in their souls, nor do they need to be. The duration of people, as we
have already seen, inheres in the continuity of the germ plasm, or
the preservation of the gene pool. And the meaning of life is
achieved by identification with the transcendent order. Nor do we
any longer need the concept of a pre-existent soul to account for
life; we know that the transmission of life is the work of the genes
in the sperm and egg cells. Still, in our Christian culture, we have

reserved the concept of the soul for human beings; now we see that insight was correct inasmuch as the peculiarly human individual we identify with a soul is a product of human culture.

A Little Lower than the Angels

We do pretty well—for human beings. This thought makes me patient with myself and with my fellow human beings at our bungling, bumptious worst. For we are not gods with absolute powers to manipulate the world. Nor are we gifted with pure reason which could bring perfect concepts to bear upon complex problems. We are product and part of the evolutionary process, gifted with an enlarged brain that makes it possible for us to understand an orderly universe. But all we can know is *how* the universe works and all we can do is facilitate its operations; we cannot impose our intellectual designs upon it. We have to honor the laws of the great living system or perish. Ralph Burhoe (1966, Ch. II, p. 19), director of the Center for Advanced Study in Theology and the Sciences, observes:

> The interconnections worked out in recent decades between psychology, anthropology, biology, chemistry, physics, and astrophysics have interlocked the history of individual men and societies of men tightly into the cosmic network of reality. There is no other possibility for man, nor for any creature, but to bow before this hidden but omnipotent reality and serve its sacred ends. Its ends or values are sacred and holy because there are none other, neither for man nor for any other contingent entity anywhere.

In the same vein, Jonas Salk (1973, p. 53) says:

> Since survival is a prerequisite for evolution to proceed, and since evolution is essential for increasing probability for survival, existence depends upon the establishment of patterns of order relevant to a dynamic evolutionary process. . . . When we speak of the survival of the wisest, by wisest we mean those who comprehend the survival-evolutionary process, . . . and who make choices such as enhance the possibility of existence rather than nonexistence, recognizing evolution as an essential and inexorable continuum of growth and development.

In humans the evolutionary process comes to consciousness, but thoughtful people have the same dependency on the ongoing process which sustains them as the human brain does on the body which sustains it. We must have greater respect and reverence for that ongoing process or we will destroy its capacity to support us. We are *part of our own environment;* we are the most creative, dynamic, and flexible part of the environment, but anything we do that affects the system in which we are involved must be done with care, lest we start a destructive chain reaction we did not anticipate. The basic structure and dynamics of the greater system are given and we are constrained to work in harmony with them. Ralph Burhoe (Ch. II, p. 17) emphasizes the chastened view of humanity which is emerging from the sciences:

> The so-called triumph and dominance of man over nature, and the doctrine that scientific knowledge now makes man more than ever the master of his own fate, is a superficial and erroneous view. Man cannot alter one jot or tittle of the cosmic law, whether it be the law of gravity or the amount of energy available to support life on earth. A more exact way of reporting the human condition is to say that the cosmos has given to man his life and his powers to know and cooperate with the laws of the cosmos, such that man can become increasingly an incarnation of what the cosmos has decreed for successful and advancing life patterns.

This is a much more humble view than the *Book of Genesis* notion that we should subdue the earth and have dominion over all of its creatures, or the religious humanist notion in the late 19th and early 20th centuries of humans as an imperious rationalist. In fact, we have come full circle and are again much closer to the view expressed by the poet who composed *Psalm VIII* (Verses 3–5), "When I consider thy heavens, the work of thy fingers, the moon and the stars, which thou hast ordained; What is man, that thou art mindful of him? and the son of man, that thou visitest him? For thou hast made him a little lower than the angels, and hast crowned him with glory and honor."

Chapter **4**

The Search for Hidden Reality

THE MOST IMPORTANT capacity of humans is reflective thinking. But how do you know that what you are thinking has anything to do with reality, with the way things really are or will be? How do you know what to believe? How do you make up your mind as to what is most probably true?

We are not asking, "What is *the* truth?" "The truth" in religion is generally a claim made that a proposition is axiomatic. The question is, is it so? A proposition is true if I act on it and my experience bears out the expectation set up by believing the proposition; the feedback must be consistent with the input.

In order to consider the question of how do you know what to believe, we have to re-evaluate some of the popular assumptions about how we acquire reliable information, the method or grounds of knowledge, or "epistemology." To reorient our assumptions about epistemology can be an emotionally disturbing experience, as our theory of knowledge affects our view of reality. It can be painful to have old certainties challenged. But the sciences have been shaping some new views about the process by which we convert experience into reliable symbols that oblige us to reconsider popular notions of learning.

113

Scientism is Dead

A classical way of establishing the credibility of a proposition was to claim that it was a "special revelation", a unique disclosure of divine will or truth. *If special revelation does not now give us guidance and new information, it never did.* Special revelation is dead as a way of knowing; it has been replaced by the epistemology of science.

The "scientism" which undermined the authority of revealed religion is dead—that is, the 19th century determinism of mechanistic materialism which held that, given time, everything could be known and controlled, is no longer the mood of science. Scientism is now the idol of only those caught in a cultural lag. Contemporary scientists are the first to disclaim potential omniscience and omnipotence; the scientific discipline has built-in checks and balances against inordinate claims of finality. Intuition, insight, and imagination are acknowledged as important in originating new concepts in science as they are in theology; now if theology will acknowledge the rules of evidence of science, the two disciplines will converge.

Charles H. Townes (1966, pp. 301-02), physicist at the Massachusetts Institute of Technology, describes scientism:

> The march of science during the Eighteenth and Nineteenth Centuries produced enormous confidence in its success and generality. One field after another fell before the objective inquiry, experimental approach, and the logic of science. Scientific laws appeared to take on an absolute quality, and it was very easy to be convinced that science in time would explain everything. This was the time when Laplace could say that if he knew the position and velocity of every particle in the universe, and could calculate sufficiently well, he would then predict the entire future. Laplace was only expressing the evident experience of his time, that the success and precision of scientific laws had changed determinism from a speculative argument to one which seemed inescapable. This was the time when the devout Pasteur, asked how he as a scientist could be religious, simply replied that his laboratory was one realm, and that his home and religion were a completely different one. There are today many vestiges of this Nineteenth Century scientific absolutism in our

thinking and attitudes. It has given Communism, based on Marx's Nineteenth-Century background, some of its sense of the inexorable course of history and of "scientific" planning of society.

Toward the end of the nineteenth century, many of the philosophical and conceptual bases of science were disturbed or radically challenged by the emergence of paradoxical problems, such as that of the nature of light. Light seemed to behave as if it were composed of small particles, and then it seemed to display the properties of waves. This paradox was resolved in the mid-1920's by the development of a new set of ideas known as "quantum mechanics," which sees the photons or light particles moving in statistical waves; that is, the steady stream of photons are more concentrated in wave forms in some parts of the stream than in others. For differing purposes, scientists still successfully treat light as either particles or waves. The apparent paradox of conceptualizing light either as waves or as particles results from relying on the old conceptual base. "The trouble was," says Townes (1966, p. 302), "that scientists were thinking in terms of their common everyday experiences and that experience encompassed the behavior of large objects, but not yet many atomic phenomena."

The eighteenth and nineteenth century assumption was that scientific concepts had a one-to-one relation with physical reality; they had a direct reference to concrete entities, as if they were mirror images. But this assumption about concepts was upset by quantum mechanics, says William G. Pollard (1958, p. 143), Executive Director of the Oak Ridge Institute of Nuclear Studies:

> We can understand something of the fundamental character of the revolution produced in physics when classical mechanics was converted into quantum mechanics by noting that this traditional relationship between our knowledge of the world and the world itself is radically altered in quantum physics. The alteration is of such a character that it is no longer possible to think of this in terms of a contact print. Rather we have to think of a complex system of lenses placed between the negative and photographic print which projects onto the print a modified image of the pic-

ture on the negative. We can have on the print, representing what we can know about the world, not a direct image in one-to-one correspondence with the world, but only a kind of a shadow pattern of reality. Thus, what quantum mechanics introduced into physics was not merely a different or alternative description of the structure and behavior of the external world, but more basically a radical modification in the relationship between the real world and our knowledge of the world.

Newton's world was a world suitable for human beings. The phenomena he dealt with were sensible; they were large enough to be confidently known through the senses. His laws dealt with objects which behaved predictably—falling bodies and planetary motions and organic fuels. It may be comfortable to live in such a world corresponding to our scale of being, but as we continue to explore it in minute detail, it becomes more obscure and unmanageable. Newton's laws are still perfectly satisfactory for gross mechanical purposes, but their clarity and predictability vanish when we dig a little deeper. The more closely we examine the world, the more it looks as if we are going to have to go along with it rather than control it.

Werner Heisenberg, a German physicist, discovered in 1927 that when subatomic particles are examined, we are not certain what is going on; just the act of observation alters the situation. This limitation in knowledge Heisenberg called "the uncertainty principle," which states that both the position and the velocity of a particle cannot be precisely specified simultaneously. Although this paradox is of no consequence in observing anything larger than the point of a pin, it does make the sub-structure of matter indeterminate. For when we get down to the fine points, we miss the point. The quantum of light necessary to observe a particle is near enough the mass of the particle to significantly disturb the position of the particle on impact. Apparently this lower limit on observation is not a consequence of human ignorance or ineptness which could be corrected in time, but a limitation built into the composition of reality. Since I am mathematically illiterate, I cannot appreciate the beauty of the mathematical equations that demonstrate this principle, but I can understand that it has significant implications not only for the nature of matter but for our theory of knowledge.

What the uncertainty principle says is that we can't know all about a particle from one point of view, or by one experiment. Concepts which seem contradictory or paradoxical when arrived at by different methods are not necessarily incompatible but *supplementary*. Niels Bohr, Danish physicist, proposed the concept of "complementarity" when apparently contradictory results in elementary particle physics forced an expansion of the frame of reference of classical physics. Bohr *(Encyclopaedia Britannica, 1970, Vol. 3, p. 857)* defined "complementarity" as follows:

> Evidence obtained under different experimental conditions cannot be comprehended within a single picture, but must be regarded as complementary in the sense that only the totality of the phenomena exhausts the possible information about the objects.

Bohr himself came increasingly to believe that complementarity was a concept that could be useful in integrating paradoxical data in other systems than quantum mechanics. Townes (1966, pp. 309-10) says:

> Niels Bohr has already suggested that perception of man, or any living organism as a whole, and of his physical constitution represents this kind of complementarity. That is, the precise and close examination of the atomic makeup of man may of necessity blur our view of him as a living and spiritual being.

Different conditions of observation, such as an analytical approach by reducing an object to its elements or an intuitive approach which perceives the patterns and relationships of elements in a whole, can result in apparent contradictions which can be resolved by recognizing that neither description is complete or totally correct, but both are complementary and necessary to a more complete understanding of reality. Thomas R. Blackburn (1971, p. 1003), associate professor of chemistry at Hobart and William Smith College, comments:

It is conceivable, then, that the notion of complementarity offers a method of including both sensuous and intellectual knowledge of nature in a common frame of reference. The result, far more than a mere compromise or amalgamation of the two viewpoints, could be a richer science, in which esthetic and quantitative valuations, each retaining its own integrity, would contribute equally to the description of nature that science long ago took for its province. Further, it may produce a scientific ethic that is less destructive toward nature.

Quantum mechanics has not only deepened our understanding of matter but, in the concepts of Heisenberg and Bohr, modified science to give us a whole new approach to understanding all of reality, which transcends and integrates partial and paradoxical observations.

The principle of complementarity, for instance, obviates the classical absolute dualism of body and mind, or of materialism and idealism. According to materialism, the body including the brain is a physical process entirely reducible to matter, subject to biological laws, and observable to others. According to idealism, the mind is an autonomous process observable only to the subject and reported to others, and as "nous," "psyche," or "soul" did not originate in and is not reducible to matter. Each school of thought, in its many permutations, claims that its position represents the fundamental constituent of the universe and that neither can be explainable in terms of the other. Idealism is based upon a subjective reference to the functioning of the body as a whole, while materialism is based upon an objective reference to an analysis of the constituents. From these different points of view, they arrive at opposing concepts. Taken as complementary, they can be seen as Taoist "Yin and Yang" concepts, fitting together to make a more complete representation of human beings.

This duality, if not absolute dualism, seems to be characteristic of the functioning of each human brain. Warren S. Brown (1975, p. 120), psychiatrist at the UCLA School of Medicine, writes:

> Over the past two decades an increasing amount of data has been accumulating which suggests that this duality in thought modes is a reflection of the concentration of different mental abilities in the

right and left cerebral hemispheres of the brain.... It is a unique aspect of the human brain that, in the case of the more complex kinds of mental processing, the right and left hemispheres appear to have quite different modes of operation.... The difference between the functions of the two hemispheres, and the fact that either hemisphere alone is sufficient for consciousness, personality, and thinking, has led to the theory that man has two potentially independent minds, a logical-verbal mind in the left hemisphere and a more image-oriented and intuitive mind in the right hemisphere.

The conflicting modes in which we picture the surround seems to be less a difference between individuals and more a matter of which hemisphere of the brain in each individual is dominant for a particular purpose.

The confidence with which laypeople expect scientists to come up with answers to all possible questions has been considerably chastened by the discovery of the limits of observation based on quantum mechanics. It may be that in many fields of human concern we will come up against an inability to control all the variables in the situation at the same time, and thus be unable, by the nature of things, to completely predict and control our environment. There may be a limit to how completely we can know.

After surveying the implications of the study of small particles, Lincoln Barnett (1962, pp. 34-35) concludes:

Quantum physics thus appears to shake two pillars of the old science, causality and determinism. For by dealing in terms of statistics and probabilities it abandons all idea that nature exhibits an inexorable sequence of cause and effect between individual happenings. And by its admission of margins of uncertainty it yields up the ancient hope that science, given the present state and velocity of every material body in the universe, can forecast the history of the universe for all time. One by-product of this surrender is a new argument for the existence of free will. For if physical events are indeterminate and the future is unpredictable, then perhaps the unknown quantity called "mind" may yet guide man's destiny among the infinite uncertainties of a capricious universe. Another conclusion of greater scientific importance is that in the evolution of quantum physics the barrier between man, peering dimly through the clouded window of his senses, and whatever objective reality may exist has been rendered almost impassable.

Quantum mechanics has also upset the old dichotomy between matter and spirit. A hard and fast distinction has classically been made between material and spiritual things on the supposition that matter was hard and inert and somehow inimical to the highest human interests. But it begins to appear that matter is no such palpable stuff. Einstein's little formula of $E=MC^2$ has terrific implications beyond the production of power; it also says that matter and intangible energy are convertible into each other. Matter is at bottom energy, and vice versa. The old solid, substantial view of matter has disappeared before our eyes. It is distressing to our old sense of certainty and reliability. William G. Pollard (1966, p. 184) suggests how far we can go in this direction:

> The recent breakthrough in the discovery of SU(6) and its capacity faithfully to delineate the whole spectrum of strange particles, anti-particles, and mesons which make up matter hints at a new underlying level of reality. It suggests that neutrons and protons along with all the other "elementary" particles are themselves structures composed of odd underlying entities called "quarks". On the other hand, nature may prove to be so constituted that quarks cannot exist by themselves. If so, the basic constituents of matter as we now know it may be systems of subunits which themselves do not exist as observable entities. Or to put it another way, what we know as matter may prove to be only a shadow formed by a six-dimensional special unitary transformation in Hilbert space.

You may not understand any more than I do precisely what that means, but both of us can at least see that if matter is "only a shadow formed by a six-dimensional special unitary transformation in Hilbert space," it is not as substantial as we thought it was.

If Quantum Theory has led us to the inner limits of knowledge, the Theory of Relativity leads us to the outer limits. As the Quantum Theory has shaped our concepts of the atom, the basic units of matter and energy, and the realities which are too elusive and too small to be perceived, Relativity Theory has shaped our concepts of space, time, gravitation, and the cosmic realities which are too remote and too vast to be perceived, says Lincoln Barnett.

When Albert Einstein, a twenty-six-year-old patent-office clerk in Switzerland, published his short paper on the *Special Theory of Relativity* in 1905, his fundamental postulate was: "all the phenomena of nature, all the laws of nature, are the same for all systems that move uniformly relative to one another." This reiterates the scientist's faith in the universal harmony of natural law if the systems and their relations are specified. Barnett (1962, p. 46) adds:

> It also advises the scientist to stop looking for any absolute, stationary frame of reference in the universe. The universe is a restless place: stars, nebulae, galaxies, and all the vast gravitational systems of outer space are incessantly in motion. But their movements can be described only with respect to each other, for in space there are no directions and no boundaries.

The reason there is no absolute frame of reference is that Einstein discarded the conceptions of *space* and *time* as self-existent frameworks within which the constituents of the universe do their "wheeling and dealing." To Newton, space was a physical reality, a fixed frame of reference against which all motion could be measured. This is a popular assumption most of us share simply because it seems obvious to us and it never occurs to us to think of it in any other way, along with the assumption that time is also an infinite passage of something self-existent, like a flowing river on whose surface events are carried away like floating leaves. Our greatest handicap in understanding the world is the obvious, common-sense notions reported to us by our senses; when Copernicus proposed that the sun was the center of our solar system, the resistance to this concept came from people whose common sense told them that the sun rose and set, as any fool could plainly see. Einstein proposes that we make just as radical a revision of our concepts of time and space. *Space*, according to Einstein, is simply "the order of relation of things among themselves"; without things occupying it, it is nothing. *Space is a void delineated only by the presence of observable objects.*

This resolves the question that used to trouble me when I couldn't sleep as a boy: what is outside of that? The infinite regression implied in this question is terminated by the answer, "literally nothing." Where there is no thing, there is nothing. Of nothing, of sheer emptiness, there is no limit.

Correlated with the conception that space is defined by the relation of things, Einstein proposed the concept of a *finite universe.* There is a limit to how large the universe is, which mathematicians have figured to be about 70 billion light-years in diameter — that's 420,000,000,000,000,000,000,000 miles, so we will get some impression of the magnitude. That's sufficiently enormous to encompass what we see. This is not a static but a dynamic universe. It is expanding into the void at an amazing rate. And the expansion began about ten billion terrestrial years ago. We don't yet know whether this expansion will continue indefinitely, or whether it will sometime start contracting and fall back into one dense, terribly hot, mass which will again explode and start the whole process over again. But we do have pretty good grounds for believing that, as Barnett (1962, pp. 102-3) says:

> . . . the substance and energy of the universe are inexorably diffusing like vapor through the insatiable void. The sun is slowly but surely burning out, the stars are dying embers, and everywhere in the cosmos heat is turning to cold, matter is dissolving into radiation, and energy is being dissipated into empty space.
>
> The universe is thus progressing toward an ultimate "heat-death", or as it is technically defined, a condition of "maximum entropy." When the universe reaches this state some billions of years from now all the processes of nature will cease. All space will be the same temperature. No energy can be used because all of it will be uniformly distributed through the cosmos. There will be no light, no life, no warmth—nothing but perpetual and irrevocable stagnation. Time itself will come to an end.

"Time itself will come to an end," said Barnett, because Einstein also dispensed with the concept of absolute time. *Time is a subjective perception of a sequence of events,* just as space is an

THE SEARCH FOR HIDDEN REALITY

order of material objects. Barnett (1962, p. 147) quotes Einstein to explain the nature of time:

> The experiences of an individual appear to us arranged in a series of events; in this series the single events which we remember appear to be ordered according to the criterion of "earlier" and "later." There exists, therefore, for the individual, an I-time, or subjective time. This in itself is not measurable. I can, indeed, associate numbers with events, in such a way that a greater number is associated with the later event than with an earlier one. This association I can define by means of a clock by comparing the order of events furnished by the clock with the order of the given series of events. We understand by a clock something which provides a series of events which can be counted.

Barnett (1962, p. 47) comments: "By referring our own experiences to a clock (or a calendar) we make time an objective concept. Yet the time intervals provided by a clock or a calendar are by no means absolute quantities imposed on the entire universe by divine edict." For instance, all the time measurements ever used by humans are geared to the rotations of our earth, but an inhabitant of the planet Mercury would have an entirely different scale of time. Mercury rotates on its axis once every 58.6 of our days — which is how long a "day" is on Mercury, while it orbits the sun once every 88 or our days, which is how long its "year" is. If we radioed inhabitants of Mercury that our spaceship with crew was arriving in 37 days, they would have to correlate their time frame with ours in order to know when to prepare for guests. "For relativity tells us there is no such thing as a fixed interval of time independent of the system to which it is referred," says Barnett (1962, p. 48).

For fixed time and for stable space, Einstein has an alternative: the concept of the *space-time continuum*. The space-time continuum is four dimensional, which means that dimensions of space and time are continuous as north and south are continuous even though they indicate different directions. To locate a moving object, it is necessary to give the three dimensions of space and the fourth coordinate of time. If you want to give the position of an airplane in flight, you have to give longitude, latitude, altitude, and time. All events transpire in this four-dimensional space-time continuum, so you can't stand still and remain in the same place. If you stand still, you may feel that the immediate space coordinates around you are not changing, but everything is in motion and the larger coordinates, whose relative change in relationship to us is measured in time, show us to be in a different position.

If you have been able, with me, to appreciate, if not completely understand, what I have reported about the transposition of matter and time and space introduced by quantum physics and the theory of relativity, you are in a position to understand the new mood of science. It is a mood not of brash self-confidence and aggressive control of the world, but of reverence before its mysteries. Barnett (1962, p. 117) comments:

> In the evolution of scientific thought, one fact has become impressively clear: there is no mystery of the physical world which does not point to a mystery beyond itself. All highroads of the intellect, all byways of theory and conjecture lead ultimately to an abyss that human ingenuity can never span. For man is enchained by the very condition of his being, his finiteness and involvement in nature.

Awareness of the boundaries of mystery is what has made so many scientists religious. Not in the sense of Pasteur's piety in a realm separate from his laboratory, as mentioned in the earlier quotation from Townes, but in the sense of awe before the grandeur and complexity the scientists contemplate. Einstein (Barnett, p. 162, p.108) once said:

> The most beautiful and most profound emotion we can experience is the sensation of the mystical. It is the sower of all true science. He to whom this emotion is a stranger, who can no longer wonder and stand rapt in awe, is as good as dead. To know that what is impenetrable to us really exists, manifesting itself as the highest wisdom and the most radiant beauty which our dull faculties can comprehend only in their most primitive forms—this knowledge, this feeling is at the center of true religiousness.

The world does not now appear to us like a great mechanism which can be redesigned to suit our purposes. The certainties of Biblical cosmology, where everything was created and sustained by a benevolent Creator, were replaced in the eighteenth and nineteenth centuries by the certainties of science, where everything was shaped by inexorable cause and effect and thus could be precisely predicted and effectively controlled. By the middle of the twentieth century our scientific research had revealed that we understood only a small segment of the nature of reality and that there were outer reaches in the microcosm and the macrocosm which elude our comprehension and control. Barnett (1962, p. 115) comments that ". . . Relativity, like the Quantum Theory, draws man's intellect still further away from the Newtonian universe, firmly rooted in space and time and functioning like some great unerring, and manageable, machine." Consequently, knowledge produced by the sciences is held much more tentatively by scientists than by many laypeople, tremendously impressed by the triumphs of technology. Science cannot be expected to solve all problems.

The Middle Range

We live in the middle range. The problems we confront, the challenges to which we have to respond, and the questions we have to answer come to us from a level of concreteness where our senses and intelligence are adequate to report what is going on so we may appropriately respond. We live in the middle range between the elusive microcosm and macrocosm, but the range in which we live is as real and substantial as we are. In fact, it is interesting that in the order of magnitude, we human beings stand just about half way between the smallest and the largest entities in the cosmos. Physically, we are as Barnett (1962, p. 22) says as much larger in size than an electron, one of the smallest physical entities, as we are smaller than a super-giant red star, the largest material body in the universe. And the evolutionary process has fitted us to cope successfully with the relatively immediate environment in this middle range.

It is only at the extremities that things become vague; not only the extremities in space, but also in time. The scientists have nothing to say about origins or beginnings and ends or last things;

they push their speculations about the process back to the "big bang" which seems to have begun this era in the universe, or project their speculations forward to the "heat death" which may end it, but they are confident that beyond the veil of mystery in either time-direction something is still going on out of which the present processes arise and in which they will submerge. We can be content to be agnostic before what Harlow Shapley (1966, p. 281) calls the "rather hopeless unclarity" about the beginning and the end.

Our naive forebears, standing almost at the beginning of recorded history and with little perspective on time or space, spoke confidently of "original creation" and of the "last judgment" (though they did think the present organization of the world would be replaced by a better one), but the sciences have so opened up the universe of time and space that we no longer speak with certainty (nor feel the need to) of such ultimates. Only lingering habits of traditional thought impel us to try to define the extremities before we can feel secure in the known world. Actually, we can accept ultimate mysteries confident that within the known cosmic magnitude there is sufficient order and stability for our needs.

For our purposes of adequately coping with the environment, there comes a point of diminishing returns in the quest for knowledge. For instance, there are limits to what I need to know about a chair, depending upon my interests. In order to decide whether I will sit in a chair, I need to know only if it is comfortable and strong enough to support me. If I plan to buy one, I will also wish to know about the chair's design, color, construction and materials. There is available information I do not need in either case. Physicists may explain to me that the chair is ultimately composed of such intangible stuff as electrons, protons, and other elementary particles whirling in space. But they are telling me more than I care to know in order to relate confidently to the chair. Besides, they are not describing a concrete chair; they are describing the composition of all matter, which is not useful information in buying a chair. Knowledge about levels of concreteness corresponding to my own level of concreteness is sufficient for my concrete needs. Likewise, I need to know only enough about time and space to order my relations in them. I can be satisfied with understanding the middle range of phenomena, while being interested in what scientists are learning from probing the extremities to the extent that such information modifies my understanding of the middle range. In the midst of infinities, I can be content living on such a central island of stability as I can discern. From the relatively stable central island of the middle range of the knowledge continuum, I can serenely gaze toward the attenuated extremities. As we enlarge the diameter of the domain of the known, the boundary of the unknown increases geometrically, but it also becomes more remote and more inconsequential. The unknown may set limits to my predictions and confident control of related phenomena, but its immediate relevance decreases with its remoteness in time and space. The scientists have cleared an area in the universe radiating from ourselves, of the confidently and predictably known, that is more reliable than the relatively closed little cosmos of the Greeks, who instituted the categories of absolutes.

The Habit of Truth

The earth is a relatively stable system. The patterns of information we have about it are fairly reliable. But when some new insight comes to us, or a new concept is presented to us, how do we know it is reliable? What does it mean to say something is "true"? Bronowski (1965, pp. 32-33), the late scientist who composed and dramatized the 1974 NET-TV series on "The Ascent of Man," says:

> The words true and false have their place ... when the data of the senses have been put together to make a thing [a word or symbol] which is held in the mind. Only then is it meaningful to ask whether what we think about the thing is true. That is, we can now deduce how the thing should behave, and see whether it does so. ...What the human mind makes of the sense data, and thinks about, is always a created thing. The construction is true or false by the test of its behavior. We have constructed the thing from the data; we

now deduce how the thing should behave; and if it does not, then our construction was false. What was false was not the sense data, but our interpretation of them: we constructed a hallucination.

What is true is that which turns out to be so. If I tell you it is three blocks from here to Main Street and you act on it and when you come to the third corner find the sign for Main Street, you judge that what I told you was true. *A true statement is a prediction which is confirmed by experience.* A statement is neither true nor false which is not predictive of some kind of activity. Truth is judged in relation to experience in the structure of reality. The meaning of a conception, as the American pragmatists C. S. Peirce and William James taught, is to be found in the kind of activity it causes you to engage in; if it leads you to do what you intend, it is true; if not, it is false. Charles S. Peirce (Lipmann, 1960, p. 129) said, "The opinion which is fated to be ultimately agreed to by all those who investigate, is what we mean by truth, and the object represented in this opinion is the real." The truth of an idea is to be tested by its practical consequences. Thought is a guide to action and is validated by the way it works in the concrete world of events, except that a statement may be true when it is consistent with another statement which we already know to be congruent with reality.

The scientific revolution begins, says Bronowski (1965, p. 46), when no statement is allowed to remain untested:

> The habit of testing and correcting the concept by its consequences in experience has been the spring within the movement of our civilization ever since. In science and in art and in self-knowledge we explore and move constantly by turning to the world of sense to ask, Is this so? This is the habit of truth.

Although humans have wandered off into many unproductive and contentious ways of validating truth, such as claiming it came by special revelation from a supernatural unquestionable source, or came from some private mystical experience which is unconfirmable, we have always been able to conceive of new ideas and substantiate them in the same way, by insight and experience. Science has now made the process more systematic, but the validation of information or ideas has always been empirical.

In our Western culture we are so thoroughly imbued with the axiomatic logic of the Greeks and the claims of special revelation by orthodox Christianity, based upon the poetic claims of the Old Testament prophets—"Thus saith the Lord," that we miss the fact that no alleged truth has ever been valid unless it has been tested against experience. *If special revelation does not occur today, it never did.* The people of the Old Testament times knew this, and relied on the *unfolding of history* to differentiate between true and false prophets. Thus, in Deuteronomy (18:21-22), the writer asks the rhetorical question, "How shall we know the word which the Lord hath not spoken?" and then answers, "When a prophet speaketh in the name of the Lord, if the thing follow not, nor come to pass, that is the thing which the Lord hath not spoken, but the prophet hath spoken it presumptuously."

Or, in I Kings 22 the prophet Micaiah is denounced by King Ahab for prophesying that Ahab will be destroyed if he goes to battle against Syria. The King, until he returns, orders the prophet to be put in prison on bread and water. To which the prophet responds, "If thou return at all in peace, the Lord hath not spoken by me." Micaiah recognized that the validation of his prophecy would be in the outcome of the King's activity.

In another conflict of opinion, the prophet Jeremiah (28:1-9) found that during the Babylonian exile of the Israelites, he alone among the prophets was not optimistic about the early demise of Babylonian power and return of the Israelites to Jerusalem. Jeremiah defended his opinion by saying, "The prophet which prophesieth of peace, when the word of the prophet shall come to pass, then shall the prophet be known, that the Lord hath truly sent him."

What became of the prophets who prophesied falsely, whose opinions were not borne out by the events of history? Most of them are unmentioned and forgotten. Only those prophets whose judgments were vindicated by the course of events are now remembered as the great prophets of Israel. They met the test of experience. The process of arriving at truth throughout history has been by trial and error, which is very slow. Nonetheless, the conclusions arrived at empirically by our ancestors were valid and are still valid insofar as the situation has not changed.

But the discipline of science has speeded up the process of arriving at truth by making the process systematic. Science is a discipline whose possibilities Francis Bacon discerned in the seventeenth century and whose methodology and achievements developed rapidly in the eighteenth and nineteenth centuries. But like the little boy who was delighted to learn that he had been writing prose, we have unsystematically been using some of the methods of science for a long time. People have long conceived of new notions or possibilities, which we now call "hypotheses," and left them to trial and error to be justified, a process which we have now organized as *controlled experiments*. The difference is in immediately testing a new idea under controlled conditions. *Science was born when philosophers rolled up their sleeves.* One of the eighteenth century scientists was Joseph Priestley, a British Unitarian minister who discovered oxygen and the process of carbonation of water, but who called himself "an experimental philosopher." He made his own equipment and conducted his own experiments. Philosophers did not think of soiling their hands with manual labor until the time of the Protestant Reformation, which dignified all forms of labor, including the most menial. Until philosophers roll up their sleeves, they are intellectuals whose insights and conceptions may be creative but are irrelevant and meaningless until somebody tries them out. The genius of science is that the person who has a new idea then tries it out, and publishes not only the findings but the *procedures* so that others may duplicate the experiment in order to see if the findings are confirmed or not.

In the sense of controlled experiments, many disciplines cannot be scientific in the full sense of the word. The hypotheses of theology, for instance, cannot be taken into a laboratory for deliberate experiment where all the variables are under control; only history can validate many concepts of theology. Political science and sociology also work under this handicap; they must wait until the value of their theories is demonstrated in the course of time. So the disciplines of science are applicable in varying degrees to different fields of interest.

The scientific method is a tested set of procedures for analyzing various phenomena in nature, primarily for discovering the regularities and uniformities. When regularities in sequences of events are discovered, the description of these constitutes what we call a "natural law." It is important to remember that the regularities do not occur because of the law, but the *law is formulated to describe the regularities*. This is quite different from our experience with civil law, which legislative bodies have enacted in order to control human behavior. An enacted law defines what is acceptable behavior and exacts penalities; it does not describe a discovered sequence of interconnected events. Civil laws—which declare how people *should* behave, not how they *will* behave— have little usefulness for making predictions, which is the most significant function of the laws discovered by science. It is because science discovers reliable formulas, expressed as laws, that science is so successful in controlling nature. What has really happened is that the scientists have discovered laws of nature and obeyed them. Having learned how the world works, science is able to use the forces in nature to improve the human condition by manipulating the environment. Science is one of the most significant developments of our cultural evolution and is responsible for the tremendously accelerated rate of achievement of the past two centuries, but it also has, through technology, jeopardized the human and other species. Ralph Burhoe (1966, p. 6) comments:

> The sciences constitute human culture's most radical advance-ment in tools for knowing at least since the emergence of written language. . . . This does not mean that the store of information in language did not increase in the past, nor that such prescientific cumulations of information are not continuing as heretofore in the midst of the scientific revolution. In fact, science is itself dependent on the accomplishments of the earlier evolution, and it may be said that science simply increased the rate of growth of knowledge by

making conscious and systematic some of the principles of selecting or testing a symbolic system or language that had previously
operated less consciously.

Walter Lippmann (1960, pp. 233, 235) has commented, "There is
something radically new in the modern world. . . . In modern
times men have invented a method of inventing, they have
discovered a method of discovery. Mechanical progress has
ceased to be causal and accidental and has become systematic
and cumulative."

The importance of the development of the scientific method is
not only the tremendous technological progress it has produced,
but also its contribution to ways of knowing. You don't have to
don a white coat and surround yourself with laboratory
instruments in order to think scientifically, although that is the
milieu in which most precise scientific research is conducted. The
scientific method has refined our approach toward handling
information, acquiring knowledge, and solving problems.

We speak of "science" as if it were a specific body of
knowledge, rather than a method of acquiring understanding and
information, more or less precise according to the subject matter
and the state of the art in that field. Or we reify science as an idol
whose one voice speaks with authority, while in fact the scientists
speak with many voices according to the *presuppositions* with
which each scientist works. Nonetheless, the scientific method
has provided us with a way of knowing which can close the gaps in
our understanding not only of the physical world but also of each
other. It provides a basis for communication which can resolve the
conflict between ideologies. Burhoe (1966, ch. 1, p. 7) comments:

> What is of unique importance is that the world-wide acceptance of
> the linguistic coins bearing the scientific world pictures offers hope
> for a truly world-wide ecumenicism at the ideological or belief level.
> This world community of understanding of basic common values is
> essential if we are to have a rational and peaceful ordering of world
> society.

An example of the effectiveness of scientifically acquired
knowledge to bridge ideological gaps is the swiftness with which

the international atomic test-ban treaty was ratified, especially by the United States and the USSR. Recognizing the gravity of continued pollution of the atmosphere by fallout from above-ground atomic tests, Cyrus Eaton informally called together an international conference of scientists at Pugwash in Nova Scotia. These people, sharing a common discipline, could transcend the ideological differences of their nations and their own language barriers and really communicate about the seriousness of the problem. On their return to their respective nations, they could relay their own sense of urgency to influential people in their governments so the atomic test-ban treaty was ratified quickly.

You may ask why the scientific discipline cannot be used to convert the world immediately into a peaceable kingdom. We will see how even scientific understanding is greatly influenced by cultural presuppositions and personal biases as we proceed with this discussion. It is important to note here that the scientific method enjoins a habit of truth which we may use in all our inquiries and in all our communications.

Existential Questions

The questions worth answering are those that arise in existential situations. Those questions that are urgent are asked by experience. We cannot answer every question we can think of, but we can answer every important question the incongruities of experience can pose. Legitimate questions come from contradictions between what is "known" and what is experienced; some event puts a question to what we thought we understood. But when we spin out questions from some axiomatic base, we may ask what we cannot answer, nor find it even worthwhile to try. Adequately coping with the challenges of our environment depends a great deal upon asking significant questions. For questions as well as answers can be trivial; they can lead us to formulate answers which are not relevant. We may ask false questions either because the problem is artificial, arising from an erroneous vision of the nature of reality, or because they are rhetorical, designed simply to lead us to accept an answer that is already premised.

We ask questions in a frame of reference in which the answer is implied. There is a correlation between the question we ask and the answer we expect. The questions we ask presume a context which generally determines the kind of answers we find meaningful. Some presupposition underlies every question, and if we are not satisfied with the answer, it may be that we need to examine the presupposition with which we started. The hidden assumptions we make predetermine the kind of answers we are prepared to receive. Assumptions can blind us to significant new discoveries. Joseph Priestley shared with many of his contemporary eighteenth-century natural philosophers the belief that fire was caused by a material substance called "phlogiston" which was combined in all combustible materials. So when he discovered how to "dephlogisticate" air, he did not realize the significance of his discovery. The French chemist, Lavoisier, heard about Priestley's experiment and called the extracted element "oxygen" and built modern chemistry on the new element. Relinquishing cherished but misconceived assumptions about ourselves and about our environment is positively correlated with creative achievement.

We make assumptions in any inquiry. But when the inquiry seems to be unproductive, we need to look to what we have taken for granted. Many fruitless arguments revolve around unexamined premises. Though this is obvious enough, I learned about it from experience. In a railroad train in northern China which was detained by a bridge blown up by guerilla forces at the end of World War II, I shared some interesting hours discussing theology with a French Jesuit priest returning to his mission station. Finally, I realized that the priest and I were getting nowhere because we had different assumptions as to the criterion for truth in religion. No matter what we began discussing, our argument was circular, coming back to the question of how you knew what to believe. Since he accepted the authority of the teachings of the Roman Catholic church, and I did not, we were not playing in the same ball park.

A scientific attitude toward either research or dialogue requires, not that we have no assumptions, but that we be aware of them and make them explicit. In a dialogue, we can also have a much more rewarding experience if we agree on definitions of the words we use. Sanborn Brown (1966, Ch. I, p. 3), the M.I.T. physicist, says:

> One of the characteristics of the so-called scientific approach to understanding is to agree for the purposes of a discussion and argument on the definition of words to be used within the framework of a particular study. One does not have to agree with the validity of the definition to use it in discussing a theoretical construct, but only agree to the same meaning of the words within the context of the discussion.

The main human process not only for survival but to maximize security and comfort is the formulation of symbolic information in a plan for coping with a problem: if mistaken, we lose out; if successful, we persist and may even flourish. The general purpose of formulations are, say Kluckhohn and Murray (1948, p. 7):

> (1) to *explain* past and present events; (2) to *predict* future events (the conditions being specified); and (3) to serve, if required, as a basis for the selection of effective measures of *control*. The validity of a formulation is to be found in the degree to which these purposes are fulfilled.

Knowledge is the organization and integration of information or data for a purpose. Norbert Wiener (1964, p. 14) describes learning as the process by which an organized system (including computers when appropriately programmed to play a game and learn from their own experience) transforms incoming messages into outgoing messages according to some principle of transformation which is subject to a certain criterion of merit or performance. Hudson Hoagland (1966, pp. 155-56) comments:

> The ability to form meaningful configurations that encompass large segments of the environment is a property of the more highly developed brains, and a good case can be made for the view that man's concerns with science, philosophy, political ideologies, and theologies are a reflection of a basic property of his nervous system to integrate extensive configurations relating himself to his

environment. The more effectively we think we bring large
segments of our environment into meaningful relations, the more
satisfied we feel, and I believe this is the basis for religious beliefs
which are the products of brains trying to make sense of the
universe as a basic survival mechanism in the way that a
cockroach's brain makes it systematically explore its cage in order
to survive.

Walter Lippman (1960, p. 182) describes the process of
transformation of data into knowledge in a vivid way:

> A naturalist out of doors perceives a whole universe of related life
> which the rest of us do not even see. A world which is ordinarily
> unseen has become visible through the understanding. When the
> mind has fetched it out of the flux of dumb sensations, defined it
> and fixed it, this unseen becomes more real than the dumb
> sensations it supplants. When the understanding is at work, it is as
> if circumstance had ceased to mutter strange sounds and had
> begun to speak our language.

To seek to understand our environment is important to human
survival individually and socially. "An opportunity that enables the
human mind to exercise its personal powers is a person's calling
or vocation, which determines his responsibilities," says Michael
Polanyi (1965, p. 36). It is as disastrous to their future for people to fail
to think as it is for them to fail to eat.

Participation of the Knower

Purely objective fact is no longer believed to be available to us
in our quest for truth. Every observation is seen to be mixed with
personal bias. With the work of Planck and Einstein, says Wiener
(1964, p. 89),

> . . . the observer has ceased to be an innocent registrar of his
> objective observations but has, rather, come to take an active
> participation in the experiment. Both in relativity and in quantum
> theory, his role in modifying the observations is to be regarded as
> far from negligible.

This dramatic shift in our understanding of the nature of the data
which comprises knowledge is well expressed by J. Bronowski
(1965, pp. 73-74):

It is a common and cardinal error to suppose, as the nineteenth century supposed, that the facts on which science builds are given us absolutely, and call for no judgment or interpretation from us. The great discoveries in the physical sciences in the twentieth century begin from a radical denial of this philosophy. We now understand that science is built not on facts but on observations; that observation is not a passive state of reception, but an active relation between the observer and his world; and that science is therefore not a mechanical index of facts, but an evolving activity.

This means that, for us, unalloyed experience is impossible; every personal experience is shaped by memory and anticipation and is correlated with and colored by other experiences and by concepts and values. Only beings least capable of thought can have anything approximating a pure experience; for us, each experience is interpreted by a constellation of concepts.

Even the act of learning from others, rather than at firsthand from our own experience with reality, is an act of participation. The learner recreates what the discoverer created. J. Bronowski (1965, p. 20) observes:

Science, like art, is not a copy of nature but a re-creation of her. We remake nature by the act of discovery, in the poem and in the theorem. And the great poem and the deep theorem are new to every reader, and yet are his own experiences, because he himself re-creates them. They are the marks of unity in variety; and in the instant when the mind seizes this for itself, in art or in science, the heart misses a beat.

The emotional response to understanding is a personal validation of knowing. Understanding is a satisfying experience, as Michael Polanyi (1965, pp. 25-26) points out:

When we reorganize our understanding, . . . we exercise our tacit powers in search of a better intellectual control of the matter in hand. We seek to clarify, verify or lend precision to something said or experienced. We move away from a position that is felt to be somewhat problematic to another position which we find more satisfying. *And this is how we eventually come to hold a piece of knowledge as true.* Here is . . . the unavoidable act of personal participation in our explicit knowledge of things: an act of which we can be aware merely in an unreflecting manner. . . . It is this personal coefficient alone which endows our explicit statements with meaning and conviction.

It sounds as if we have arrived at a kind of subjectivism, in which all knowledge is merely a personal interpretation. If this were so, meaningful dialogue would be impossible because there would be no significant communication, no observations that could be shared. We could not learn from each other, for there would be no common referent, only private feelings. But Polanyi (1965, p. 13) says, "I deny that any participation of the knower in the shaping of knowledge must invalidate knowledge, though I admit it impairs its objectivity." Personal knowledge can have universal validity, says Polanyi, since people's own sense of responsibility prompts the knowers to submit to their own "intimations of reality" and to employ every clue available to them that points to the true nature of the object they are considering. Their intimations may be strained through their own interpretive system, but they may nonetheless be reflections reaching them from self-existent sources. "Such are the assumptions of human responsibility," says Polanyi (1965, p. 63), "and such the spiritual foundations on which a free society is conceivable."

The same distinction between, and combination of, the personal coefficient and objective knowledge which avoids subjectivism is expressed by Abraham Maslow (1962, p. 72):

While it is true that all human perception is a product of the human being and is his creation to an extent, we can yet make some differentiation between the perception of *external objects as relevant to human concerns and as irrelevant to human concerns.* Self-actualizing people are more able to perceive the world as if it were independent not only of them but also of human beings in general. This also tends to be true of the average human being in his highest moments, i.e., in his peak experiences. He can then more readily look upon nature as if it were there in itself and for itself, and not simply as if it were a human playground put there for human purposes. He can more easily refrain from projecting human purposes upon it.

Thus, though you and I color everything we see with our own selective interpretation, there does exist between us an objective reality which, if we responsibly try to report it, does make possible genuine communication.

The Fallacy of Misplaced Concreteness

If you and I had to pay attention to everything that was going on around us, we would be so overwhelmed by details that we would be bewildered. We would not be able to process so much data. Our senses would be jammed and our mind would be immobilized by the input overload. So our central nervous system, like the electric wiring system in a home, has breakers which adjust the flow of stimuli that are allowed to activate the system. *Selective attention* seems to function at every level of our internal communications system, beginning with every nerve-ending and synapse. The eye, for instance, focuses on specific objects in view, though the rest of the view may be recorded subliminally. Thus, what we are aware of in our surroundings is only a report of events that *interest* us; the rest we ignore. It is a sufficiently complete and reliable impression for us to respond adequately to our environment, but it is not complete. It is these selected data that we associate with words to build up a language. Words which begin as names for objects are transformed into symbols for ideas. Symbols are high-level abstractions which give the remarkable flexibility to human language. We have a symbol system by means of which we store experience and postpone responses. C.F. Hockett (Dobzhansky, 1962, p. 209) calls this capacity "displacement," which means that human beings can think of events, and respond to them, regardless of their distance in space and time.

Vocal sounds become symbolically meaningful when functioning as constituents of words. And the meaning of words is a social convention. The meaning of a word is arbitrary, having been agreed upon through usage in a society and is not deducible from the component sounds. Although the usefulness of words is dependent upon their ability to orient the user or the hearer to what is intended, words are fortunately generally imprecise. Many words carry overtones or are freighted with connotations which suggest other possibilities so they make serendipity possible. A combination of words can reveal to us something unexpected which is not denoted by any of the particular words in the combination. A finite number of words can express an infinite number of ideas simply by their rearrangement. We can use words whose meaning is associated with one set of experiences to help us understand and determine our attitudes toward a completely unfamiliar set of experiences. We can even by definition set up a symbolic language called "mathematics," whose symbols we can manipulate in order to find the answer to some problem in reality and, if the initial definitions of the symbols were precise enough, find that our answers are amazingly accurate. Isaac Newton reports that in the year 1666, "I began to think of gravity extending to the orb of the Moon . . . having thereby compared the force requisite to keep the Moon in her orb with the force of gravity at the surface of the earth and found them to answer pretty nearly." When our manipulation of mathematical symbols does not "answer pretty nearly," it is generally because of errors in our observations. Although the development of more precise measuring instruments has greatly facilitated measurement in some of the sciences, we are often still left with imprecise observations, which can be averaged out to give us a near enough approximation to be normative. So we close up many gaps in our knowledge by the use of symbolic language.

Some language systems, such as mathematics, are universal in that the same definitions and usages are employed by agreement in many cultures. But the symbols we use in our everyday speech are "given"; that is, we find them already current in the community where we were born and we know they will still be in circulation when we die, plus or minus additions or subtractions made while we live. Significant symbols include, says anthropologist Clifford Geertz (1965, pp. 107-08):

> . . . words for the most part but also gestures, drawings, musical sounds, mechanical devices like clocks, or natural objects like jewels—anything, in fact, that is disengaged from its mere actuality

and used to impose meaning upon experience. From the point of view of any particular individual, such symbols are largely given.

Since significant symbols are given by the culture, whether they are used in everyday language or in the specialized language of mathematics, they are wholly acquired by learning. One of the advantages of learning a second language is that we become more consciously aware of the arbitrariness of our native language and then are sophisticated enough not to employ the symbols of our native language as absolutes. Contemporary linguistics is showing us that what we are capable of thinking is conditioned and limited by the symbols that happen to be available in the language which we inherit. Within the structure of some languages, some ideas are inaccessible. Thus what we know is in part determined by the symbol system in which we happen to be reared.

When we are aware of the arbitrariness and social givenness of most of the words and symbols which we use, we can better appreciate what Alfred North Whitehead (1948, p. 54) means by the often quoted phrase, "the fallacy of misplaced concreteness." The fallacy is when we take our words and symbols as concrete in themselves, instead of as referents. What is concrete are the events to which the symbols refer, not the symbols themselves.

Time and space are symbolic concepts by which we conveniently orient ourselves to the ongoing process, including coordinating our activities with each other, but they have no substance in themselves. If we assume they are concrete, we lose part of their usefulness. Michael Polanyi (1965, p. 30) helps to make this clear:

> Take words, graphs, maps and symbols in general. They are never objects of our attention in themselves, but pointers towards the things they mean. If you shift your attention from the meaning of a symbol to the symbol as an object viewed in itself, you destroy its meaning. . . . Symbols can serve as instruments of meaning only by being known subsidiarily while fixing our attention on their meaning.

The intellectual structures we build with symbols are valuable insofar as they help us cope with concrete reality, but the symbolic systems are devoid of substance.

"The path to human knowledge . . . goes by way of the making and correcting of concepts," says J. Bronowski (1965, pp. 36-37). "The symbol and the metaphor are as necessary to science as to poetry. We are as helpless today to define mass, fundamentally, as Newton was." A *concept* is an abstraction from reality. It is as useful in examining reality as is the lens of a microscope. A concept is to reflective thought as a lens is to microscopic observation; both are instruments for restricting the field of attention and focusing on details. A concept focuses by abstraction. Selective attention abstracts from the flow of experience and gives us manageable units. We let the rest go, but the rest is still going on, is still affecting us. This is the reason some of our most brilliant achievements meet their nemesis. What we paid attention to we managed very well, but what we ignored accumulated its own fate for us. Not that we should cease pursuing the advantages in dealing with the environment offered by abstract concepts, but that we be aware of their partiality and beware of the dangers accruing in what we have overlooked. Some of what we call misfortune stems from oversight.

Abraham Maslow (1962, p. 84) says of the process of concept making:

> Abstracting is in essence a selection out of certain aspects only of the object, those which are of use to us, those which threaten us, those with which we are familiar, or those which fit our language categories. . . . Abstractions, to the extent that they are useful, are also false. In a word, to perceive an object abstractly means *not* to perceive some aspects of it. It clearly implies selection of some attributes, rejection of other attributes, creation or distortion of still others. We make of it what we wish.

This book is an example of abstractions from the continuum of life. What is a continuous experience of reality is broken up into concepts and categories so we can consider it in intellectually manageable units. I cannot concentrate on the whole life spectrum at once, so I follow my interests in defining areas to which I pay selective attention. But the realities we are discussing are not thus fragmented. The way I perforce think should not mislead either you or me into assuming that the world as a whole also is organized precisely this way. We can achieve new perspectives on the world through such abstractions, but the world is much more complex than these abstractions represent.

The selectivity and cultural relativity of our conceptual abstractions mean that we do not have in mind a picture of what is really there in reality, but only a more or less adequate representation or map of what is there. Lawrence K. Frank (1966, p. 164) says:

> Each cultural group has developed its own highly selective awareness and its patterned perception of the "surround" in accordance with its basic concepts about nature and man. Each culture, therefore, has created its own selected version of the world and all its events as its "reality" and established that as the objective world. What we call scientific knowledge of the world is also a highly selected symbolic formulation of the order of events as nearly as they can be observed and formulated according to contemporary scientific assumptions and symbolic expression, such as mathematics.

Hence, even scientists are "culture bound." For instance, a realistic conception of human nature has been retarded by the limitations and distortions of perception and conceptualization because of the blind spots, rigidities, and defensive rejections in the personality of the social scientist himself. Since our self-image is constructed of the same culture-bound conceptions as those that limit our realistic appraisal of humans, any challenge to our conceptions is a challenge to our personal identity. "Only recently," observe Kluckhohn and Murray (1948, p. 5), "has a cross-cultural perspective provided emancipation from these values that are not broadly 'human' but merely local, in both space and time." By realizing that concepts are culture specific, we can minimize culture conflicts and misunderstandings.

We cannot get along without concepts. One of the great

contributions of science to our way of knowing is its conscious and knowing use of hypotheses, theories, and models. When scientists are confronted by a problem, the first thing they do is formulate an hypothesis, or a set of hypotheses comprising a theory. It can be an educated guess or a hunch, but generally the more a scientist knows about the field in which the problem emerges, the more insightful the hypotheses are apt to be— except that a thorough knowledge of a subject may so trammel the imagination that possible hypotheses are precluded as supposedly impossible. The imagination needs free rein in projecting hypotheses. Out of the welter of possible avenues to explore in seeking an answer to a problem, an hypothesis focuses the search and guides us in anticipating what to look for; otherwise, the significance of clues which turn up can go unnoticed. We can then devise an experiment to see if our hypothesis is borne out in experience; if it is, it becomes knowledge which can reliably guide us to future action.

In constructing hypotheses, we especially engage in the pursuit of what Bronowski calls "hidden likenesses" by taking a phenomenon that is better understood as a model for a more problematic phenomenon. Not that the model can be transposed point-for-point to the problem area, but the concepts and laws defining the model can guide us in exploring the unknown phenomenon. The fairly well-known solar system was once taken as a model for the structure of the then unknown atom, and what we knew about the solar system provided clues for what we should look for in the atom. A model need not precisely fit the new situation in order to throw considerable light upon it. When we find that the hypotheses cannot be vindicated, or the model cannot be fitted without doing violence to the original, they are abandoned. There is danger of smuggling in the verifiability of the concepts of a model and implying they have equal validity in the different frame of reference, which usually cannot be justified. However, the use of models is one way of coming to know.

The use of models is an old way of knowing dressed in new, more systematic garb. We have throughout recorded history closed the gaps in our knowledge through reasoning by analogy. "As little, so big" has been one of the basic principles of reasoning since we first began taking thought. The neurophysiologist R. W. Gerard (1962, p. 110) observes that "one might just as well accept thinking by analogy because that is the way we think, that is the way the brain is made. The only problem is whether we use analogy well or stupidly."

For instance, Jesus of Nazareth both learned and taught by analogy. He often taught in parable, a story illustrating a point. "Parable," in its Greek derivation, means "comparison." He taught by using familiar analogies. William Wallace Fenn (1938, p. 33), former Dean of Harvard Divinity School, says of Jesus, "He taught in parable, because the truth came to him in parable." The moral and religious insights of Jesus did not come entirely from the scriptures and traditions of the Jews, nor from a transcendent source, but from his personal experience. "That experience," says Fenn, (1938, pp. 74, 29), "was not in ecstatic moments but in the normal ways of nature and the ordinary paths of men. By a most simple, logical method he argued from the facts of his experience up to the will of God." Jesus saw the "divine meaning in common things." He frequently quoted from the Old Testament, of course, especially when he was hard pressed by his legalistic adversaries who recognized the authority of only the Old Testament, or when "the wisdom of the dead"—his memory of beautiful phrases from psalm and prophecy—came to his lips to express his feelings; even then, as Bossuet (Fenn, 1938, p. 25) has said, "The Scriptures spoke to him with an authoritative voice, but he heard only that to which his ear was attuned." He used the Scriptures selectively. "Ye have heard that it hath been said, but I say unto you," said Jesus, and he appealed to the people who heard him with the challenge, "Why do you not judge for yourselves what is right?" (Luke 13:57).

Thus has reasoning by analogy been a time-honored way of increasing knowledge, still useful to us today, especially as it has been systematized in the scientific method.

"But the irony of man's quest for reality," says Lincoln Barnett

(1962, p. 113), "is that as nature is stripped of its disguises, as order emerges from chaos and unity from diversity, as concepts merge and fundamental laws assume increasingly simpler forms, the evolving picture becomes ever more remote from experience. . . ." As the scientists have probed the depths of reality in all dimensions, they have had to leave some experiences behind and spin out hypotheses and propose models which, though they helped us understand, made us feel as if we lived in an alien world. The sciences have been very successful in going beyond the senses, says Lincoln Barnett (1962, p. 113):

> But its highest edifices, Einstein has pointed out, have been "purchased at the price of emptiness of content." A theoretical concept is emptied of content to the very degree that it is divorced from sensory experience. For the only world man can truly know is the world created for him by his senses. If he expunges all the impressions which they translate and memory stores, nothing is left.

Perhaps this accounts for the malaise of modern people; as their understanding of the universe improves, their sense of the reality and meaningfulness of the world they inhabit diminishes. Perhaps we need to root ourselves firmly in our human perspective, accepting the world of appearances reported by our senses as the most immediate and relevant to our sense of well-being, while recognizing and using the knowledge made available to us by the explorations of the sciences. We can appreciate the world of color and sound and beauty and form which appears to us concretely, while taking into account the impalpable, colorless, soundless system of symbols which the scientists use to predict and control the reaches of reality which do not appear. The symbols and models we use to explain the mysteries of the remote environment have something real in mind, but this level of reality interests us only as it is manifest in what happens. Lincoln Barnett (1962, p. 116) describes how the suprasensible comes to be concrete and of direct personal interest:

> "The event," Alfred North Whitehead declared, "is the unit of things real." By this he meant that however theoretical systems

> may change and however empty of content their symbols and concepts may be, the essential and enduring facts of science and of life are the happenings, the activities, the events. The implications of this idea can best be illustrated by contemplating a simple physical event such as the meeting of two electrons. Within the frame of modern physics one can depict this event as a collision of two elementary grains of matter or two elementary units of electrical energy, as a concourse of particles or of probability waves, or as a commingling of eddies in a four dimensional space-time continuum. Theory does not define what the principals in this encounter actually are. Thus in a sense the electrons are not "real" but merely theoretical symbols. On the other hand the meeting itself is "real"—the event is "real."

The extensions of our understanding may be devoid of experience, but reality becomes concrete when something occurs. "All real living is meeting," says Martin Buber (1958, p. 11). At all levels of existence, the interesting and creative event is meeting, is an encounter, is establishing mutual relations. At levels of concretion in the microcosm and macrocosm where we cannot participate, it is less directly interesting to us, but still something significant happens.

The "Aha Phenomenon"

Everything we know does not have to be proved. We understand a great deal without having it demonstrated to us. That is because we bring to each new experience a great deal of past experience in the same world. We recognize the similarities in the new situation by implicit comparison with the familiar. J. Bronowski (1965, p. 19) calls it discovering a "hidden likeness":

> The discoveries of science, the works of art are explorations—more, are explosions, of a hidden likeness. The discoverer or the artist presents in them two aspects of nature and fuses them into one. This is the act of creation, in which original thought is born, and it is the same act in original science and original art.

What we are capable of recognizing depends upon how much we already know. If events are to come alive for us, we have to bring something to the experience. What we can learn is enhanced by background we already have to which we can relate new experiences. Polanyi (1965, p. 23) calls the implicit act of recognition a "tacit feat of intelligence":

> The facts of biology and medicine . . . can be recognized as a rule only by experts possessing both special skill for examining the objects in question and a special connoisseurship for identifying particular specimens. The exercise of such an art is a tacit feat of intelligence which cannot be fully specified in terms of explicit rules.

What we are speaking of is knowing by intuition or insight, by immediate apprehension of the relation of things. Hudson Hoagland (1966, p. 155) says that insight "refers to the fact that novel, puzzling situations, at first devoid of meaning, suddenly come together to make sense," and comments:

> This sudden precipitation of significance out of a puzzle has sometimes been called the "aha phenomenon," and the experiencing of "aha, that's it" associated with the clothing of a situation with meaning is emotionally satisfying, and is the major charm of scientific research and of artistic creation, as well as in the solution of crossword puzzles.

To illustrate the "aha phenomenon," Hoagland (1966, p. 155) tells the story of Wolfgang Kohler's experiment of putting a banana out of reach beyond the cage of a hungry chimpanzee and then putting a stick in the cage. After various vain attempts to reach the banana, the chimpanzee suddenly took the stick and fished the banana, within reach of its hand. "It happened all at once," comments Hoagland, "the problem was solved by a flash of insight—by closure of a meaningful configuration of patterned messages in the brain, the relation of the stick to the banana was perceived."

The capacity to see things in relations, to see configurations or patterns is an important way of knowing. Intuition is really seeing the whole picture. Michael Polanyi (1965, pp. 29-30) describes it thus:

We may say when we comprehend a particular set of items as parts of a whole, the focus of our attention is shifted from the hitherto uncomprehended particulars to the understanding of their joint meaning. This shift of attention does not make us lose sight of the particulars, since we can see a whole only by seeing its parts, *but it changes altogether the manner in which we are aware of the particulars. We become aware of them now in terms of the whole on which we have fixed our attention.* I call this a *subsidiary awareness* of the particulars, by contrast to a *focal awareness* which would fix attention on the particulars themselves, and not as parts of a whole.

Polanyi illustrates the difference between the two levels of reality, the level of the parts and the level of the whole, by pointing out that no amount of physical and chemical analysis of the parts of a watch will ever tell you how a watch keeps time; only when the pieces are assembled as a functioning whole can you understand its time-keeping operation. The principles by which a watch keeps time can be discerned only by a comprehensive view of the whole in which the interaction of the parts can be seen. In our personal knowing, each of us recapitulates the sequential development of "scientific specialities" described by Ralph Gerard (J.G. Miller, Autumn 1965, p. 107):

Most of them pass from observation to description to classification to concern with structure to concern with dynamics to recognition of the intricate interaction of the total system. And at that stage "the units in their variable relations are returned to the whole, the Gestalt is recognized, the planet or organism returns to the center of focus."

The imagination makes it possible for us to shift our perspective and see relations in a different configuration. Copernicus visualized the heliocentric solar system by a leap of imagination; he wondered what the orbits of the planets would look like if he were standing on the sun. Once having adopted this speculative point of view, he found that the orbits looked simpler and "more pleasing to the mind."

We engage in essentially the same act when we try to understand another sentient being. Michael Polanyi (1965, pp. 57-

58) points out that we decide when we think a rat has learned a maze by "indwelling": assuming that the rat is displaying the same mastery of the maze as we ourselves would show if we were trying to master it without linguistic clues. That is, we understand what the rat is doing by imaginatively dwelling in the mind of the rat. It is the same process of identification with the other which the social psychologists mean when they speak of "taking the role of the other" by adopting the prejudices and purposes of the other in order to understand what is going on in the other mind. It is like the story about the boy who was asked how he found a lost mule: "I asked myself where I would go if I were a mule, and I went, and there he was."

An unusual experience can give us an insight which conditions our attitudes thereafter. Such an experience is called by Abraham Maslow a "revelatory event" or a "peak experience." One such revelatory event seemed to give me a glimpse into the heart of the universe, and colored my feelings about it thereafter. At Beloit College, the astronomy professor loaned keys to the observatory with its fifteen-inch telescope to students in his classes. One brisk October evening my roommate and I went over to have a look on our own. As we opened the dome and set the telescope's coordinates for the Ring Nebula in Lyra, a constellation we had chosen at random, the wind sighed through the aperture and we could hear the rush of traffic on the highway below the hill. I put my eye first to the finder and then to the eyepiece of the telescope and was quite astounded; there in silent splendor in the depths of space hung a softly glowing smoke ring with a star in the center. It was beautiful, but what really impressed me was that nobody had put it there, and it had been there all the time without my knowing it. At that instant, I felt my relationship to the cosmos because I had seen into it. And it also amazed me that somebody could prepare a little manual of where to look at a certain time and date, and there find the constellation just as I expected. A whole new dimension of existence then became real to me. Peak experiences, such as this, help us have entirely different views of our situation, and have enduring consequences. Mountain climbing or flying in an airplane can be more than emotional peak experiences; they can change your whole point of view. A weatherman told me that he could not get excited about air pollution until he saw a photograph of the whole earth taken from a space rocket. It had always seemed to him obvious that the vast movement of the air masses he daily plotted would dissipate the wastes we spewed into the air, until the picture of the whole earth with its thin layer of cloud formations drove home to him that our weather was a finite system.

The "aha phenomenon" is the meaning of legitimate "mystical" experiences. Long before we understood the process, people were blessed by insights into the patterns of reality. Some significant relationships were intuited, but since the process was mysterious, it was called a mystical experience. Because such experiences still occur, we cannot doubt that they always did. But to be legitimate, to be a disclosure of a truth, they had to meet the same conditions they do today, namely, to have been a recognition of a hidden likeness or an integration of previously disassociated bits of information. Always there has to have been some existing knowledge to be brought together; insights do not occur in an information void.

Another kind of peak experience once clarified this for me, an experience which in a less critical culture I might have called a mystical experience. Traveling under Navy orders during World War II, I was trying to return to my home base in South Carolina by hitch-hiking rides in military airplanes. All large plane traffic had been grounded by fog in New York, but a Navy chief was getting clearance to fly to Norfolk in a small two-place Navy training plane. He agreed to take me along and strapped me in the back seat and stuck earphones on my head. After we had broken through the fog and were wafting along at about 5,000 feet, he switched the radio from the air traffic control band to a commercial radio station. For a while I enjoyed listening to a choir singing, until he snapped off the set entirely. But I could still hear the choir singing, and the sound, in that unearthly disorientation over the sea of clouds with the motor noise and whistling wind ringing in my muffled ears, was convincingly loud and clear. I discovered to my amazement that the choir would sing my request numbers, so I willed that it sing the air from Finlandia, of which I knew only a few opening bars of the melody. The choir opened strong and then faltered and stopped at just about the point where I no longer knew the tune. It struck me that the voices I was hearing knew no more than I did.

This experience left a big question in my mind about any mystical revelations of wholly new knowledge, now including the glorious new insights that allegedly come from the use of so-called "mind-expanding" drugs. My reading of *The Glorious Cosmology* confirms that Alan Watts knew no more after he had experimented with LSD than he had already transcribed in his previous excellent books. No matter how glorious his feelings may have been while on an LSD trip, his report was less cogent than his earlier reflective insights. It remains possible in my mind that artificial stimulants may relax inhibitions to insight, but they can't teach me anything new which can be intuitively integrated. Without ideational content, a mystical experience can be a ride on a psychic roller coaster, very thrilling but devoid of significance. A mystical intuition, like any other conception, needs to be tested in order to distinguish valid insights from hallucinations.

The Search for Hidden Reality

The criteria of what is credible and what is incredible depend upon the nature of the ideas which are at the threshold of our belief. In the natural sciences, an hypothesis can be put to the test of controlled experiment. Where results of experiments can be measured, the tests can yield precise "yes" or "no" answers. We can, as Charles H. Townes (1966, p. 308) says, "'prove' it by making some kind of test of the postulate against experience. We devise experiments to test our working hypotheses and believe those laws or hypotheses which seem to agree with experience." However, when the concepts cannot be subjected to manipulation and control, their validity is measured against other norms. Says C.I. Lewis (Hartshorne, 1941, p. 57):

> A philosopher can offer proof only in the sense of so connecting his theses as to exhibit their mutual support, and only through appeal to other minds to reflect on their experiences and their own attitudes and perceive that he correctly portrays them.

If a concept presented to you makes sense of your experiences, if it gives coherence to what had previously been disparate fragments of experience for you, you readily believe the concept simply because it makes your experiences more meaningful. But a concept must not only make you feel better in the midst of your present and past experiences but also help you orient yourself toward future experiences. Sanborn C. Brown (1966, p. 19) says, "One of the most important criteria for a valid theory is that not only must it agree with the data within the limits of observation but it must predict sensible results elsewhere." Michael Polanyi, in a lecture at The University of Chicago, May 13, 1967, suggested the following criteria by which useful concepts will validate themselves:

1. By revealing the hidden coherence in nature.

2. By making a meaningful pattern of what is otherwise a random aggregate, as speech does of noise.

3. By having consequences for making concrete choices.

4. By making it possible to anticipate future events.

5. By raising new questions which lead to further explorations and the discovery of new answers.

A concept is not useful if it closes off further speculation because any concept which proposes to be final does violence to the dynamic and complex nature of reality. Too neat an answer is suspect of oversimplification.

Still, credibility is not simply a matter of integrating thought with thought, but of *integrating thought with reality*. A valid concept discloses what is already there. Michael Polanyi (1965, pp. 34-35) comments:

Discovery, invention—these words have connotations which recall what I have said before about understanding as a search for hidden reality. One can discover only something that was already there, ready to be discovered. The invention of machines and the like produces something that was not there before; but actually, it is only the knowledge of the invention that is new, its possibility was there before. . . . I am merely referring to the important fact that you cannot discover or invent anything unless you are convinced that it is there, ready to be found. The recognition of this hidden presence is in fact half the battle; it means that you have hit on a real problem and are asking the right questions.

The existence of the hidden reality gives viability and verifiability to our concepts. It is an aspect of the scientists' faith that there is "an objective and unique reality which is shared by everyone," says Charles H. Townes (1966, p. 305). There may be different interpretations of reality according to the cultural categories we have accepted, but if we take the same point of view, both of us can reach agreement about it. For the hidden reality, when viewed through shared concepts, substantiates universal truths which can be held in common. Michael Polanyi (1965, p. 36) asserts:

The sense of a pre-existent task makes the shaping of knowledge a responsible act, free from subjective predilections. And it endows, by the same token, the results of such acts with a claim to universal validity. For when you believe that your discovery reveals a hidden reality, you will expect it to be recognized equally by others.

A person who has learned to respect the truth will feel entitled to uphold the truth and find it honored in a society which has taught respect for the truth, adds Polanyi. Of course, in a society which has not cultivated the habit of truth, the truth cannot be mutually established. And in a sense, a truth is not of much value unless it is shared, unless someone else believes it. The suitability of a proposition to be shared is part of its validation. The compulsion to share a cherished concept arises from the need to reinforce it by seeing it mirrored in the minds of others, as well as to make it operable by having others share the same motivation.

Another test of the validity of a proposition is that it is self-evident to other people. If a proposition has to be enforced, it evidently lacks the support of the hidden reality. Unless other people can voluntarily share in the "aha phenomenon," imposing a truth is vain. For a concept is valid to the extent that it gives "an unforced unity to the experience of men," says J. Bronowski (1965, pp. 41-42). "Does the concept make life orderly, not by edict but in fact?" Concepts are valuable, and are selected in the evolutionary process if they help make a society work of itself, says Bronowski, "without force, without corruption, and without another arbitrary superstructure of laws which do not derive from the central concepts." Authoritarianism in any form does not confer survival value upon the society thus controlled because it does not rely upon the continuity and integration supplied by the hidden reality. Resort to force to achieve an end is an admission of failure to be correlated with the processes of the world. Force is destructive and can be reasonably resorted to only as a counter-force to ward off destruction.

You and I cannot test every concept which we might helpfully adopt, so we believe in concepts on the authority of other people's competence. In the sciences, the principle of "mutual authority" operates to fill the interstices in one's personal knowledge of truth. The scientists have agreed upon the nature of evidence and upon procedures, and keep watch upon each other within their own disciplines, says Polanyi, but in disciplines more remote from their own experience they accept each other's conclusions. In much the same way we carry on our mutual search for truth in our daily social relations. Michael Polanyi (1965, p. 68) comments:

> In an ideal free society each person would have perfect access to the truth: to the truth in science, in art, religion and justice, both in public and private life. But this is not practicable; each person can know directly very little of truth and must trust others for the rest. Indeed, to assure this process of mutual reliance is one of the main functions of society.

The sciences have also taught us that when we are dealing with a large assemblage of data, the generalizations or laws we arrive at as a result of our observations are not certainties or absolutes, but *probabilities*. The laws of classical physics described the operations of matter at a sufficiently large scale to give certainty for all practical purposes; at the micro level of concretion, however, the laws are statistical probabilities. That is, a sufficient quantity of examples give reliable answers. In laws of probability we are implicitly dealing with percentages; the greater the population being considered, the more reliable the findings in percentages. What seems a predictable, solid event is really the consequence of the indeterminate influence of multiple entities, each in itself autonomous and unpredictable, but collectively making a highly reliable pattern. What we have, therefore, is not a determinate certainty, but a statistical probability. William G. Pollard (1958, p. 55) explains:

> Large scale phenomena involve enormous numbers of atoms and molecules all acting together. But in every case in which individual behavior is indeterminate, but the probability of alternative possibilities is known, such probabilities approach certainties when sufficiently large numbers are involved. The moment at which an individual radioiodine atom will decide to radioactively change into xenon is completely indeterminate. A dose of radioiodine administered by a physician to a patient contains, however, a hundred million billion radioiodine atoms. With such enormous numbers involved, it is possible to predict with considerable precision exactly how many atoms will have decayed radioactively at any time after administration of the dose. So it is also with the properties of substances such as melting points and boiling points, hardness, compressibility, specific heat, and the like. All such properties are the result of tremendous numbers of atoms and molecules acting together. A prediction from quantum mechanics of the probabilities governing the indeterminate behavior of individual particles becomes, with such large numbers involved, practical certainty in the behavior of the entire group.

What is significant about this new understanding of the nature of our knowledge is not that there are no reliable generalizations, but that the generalizations are not disqualified when we find that every case in the statistical sample does not conform to the probable prediction. We should remember this when considering the behavior of populations of human beings. Human behavior patterns are predictable even when there are flagrant exceptions which may be much more newsworthy. George Wald (1965, pp. 34-35) points out:

> When we are dealing with many millions of molecules, and hence the statistics of large numbers, one has a show of smoothness, predictability, and complete determinancy. The moment one's attention is fastened on one molecule in a population—one need not isolate that molecule but only concentrate one's attention upon it—all that regularity and dependability disappear. Now it's all-or-nothing: it's either A or B and goes from one to the other in an instant. What is a smooth and predictable process in large numbers of units becomes an all-or-nothing, explosive and unpredictable transition in a single unit.

Too often we are tempted to be guided by the exception, which interests us and reinforces our preferences, rather than by the statistically probable successful behavior. It is the latter which gives us a norm by which to guide our decisions.

Edmund Sinnott (1966, pp. 82-83) nicely summarizes the polarity of individual unpredictability and group dependability:

> Although the behavior of a single particle cannot be predicted, the behavior of a large group of them can be; not with certainty, indeed, but with a very high degree of probability. This is in harmony with the now generally accepted idea that most natural laws are statistical ones. They are not inflexible, grounded on mathematical certainties, but are the sort of predictabilities on which an insurance company stakes its money or the ones with which a student of Mendelian genetics deals. The length of an individual life, or the presence in a genetic population of an individual with a particular combination of characters, cannot be predicted with certainty, but its probability can. The larger the number of individuals, the closer will the result be to the expectation and the greater the probability of a given outcome. In the relatively large bodies dealt with in classical mechanics probabilities are so high that the results, for all practical purposes, are certain, and laws drawn up from them can be relied upon with safety. Nevertheless, at the foundation of things there seems to be no certainty. What an individual particle will do no man can tell. The very important fact emerges, however, that its course is not a purely random and aimless one, for it has a tendency, a *potentia*, as the older writers called it, to move in a given way. It is about this

tendency, here and elsewhere in nature, that laws can be formulated. This is the fact that makes the world dependable, and science possible.

Unfinished Views

One of the generally recognized contributions of the scientific discipline to the theory of knowledge is the willingness to hold opinions tentatively. This does not mean that scientists hold their beliefs in suspension, refusing to act upon them until they are absolutely certain. It does mean that even while they are having stunning success in applying an idea, they still hold their convictions open to change. Tales can be told, of course, of the resistance of scientists to new ideas which threatened their established ways, such as the slowness with which Pasteur's germ theory of disease was generally accepted, or the resistance of Dr. Oliver Wendell Holmes' medical contemporaries to accepting their own responsibility for carrying the infection of "child bed fever" from new mother to new mother. But since the conscious formulation of the scientific method, a built-in quality has been a regularized method for testing and adopting new ideas. Joseph Priestley once wrote, "I have steadily endeavoured to keep my mind free so as to give up any hypothesis, however much beloved (and I cannot resist forming one on every subject), as soon as facts are shown to be opposed to it."

A beautiful corollary of the tentative scientific attitude is the ability to *incorporate previous knowledge* into new knowledge. People traditionally have been dominated by the notion that a new concept could be established only by eradicating the old. Especially has this been true of religious ideas allegedly founded on special revelation. "We must recognize the tentative nature of knowledge," says Charles H. Townes (1966, p. 309), and adds,

> Our present understanding of science or of religion is likely, if it agrees with experience, to continue to have an important degree of validity just as does the mechanics of Newton. But there may be many deeper things which we do not yet know and which, when discovered, may modify our thinking in very basic ways.

The reason the scientific approach to knowledge can be hospitable to new ideas while recognizing the continuing validity of some of the old ideas is that its philosophy and methods are secure without claiming finalities or absolutes.

Such view as these cause Herbert Feigl (1966, p. 198), Director of the Minnesota Center for Philosophy of Science, University of Minnesota, to conclude:

> Surely, we have to live—and get used to living—with an unfinished view of the world. We shall never cease to ask new questions, we shall—in all probability—continue to be confronted with all sorts of new problems, theoretical as well as practical. There is no philosopher's stone, there are no ultimate answers. But the endless quest of science; the candid search for knowledge and clarity; and the morally humane application of scientific knowledge are surely something that mankind can and, in all humility, should pursue.

An unfinished view of the world has important implications for the kind of answers we can expect to religious questions, as Norbert Wiener (1964, pp. 7-8) points out:

> The fact is that the superlatives of Omnipotence and Omniscience are not true superlatives but merely loose ways of asserting very great power and very great knowledge. They express an emotion of reverence and not a metaphysically defensible statement. If God surpasseth the human intellect, and cannot be encompassed by intellectual forms—and this is at least a defensible position—it is not intellectually honest to stultify the intellect itself by forcing God into intellectual forms which should have a very definite intellectual meaning. Thus, when we find limited situations that seem to cast light upon some of the statements generally made in religious books, it seems to me disingenuous to cast them aside because they do not have the absolute, infinite, and complete character which we are wont to attribute to religious utterances.

Now we can see that answers to questions in religion, including this chapter on how you know what to believe, will not and cannot have the certainty and alleged finality to which we have become accustomed in our religious tradition. Such answers as we may arrive at from this point of view are no less valid or religious for sharing in the unfinished nature of all knowledge. Religious beliefs have no better grounds than beliefs in any other area of human concern, since all beliefs are involved in the same spectrum of reality and conceptualization.

Our recognition of the incompleteness of any ideas we come to hold should make us cautious about trying to impose our personal biases upon future developments. Our faculty of reflective thought is supremely valuable in problem solving; that is, in devising alternative responses to present challenges to our continued existence which arise from the environment. But when it comes to planning for future contingencies, what we now know about the indeterminacy and probability of knowledge and the burgeoning nature of the evolutionary process should make us wary of unalterable plans. Wherever social institutions, whether political or religious, have tried to impose a final plan upon society, that society has atrophied. Not that we should not use our intelligence to organize and direct our activities, but that no blueprint for personal or social development can anticipate the consequences of present changes upon further evolution.

Robert S. Morison (1962, p. 41), Director of Medical and Natural Sciences, The Rockefeller Foundation, observes:

> There have always been those who feel that they have a clear idea of what man and his society ought to be like and they have devised means for molding them closer to the idealized images. Characteristically, and doubtless necessarily, these images have always been more limited than the actual results later brought about by undirected cultural evolution. The thing that has saved man from his limited visions in the past has been the difficulty of devising suitable means for reaching them.

Since we are not omniscient, it is fortunate that we are not omnipotent.

The Judeo-Christian tradition has long recognized that not all unanticipated contingencies brought bad luck, but that they also brought good luck which was called the "Grace of God." By stressing humility, the Judeo-Christian tradition has tended to keep the situation open so that an unexpected congruence of events could bring unforeseen blessings. Whereas humility has been traditionally a virtue which was enjoined, it is now seen to be a necessary corollary of our unfinished views.

Morison (1962, p. 42) adds a warning:

> At its deepest level, the problem is not one of differentiating the bad from the good visions, although at any given point of time it is up to all of us to try. The real point is to recognize that all such visions are in the long run inadequate. To cite a biological analogy, all known visions of man and his future suffer from the evolutionary defect of overspecialization. From the biological standpoint, man, as Huxley delights in pointing out, is one of the least specialized of all organisms. This is one of the reasons he has survived so long. But the cultures man has made for himself have all ultimately failed because of their overspecialization. In this sense, it is perhaps fortunate that, in general, cultures have had a restricted geographical coverage. As our common culture gradually extends to include our entire gene pool (a desirable development in many ways), we must give increasing attention to the dangers of overspecialization, for, in this case, failure of the culture will mean failure of the entire human race.

Since our reading of reality is inadequate and often mistaken, it is amazing that we get along as well as we do. Only the generous tolerances of nature have given us sufficient latitude for error so that we have not gotten ourselves into more serious difficulties. Nature has back-up mechanisms which provide alternate routes for development when human arrogance has blocked one route. The tolerance of nature puts to shame our intolerance toward differing opinions. This tolerance in nature the Judeo-Christian tradition has recognized as the mercy and forgiveness of God, offering another chance for growth to us when our own error or intransigence has stymied one line of development. But tolerance is not indifference, and there are limits to our scope for error.

The Counter Image

I don't know whether the excursion we have taken through

kaleidoscopic changes in our theory of knowledge, reflecting radical changes in our concept of reality, has meant anything to you or not. For me, it has issued in a breakthrough in my understanding of modern art. I have long been troubled by a contradiction in my own feeling about modern art. On the one hand, I believe the artists' sensibilities are often aware of the implications of changes before mundane people are. Poets and artists often sense new drifts in a culture before the philosophers do, and try to tell the rest of us about them in their art. On the other hand, as I looked at modern paintings, I could see only "sound and fury, signifying nothing." Modern art, instead of being prophetic, seemed to me to be decadent and meaningless.

Now it occurs to me that the artists are reflecting their awareness of the altered system of reference which began taking form in Western culture about the turn of this century. The new theory of knowledge casts artistic expression in a new function. Instead of reproducing nature, it reflects a new perspective on nature. Just as reality is now reflected in highly abstract verbal concepts, so is it also reflected in abstract visual representations. Werner Haftmann (1965, p. 8) points out that the radical reorientation in the sciences occurred at about the same time as the changed style in the arts:

> Dates seem to suggest that some kind of connection exists between science and painting. The radical change in painting took place between 1900 and 1910. Significant dates are: 1905 Fauvism; 1907 Cubism; 1910 first abstract painting. A concordance of dates important in the history of science runs thus: 1900 Planck's quantum theory; and Freud's *Interpretation of Dreams*; 1905 Einstein's special theory of relativity; 1908 Minkowski's mathematical formulation of the dimensions of space-time.

This must be the reason that F.S.C. Northrop says that when contemporary scientists and artists get together, they find themselves empathetic. The scientists, particularly the physical scientists, have already moved on to the ground of reality which the modern painters are trying to depict. We humanists and classicists are so stuck with the traditional view of reality that we cannot see what is going on in the world of modern art. When I look at a painting, I want to know what it is a picture of. But the artists, who are independently aware that objective reality is not so concrete as it seems, have taken off and are presenting colors for the sake of the emotions they arouse, not as reproductions of the colors seen in nature, or they construct figures as objects in themselves, not representations of other objects. "A modern painting," says Haftmann (1965, p. 15), "is one which embodies in the formal categories of the evocative painting a counter-image corresponding to the emanations of the changed system of reference of our century, which is the foundation of our radically changed attitude toward reality." I don't understand all modern paintings any more than I respond favorably to all classical paintings, but I do begin to get a glimmer that the modern painters have anticipated a new view of reality which the scientists are disclosing. And I can begin to understand the violent reaction to much of modern art. Haftmann (1965, pp. 15-16) says:

> We can now also appreciate the inner causes of the controversy over modern art, a controversy whose bitterness proves that the issues at stake are truly fundamental to our being. This controversy is an entirely natural accompaniment of the painful processes by which a system of reference which has long been valid and has splendid achievements to its credit is being dissolved and replaced by a new and entirely different system of reference. To one who does not stand within this new system or who takes up an embattled position, championing the old ideas against the new, changed, dislocated system of reference, the workings of this system must seem to be, literally, "out of joint." His natural reaction is, quite understandably, the old laments about the degeneration of art.

Perhaps the popular current complaint about the degeneration of morality and of religion also stems from our failure to appreciate the new situation. As we adopt the new way of understanding what is going on, we may find that many things we are doing are all right, are creative responses rather than signs of degeneration.

The Spiritual Dimension

Sometimes I wonder whether people will be overwhelmed by the sheer quantity of information we are amassing. We are garnering knowledge at an increasing rate of speed which raises the possibility that in a few generations, we will no longer be able to master it. Any organism can suffer from "excess stress or information input overload," as J.G. Miller (1965, pp. 121-22) calls it. He reports that studies of the performance of nerve cells shows "the output (in bits per second) rising as a more-or-less linear function of input until channel capacity is reached, then leveling off, and finally decreasing in a 'confusional state.' " The studies also found indications that "channel capacity decreases from cells to organs, to individuals, to groups, to social organizations." For instance, it was found that a neuron can handle 4,000 bits (pulses from an electronic stimulator) per second; the channel capacity of a rat's optic nerve was of the order of 50 of the same bits per second, while human beings in pairs responding to light flashes could handle only 5.75 bits per second, and three people responding in a series to light-flashes had a peak channel capacity of only 3.60 bits per second. This may throw some light upon the lag between theories for correcting social problems and their execution; it takes much longer for an idea to filter through a large group of people than it does for one person to dream it up. What we sometimes bemoan as "immoral society" or social indifference may be no more than the function of this delayed reaction as the channels of communication become more complex.

However, as society becomes more complex and the information input increases, we develop procedures and mechanisms to increase our capacity to deal with them. The communications media, especially television and radio, disperse information at such a rate that people become anxious over problems before they have had time to develop processes for dealing with them. At the same time, the electronic media provide such instant channels of communication that the lag between the discovery of a new solution and its popularization is being cut down considerably. We cope with the flood of information by computers, which process data faster and more efficiently than a host of bookkeepers. And we develop fields of specialization so that one person no longer masters all the techniques of even his or her own profession. Besides, we are now beginning to see that some knowledge can become useless and be discarded like outmoded machines. Wiliard F. Libby (1965, pp. 10–11) points out:

> As we come to a fuller understanding of the various branches of science and the various aspects of nature of which they treat, we shall be able to dispense with the bulk of substantiating material which led to the discoveries. Newton's laws of motion made it possible to state on one page facts about nature which would otherwise require whole libraries. Maxwell's laws of electricity and magnetism have had a similarly abbreviating effect. So it would seem that, as we continue to make progress in scientific understanding we can expect the great bulk of material which we now stare at in our libraries to become unnecessary. . . . It is hard to imagine that we could go on forever working on human genetics, for example, without coming to some general conclusions. These conclusions would be simplifying and would then allow us to compress the enormous bulk of literature which is necessary now only because of our ignorance.

You may have wondered where the emotions come into this picture of how you know what you know. The *dichotomy* between *reason* and *emotion* is another arbitrary and false distinction which we inherit in our culture but which has died by the wayside in the development of our understanding of ways of knowing. You recall that earlier in this chapter I quoted Polanyi as saying that we believe we know an answer to a question when we find an answer that is satisfying. This is an emotional experience. We feel satisfied when we resolve the problematical by integrating an unknown phenomenon with a known phenomenon. You can become tremendously excited when you discover the answer to a problem, like the exultant cry of Archimedes, "Eureka" or "I have found it," as he inadvertently ran home naked from the bath after thinking of a way to measure the alloy in a golden crown. Polanyi asserts that a motive to research is "intellectual passion," which is rewarded by the beauty of a solution to a problem. James D.

Watson (1968, p. 131) reports that when he and Francis H.C. Crick conceived of the double helix structure of the DNA molecule in the genes, they thought they must have hit upon the right solution: ". . . our idea was aesthetically elegant . . . we had a hunch, telling each other that a structure this pretty just had to exist." The continuity of facts and values is seen as soon as intellectual passion is acknowledged as a proper motive to comprehension, says Polanyi (1965, p. 38).

> The moment the ideal of detached knowledge was abandoned, it was inevitable that the ideal of dispassionateness should eventually follow, and that with it the supposed cleavage between dispassionate knowledge of fact and impassioned valuation of beauty should vanish.

However, physical passions differ from mental passions, and thereby hangs the distinction between "material" and "spiritual" values. Polanyi (1965, p. 61) says:

> By contrast to his bodily passions, which man shares with animals, the satisfaction of his mental passions does not consume or monopolize the objects which gratify it; on the contrary, the gratification of mental passions creates objects destined to gratify the passions of others. A discovery, a work of art, or a noble act, enrich the mind of all humanity. Man, hitherto self-centered, enters thereby on a participation in timeless and ubiquitous things. This process determines the spiritual grounds of the human mind.

Thus, our highest achievement, but little shared with the rest of the animal kingdom, are works of the mind of a spiritual nature which are not consumed or monopolized in the enjoyment. While the gratification of most passions depletes the quantity of gratification available to others, the works of the mind enrich humanity. Organized religion has no corner on spiritual activity; creativity, whether in the arts, sciences, or religion, is a spiritual activity.

Beyond the Evidence

In our quest for truth, for reliable propositions by which to guide our adaptations to the environment, we are relating to a single unified system of reality. We may be dealing with levels of complexity and magnitude, but we are not dealing with different kinds of being. Therefore, we will not expect to find different kinds of truth. *A proposition believed to be true by theologians cannot be incongruent with propositions believed to be true by scientists.* Now that the science of mechanistic determinism is dead and the theology of special revelation is dead, the alleged conflict between science and religion of the past few centuries is dead. Science and theology converge, as do all the arbitrarily specialized fields of interest pursued by men. Science is not an activity only scientists engage in; it is a way of looking at the universe systematically. People were discovering truth empirically long before the procedure was regularized in a methodology. The Greek Archimedes was behaving scientifically in the third century B.C. when he placed the king's crown, and then an equal weight of gold, in a water-filled basin to determine whether each displaced the same amount of water, and hence whether the crown was pure gold. Joseph Priestley in the eighteenth century scientifically conducted his experiments that led him to the discovery of oxygen, but he called himself a "practical philosopher." And you and I seek the answer to some of our questions more or less scientifically, depending upon the nature of the phenomena we are examining.

R.B. Lindsay (1959, p. 376), physicist at Brown University, who believes that the modern methodology of science is relevant to the study of values, says of science:

Science is a method for the description, creation, and understanding of experience. . . . Science *describes* by endeavoring to find order among certain human sense perceptions and making statements about these with the smallest possible number of distinct terms. . . . Science *creates* experience by devising experiments to channel and control experience, to make it active instead of merely passive. . . . Finally, science *understands* by building theories which are imaginative creations of the mind or postulated pictures from which, by logical reasoning, the observed regularities of experience or "laws of nature" can be derived.

Peter Caws (1967, p. 41) of Hunter College puts it another way: "The function of science is the explanation of nature in its own terms; its method is that of imagination controlled by evidence." It is in the gathering of supporting evidence that propositions are more or less susceptible to the more rigorous disciplines of the scientific method. In chemistry, where the variables can be isolated and controlled, both the experiments and the findings can be precise. But some of the experiences we seek to understand occur in larger fields where the variables cannot be so much con-trolled as accounted for. When we are dealing with larger orders of reality, we can't set up an experiment, we have to wait for it to happen. For instance, to verify part of Einstein's General Theory of Relativity that light would be deflected by the gravity of a large mass, astronomers had to wait for eclipses of the sun so they could take the necessary photographs. Sometimes our proposi-tions can never be proved. Archimedes said, "If you give me a lever long enough and a place to stand, I can move the world." So far, we have not been able to provide a lever long enough and a platform on which to test that proposition; yet, by extension of our knowledge about the force exerted by levers, we believe it. We know a good deal about the law of falling bodies when it comes to apples, but we have not been able to demonstrate how gravity affects tremendously heavy bodies in the universe, for they, as Caws (1967, pp. 44-45) points out,

> . . .could never have been, never will be, and indeed never could be released from rest and allowed to fall freely near the surface of the earth, so that to assert what would happen if they were so released (which is what the generalization amounts to) goes far beyond the evidence.

There are many generalizations which have not been demonstrated to be true because the evidence is not in, and we can't wait to get the evidence. As we anticipate the future, we have to commit ourselves to courses of action of whose outcome we cannot be sure. We can only guide our behavior by hypotheses about the nature of reality which go beyond the evidence, but which at least are satisfying because they make sense out of experience, and because they are not incongruent with propositions for which the evidence is available. It may have occurred to you by now that I am speaking of the realm of *faith*, the realm of belief which relates to the largest orders of being, that is, the nature and will of the supreme being. We cannot have a "scientific faith" because the transcending order of being cannot be brought into a laboratory for controlled experiments, nor arbitrarily rearranged to see what would happen. Neither can we have an incredible faith, whose propositions are inconsistent with what we know to be so. The little boy's definition of faith is not satisfactory: "believing what you know ain't so." An incredible faith will not successfully serve to orient people to the "commanding, transforming reality." Faith should not be confused with credulity. A mind-bending theology, which requires mental contortions in order to commit oneself to doctrines that are incongruent with propositions which we find to be reliable in daily experience, unfits one to live in harmony with the great living system. A credulous faith eventuates in a religion which is not taken seriously but will be, as Whitehead said religions tend to become, "an embellishment on a comfortable way of life." Or, in order for a person to be acceptable to a closed religious sect, a credulous faith requires the costly sacrifice of knowledge available about the conditions of existence, such as Jehovah's Witnesses' refusal to accept blood transfusions in surgery.

If we are to have life, and have it more abundantly, our faith must be congruous with the continuity of being as best we can visualize it. Faith should be reserved for doctrines which are beyond rational demonstration, beyond immediate evidence, such as myths and hypotheses not reducible to laboratory testing; it should not be required regarding phenomena whose structure and dynamics we understand. An incoherent religion cannot make our experiences coherent. Since religion is one of our necessary survival processes, faith projected from true concepts is essential to the survival of the human race.

Michael Polanyi (1965, p. 89) points out that we can avoid three fallacies in epistemology as follows: (1) The rationalist fallacy — by admitting the indispensable biological and cultural rootedness of all free action; (2) the relativist fallacy — by acknowledging that each person has some measure of direct access to the standards of truth and rightness and accordingly must limit arbitrary personal truth claims; and (3) the determinist fallacy — by committing oneself to a personal knowledge of the human mind as a seat of responsible choice.

The human capacity for adapting to our environment depends upon the adequacy of our epistemology; if our knowledge is incorrect, our behavior will be inappropriate. Moreover, the ability to communicate is confused by different epistemologies. Understanding and agreement are reached by people who share not only the same information but also the same way of determining what to believe as true. Ultimately, the integration of the human race depends upon sharing a theory of knowledge. This does not mean that we have to share the same culture, since there are as many ways of structuring human behavior as there are ecological niches. Nor does it mean that we have to share the same hypotheses and concepts, since different concepts reflect different points of view. It does mean that in our search for hidden reality we share the same way of validating our concepts. Then, instead of conflict, we can live in a harmony of different cultures, in unity if not uniformity.

Chapter 5

The Knowledge of Good and Evil

SINCE we are an unfinished animal, very few of our responses to the challenges of our environment are pre-programmed in our genes. We are, therefore, constantly confronted by the necessity of making decisions and choices. We consciously direct the course of our living careers not so much in direct response to stimuli from our environment as in terms of a constellation of symbols with which our minds have been furnished by our experience, including the experience of others which has been communicated to us. We as individuals have not passed this way before and from our personal knowledge do not know where the choices we make will take us. Choices that are acted on are irrevocable, like the choice of roads in Robert Frost's poem "The Road Not Taken" . . . "way leads on to way" and the choice makes "all the difference." The quality and duration of life are determined by a person's choices; nothing one does is inconsequential. Since so few of a person's reactions are instinctive, we need guidance from the experience of other people who have gone down the road before us. In short, we need a "value system," an ethic, or a knowledge of good and evil. How do we know what is good and evil, not only for ourselves but for our children and our grandchildren?

Social organization is one of the most successful processes we have developed for coping with the environment. Organization requires a structured ordering of relations and conduct, which we provide by constructing a symbolic system of normative practices. "Every social order necessarily contains within it a moral order," says anthropologist Ward Goodenough (1967, p. 64). Ralph Burhoe (1967, p. 92) comments that ". . . a human society cannot long endure in a state of anomie, in the absence of a more or less coherent culturally transmitted norm or hierarchical system of values." These values, to be effective integrators of human behavior, need to be not only coherent but also credible. A psychologist, Seymour L. Halleck (1969, p. 24), who counsels college students, observes that youth as well as adults find life more comfortable and meaningful when structured by a value system, and adds, "We are in obvious need of a value system based upon the realistic assessment of man's biological and pragmatic needs."

Unfortunately, many people do not believe that there is available wisdom about how to live. They blunder through their years as if no information or directions were acceptable. They back through life, as if one way were as good as another, like the driver of an automobile who careened through the woods at night backwards, only to discover by his receding headlights the stump that crumpled a fender or the boulder that cracked his oil pan. Then these people are apt to announce that life is absurd.

Living is hazardous, just as driving any freeway is hazardous. But many people have learned the art of defensive driving, of anticipating where danger lies and trying to avoid it. Defensive driving minimizes self-exposure to conditions and places where accidents can happen; not by staying home, but by a careful choice of routes, speeds, and lanes. We can also learn the art of defensive living in order that we may have life and have it more abundantly. The principles of ethics define ways which people have discovered whereby they may live more abundantly, even though accidents can happen.

Moralism is Dead

In this last quarter of the twentieth century, too many people in our society are suffering from meaninglessness manifested in a failure of nerve. The personal and social disorganization resulting from amorality is more threatening than the statistics of crime. We have again reached a state of society in which normative standards of behavior are not generally believed to be imperative. The moral fabric of societies before us has broken down; one of the earliest records of "anomie" (without law) is in the Old Testament Book of Judges (17:6), "In those days there was no King in Israel: every man did what was right in his own eyes." Many people today feel that they may with impunity do what is right in their own eyes because they recognize no other sanction for moral behavior than public opinion, particularly the opinion of their own peer group. A popular assumption seems to be that morality is dead, that traditional codes of conduct are no longer valid. The "Puritan ethic" is blamed for feelings of remorse and guilt, the implication being that if only our society would banish the Puritan ethic, everything would come up roses no matter what a person did. It is paradoxical that the more people proclaim the "new morality"—by which they mean sexual permissiveness, rather than theft, deceit, and murder—the more people feel alienated and anxious. Instead of being carefree and happy in the new morality, people turn in droves to faddish group experiences to increase "intimacy" and "sensitivity." As long ago as 1929, Walter Lippmann (1960, p. 306) observed that:

> . . . in one breath it is said in advanced circles that love is a series of casual episodes, and in the next it transpires that the speaker is in process of having himself elaborately psychoanalyzed in order to disengage his soul from the effects of apparently trivial episodes in childhood. On the one hand it is asserted that sex pervades everything and on the other hand that sexual behavior is inconsequential.

The practical consequence of the demise of respect for morality seems to be not a new freedom but a deeper sense of uneasiness. The rising popularity of old cults of mysticism, spiritualism, and occultism are symptoms of the quest for meaning in lieu of an ineffective traditional morality.

Three factors seem to me to have contributed to the

deterioration of traditional morality in our society: *disenchant-ment with Biblical authority,* the *half-truths from cultural anthropology,* and the *theory of relativity from physics.* When it was generally realized that the Ten Commandments were not inscribed by the finger of God on tablets of stone and handed to Moses on Mt. Sinai, confidence in the validity of the Ten Commandments was undermined. The foundation for moral norms is presumed to have crumbled when it is discovered that they are not edicts from on high. The assumption seems to be that if the Ten Commandments are not supernaturally revealed, not only they but all moral injunctions are nothing but arbitrary social conventions and are not necessarily sound.

Secondly, cultural anthropology has been substantiating the relativity of morals announced in the eighteenth century by Voltaire when he observed that what was moral on one side of the Pyrenees mountains was immoral on the other. In our times, Ruth Benedict has documented the cultural relativity of morals by reporting in her *Patterns of Culture* (1946, p. 257) that among the Zuni Pueblo Indians, humility, politeness, and cooperation are virtues, while among the Dobu Islanders off the coast of New Guinea, ill-will, treachery, and hostility are virtues. She concludes by suggesting that cultural relativity provides "as new bases for tolerance the coexisting and equally valid patterns of life which mankind has created for itself from the raw materials of existence." In 1906, Graham Sumner published a study of *Folkways* which concluded that "the standards are in the mores . . the mores can make anything right."

Awareness of the wide variety of successful human behavior patterns has the salutary effect of tempering "moralism"—the inclination to impose a narrow and conventional pattern of behavior specific to a particular culture, or subculture, upon people of other cultures, such as the drive of missionaries to clothe Hawaiian maidens in muumuus; or the effort to enforce the moral principles of some people as legal requirements upon all people, such as the Roman Catholic strictures upon birth control; or the Methodist opposition to the consumption of alcoholic beverages; or the contemporary campaigns against pornography. As a consequence of cultural anthropology, many of us have realized that the moral prescriptions of our culture are not universal or absolute, which has done more for tolerance than centuries of exhortation. The moralism which claimed absolute and universal validity is dead, not morality.

But the moral relativism substantiated by cultural anthropology is only a half truth; the other half is that *every society has some pattern of morality.* The structure and integrity of each society is maintained if a majority of the citizens honor the ethic of that society. It is one thing to discover that the moral principles of no society have universal validity, and quite another to conclude that in our society no moral principles are necessary. Anthropologist May Edel (1959, p. 30) writes:

> There is room for wide variety in the kinds of lives men build for themselves, but certain minimal standards must be met if their "experiments" are to be successful at all. Each culture must provide patterns of motor habits, social relations, knowledge and beliefs, such that it will be possible for men to survive.

And anthropologist Ward H. Goodenough (1967, p. 62) comments:

> . . . systems of definitions and rules have the effect of allocating among people the ways in which they may gratify their wants and pursue their goals. They also have the effect of entirely disallowing some behavior as contrary to the interests of all. Anthropologists know of no society that lacks such rules. . . . .

Not only does a moral code regulate relations among people in a society, but it also helps define the successful relationship of people to their environment as an ecological system, and to the universe as a living system. Cultures may vary with the nature of immediate environments, but encompassing all societies is the cosmos with its own requirements supervening upon all its constituents. "For whether we believe or not in God and his greater glory," says mathematician Norbert Wiener (1964, p. 52), "not all things are equally permitted to us." A viable ethic takes into account our relation to the whole of being. The fact that all human societies are mutually dependent upon a larger integrating system makes ethical systems converge on basic moral principles. "Common human nature sets limits to the forms that any experiments in living take," says May Edel (1959, p. 45), in addition to the "common requirements imposed by common problems." For instance, she says that incest is universally banned, although the definition varies with societies as to who is too close a kin for sexual relations. "But everywhere, behind all variations, lies a common core: a ban on marriage and sex relations within the nuclear family," she says. "It is within this small unit that stringent incest tabus are to be found virtually everywhere." As the realization spreads that societies do not serve different gods but serve the same commanding, transforming unified reality no matter what their traditions are, the human species may be able in the future to coordinate its various life styles less abrasively. The ethics of various societies converge, even if they are not universal and identical.

When such a basic science as physics promulgates the General Theory of Relativity formulated by Albert Einstein, laypeople are inclined to generalize that if relativity is characteristic of the laws of physics, then moral laws must also be only relative. But moral relativists misapprehend the theory of relativity if they conclude that morals have no validity. Henry Margenau (1966, pp. 281-82) carefully defines relativity:

> In the moral field the word relativity is often used with a meaning entirely different from that employed by physicists. For it denotes permissiveness, the right of a person to select his principles of behavior in accordance with his special circumstances, or in a milder sense the evident cultural dependence of moral norms. In physics, however, relativity means the *invariance* of nature's basic laws with the consequence that *special* observations, like the recording of distances, time intervals and speeds are conditioned by the system of reference in which they are made. Physical relativity does *not* entail that one person's laws are different from those of another, that an observer in motion sees the world differently than as observer at rest; quite the contrary: relativity

denies that motion has an effect on the nature of things and it makes appropriate provisions in stating its laws to make that denial true.

Lincoln Barnett (1962, pp. 54-55) says that Einstein's relativity axiom states that the laws of nature preserve their uniformity in all systems when related by the "Lorentz transformation." The Lorentz transformation relates distances and times observed in moving systems with those observed in systems relatively at rest. This mathematical formula makes possible the correlation of information from systems in different states of motion. The laws of physics are universal once allowances are made for the relative movement of different systems. In the theory of relativity, laws are *relative to something,* not irrelevant. It seems to me that the same kind of transformation formula needs to be defined for ethical systems.

There are a great variety of languages, too, but when we realize the cultural relativity of language we do not decide that, since the meaning of no language is absolute, we will not speak any language, or will devise our own. To refuse to honor the ethic of a culture because the ethic is culture-specific is as absurd as to refuse to speak English because it is not a universal language. As we have learned to translate languages, thereby enriching our ability to communicate, so can we learn to translate moral systems and enrich our capacity for living.

Morality may not be universal, but it is a universal phenomenon among human beings, which seems to indicate that moral norms "always serve some functional role in human living," says philosopher Abraham Edel (1955, p. 149). Ethics are the principles of behavior whereby people more successfully cope with their environment, of which *other people* are a most important part, and thus are a necessary adjunct of successful living for any people. Rather than merely inhibiting the full enjoyment of life, ethics are vital to the quality of living. Zoologist Alfred E. Emerson (1968, p. 154) says that ". . . concepts of right and wrong enabled man to control his behavior more effectively for optimal living." Paleontologist George Gaylord Simpson (1958, p. 179) well summarizes the uniqueness and importance of human ethics:

> . . . in man a new form of evolution begins, overlying and largely dominating the old, organic evolution which nevertheless also continues in him. This new form of evolution works in the social structure, as the old evolution does in the breeding population structure, and it depends on learning, the inheritance of knowledge, as the old does on physical inheritance. Its possibility arises from man's intelligence and associated flexibility of response. His reactions depend far less than other organisms' on physically inherited factors, far more on learning and on perception of immediate and of new situations.
>
> This flexibility brings with it the power and the need for constant choice between different courses of action. Man plans and has purposes. Plan, purpose, goal, all absent in evolution to this point, enter with the coming of man and are inherent in the new evolution, which is confined to him. With them comes the need for criteria of choice. Good and evil, right and wrong, concepts largely irrelevant in nature except from the human viewpoint, become real and pressing features of the whole cosmos as viewed by man—the only possible way in which the cosmos can be viewed morally because morals arise only in man.

Morality is thus not only essential to us, it is unique to us. It is essential to guide personal development and to integrate interactions among people and between people and their living environment. Though some individuals may honor moral norms in the breach, and though such aberrations can and should be tolerated as avenues through which a society's ethic evolves, the ethic of a given society must be observed by a sufficiently large majority of the people in it to stabilize the structure of that society as a functioning whole. The problem for each individual is to know which moral maxims are not important, which are essential to maintain the benefits of a particular culture, and which are cosmic imperatives.

The Knowledge of Good and Evil

Adam and Eve were driven from the Garden of Eden, according to the Genesis myth, because they ate the forbidden fruit of "the tree of knowledge of good and evil." A better understanding of human nature makes it clear that knowledge of good and evil is essential to us to provide criteria by which we may direct our behavior if we are to achieve the quality of life symbolized by the Garden of Eden. Since we lack predetermined behavior patterns programmed in our genes, we need the help of moral codes in exercising responsible choice in order to maximize the experience of living, both for ourselves as individuals and for the species.

A concern with ethics is only human, not shared with other animals. ". . . Good and evil do not exist apart from choice," says biologist Oscar Riddle (1967, p. 35). ". . . They are narrowly limited to a part of the animal world — and wholly absent from the entire gamut of plant evolution. 'Choice' is tightly associated with the fully expanded nervous system and quotas of special hormones." Other animals whose interation with the environment is much more an instinctive response to stimuli, although they too have some learned responses, have less occasion to make choices than we whose interaction with the environment is flexible and is complicated by alternatives present symbolically in our mind. We are confronted with many more opportunities for making decisions than are our fellow creatures, and need the information and principles from previous experience, and embodied in a system of morals, in making our decisions. A knowledge of good and evil is essential for human beings to live successfully.

Good and evil have become so personally relative in our culture that many of us are not sure the concepts have definite meaning, and choose to use the more subjective word "value." There is, of course, a highly subjective element of preference in any choice. Each of us is inclined to choose to experience what we feel to be of worth, so we are guided by what we value. However, our humanity gives us a shared basis for making evaluations which are *inter-subjective*, or verified in the experience of more than one person, so that we can mutually identify specific experiences as good or evil. Good and evil can have definite meaning, even though judgment in acting on them is relative to a specific situation, as we will see later.

The problem is not how did people fall into evil ways, but how did people rise to good ways unmatched by any other animal; how did it happen that there emerged in us the unselfish ways in which human beings so often act with cooperation, compassion, love, friendliness, self-sacrifice, and the desire to mitigate human suffering?

The knowledge of good and evil is not just a matter of memorizing the proverbial maxims of a culture; they won't serve to orient behavior unless people believe, at least implicitly, that they are imperatives sanctioned by some overriding power. "I share the realization which grows alarmingly in many minds," says Henry Margenau (1966, p. 142), "that ethics, moored in a stagnant but pleasant pool of values, amid the enchanting phosphorescence of decaying ideals, is practically ineffectual. . ." The mores of a culture function axiomatically to guide behavior only so long as they are assumed to be supported by the structure and dynamics of ultimate reality. This confidence obtained for people in the Judeo-Christian tradition for generations, and is still true for Fundamentalist believers, so long as they believe that the moral order was instituted by the will of God. But when the traditional theological foundations of ethics are convincingly challenged by emergent knowledge and a more persuasive epistemology, exhortation to honor traditional moral maxims does not suffice to influence behavior. Not that the maxims have become invalid, but that the sense of urgency formerly associated with them has waned. Without "divine sanction," moral laws are not imperative, and hence not determinative, until a new authority is recognized.

What is at issue in the new morality is the nature of "authority." Moral teachings are useless unless people feel some compulsion to accept them as guides to their own behavior. Walter Lippmann (1960, p. 227) suggests that what Moses "obtained on Mt. Sinai was not the revelation of the moral law but divine authority to teach it." The authority appealed to by the Old Testament prophets to win compliance for their precepts was "Thus saith the Lord," a claim of special divine communication which is not persuasive to many people today. Nor have they yet accepted the disclosure of the sciences of a supervening order which does define conditions for successful living, an imperative which operates not by duress but by interaction and feedback processes including natural selection, such as I suggested in chapter 2 on "The Great Living System." My thesis is that earlier people had inadequate notions of the nature of moral authority, and that there are *imperatives to moral behavior innate in the living system of which we are a part.*

In discussing good and evil, we often use the words "moral" and "ethical" interchangeably. For purposes of this discussion, let us keep the distinction between the two. "Moral" is an evaluative word applied to specific acts; an act is moral if it is good or right, while an act is immoral if it is evil or wrong. "Ethic" is a set of moral principles, a coherent system of norms related to the ethos or fundamental values of a society. A code of morals, such as the Ten Commandments, is part of an ethic since it was a covenant between the people of Israel and Yahweh, their God. The decalogue is not enacted law, it is simply the description of the conditions accepted by the community in its favored relationship with Yahweh. As a philosophy of morals, an ethic is a frame of reference which gives meaning and urgency to a particular set of morals. *In my usage, "moral" and "ethical" evaluate interactions with the total environment as well as private behavior.*

For purposes of this discussion, let us also define the adjectives "good" and "evil" according to the probable consequences of such acts. An act is "good" if it leads to the fulfillment of one's being individually and in relation to the environment now and in the future, if it stimulates growth and opens further opportunities, if it enhances appreciation of living, if it negates entropy and preserves or increases the order of one's being and of the environment, if it benefits the human species, and if it is in harmony with the fundamental laws of growth and change which pervade the universe. An act is "evil" if it damages one's essential nature, if it limits future choices, if it diminishes the capacity for appreciative awareness, if it betrays confidence or disrupts inter-action in relationships, if it exploits people, if it squanders the

natural heritage of humanity, if it increases disorder, and if it violates the laws of being. Alfred E. Emerson (1968, p. 153), using the
word "ethical" where I would use "moral," says:

> Other things being equal, any controlled behavior that leads
> toward individual disintegration may be considered unethical, and
> any behavior leading toward personal balance, control, and greater
> effectiveness may be considered ethical. Overindulgence in
> narcotics, tobacco, or alcohol, for instance, might be considered
> unethical at a personal level. In contrast, any behavior aimed at
> personal integrity would increase individual homeostasis and would
> be considered ethical.

Botanist Edmund W. Sinnott (1966, p. 181) defines moral, good,
or right as "that which is in harmony with the innate goals of man's
behavior," while immoral, evil, or wrong (1955, p. 151) is:

> . . . the pursuit of goals that are attractive but in their attainment
> conflict with more deeply seated and elemental ones, and thus
> exact inexorable retribution because they run counter to some
> fundamental biological norms. They are the forerunners of more
> serious violations, at a higher level, of other laws of life.

The retribution of which Sinnott (1955, pp. 152-53) speaks is not
some vague future punishment, but is registered concretely in
one's feelings. He says:

> In the simplest cases, that act is "right" which helps maintain the
> normal and essential goals of life and thus leads to feelings of
> satisfaction and pleasure; "wrong" is whatever tends to prevent the
> attainment of these goals. It can be recognized by the fact that it
> results in physical or mental pain. . . . This concept, in its simplest
> terms, regards as right *whatever helps to realize the possibilities of
> life most fully.* The moral imperative, the "ought" is thus related to
> a norm inherent in the protoplasm itself.

He points out that there are different levels of evil according to the
significance of our goals; overeating which injures the self is not as
destructive as lying which injures relations.

In the same vein, chemist Frank L. Lambert (1968, pp. 116-17)
says that "Evil, as seen by an individual, is a deeply unwanted
interruption of his own preferred dynamic patterns of life and

thought. . . . Such interruptions of our desired order amount to an unsettling randomization of our patterns." On the other hand, he points out that incarceration in a Nazi concentration camp is experienced as evil, not because it disorders the life process but because it severely restricts the possibility of order by reducing "life into what can be a deadening subhuman order. . . . a crystallization into less mutable, less free patterns . . . life is confined to what we see as a rigid and stifling order." Thus evil is any disruption of self-ordained order, whether by randomization or imposed restriction.

In some contexts, good and evil are quantitative. Oscar Riddle (1967, pp. 34-35) writes:

> The purely natural and quite inevitable characteristics of good and evil are well illustrated by some qualities which are merely the extremes of one and the same thing. They are good when present in small or moderate amount; evil when present in excess. They are qualitatively the same, and only quantitatively do they differ.

The illustration he gives is anxiety: appropriate when it causes one to do something to remove the possible source of danger, but destructive in excess when it breaks one's own mental health or infects social relations. Another example was in the tragic newspaper story a few years ago about a number of infants in a hospital nursery who died inexplicably—until it was discovered that salt instead of sugar had accidentally been mixed in the babies' formula. Salt is so essential to the human body that a salt deficiency can bring on heat prostration, yet in excess it is a poison. Salt is not intrinsically good or bad; it is only the amount imbibed that affects an organism as good or bad.

I once heard a psychologist suggest that to relieve mental tension it was good to daydream about an imaginary vacation with somebody else's spouse. Such a suggestion ignores how highly motivating vividly-held ideas are; "the wish is the father to the deed" is a valid bit of folk wisdom. Jesus (Matt. 5:27) said, "You have heard that it was said, 'You shall not commit adultery.' But I say to you that every one who looks at a woman lustfully has already committed adultery with her in his heart." Edmund

Sinnott (1955, p. 152) reaffirms that morality is a matter of the mind as well as of the deed when he says:

> To "sin," it seems to me, is not simply to do a particular thing that is called wrong but—deeper than this—to seek an end which, if reached, will betray the seeker, for it will prevent attainment of the only goals that finally will satisfy him. The moral life consists of *wanting* the right goals so much that lesser ones no longer are attractive. Character is the constant habit not simply of doing right deeds, but of desiring right ends.

Danish existential theologian Soren Kierkegaard has written, "Purity of heart is to will one thing." Morality is as much a function of our intentions as it is of our actions, since intentions are so influential in what we do.

This conception of ethics can be summarized in the words of Alfred E. Emerson (1968, p. 153):

> . . . as a learned integrated cultural system symbolizing human experience of success and failure in striving for a better life, . . . a set of customs pertaining to responsibility, duty and right, and . . . right is conceived as conduct leading toward increased optimal living and homeostatic control.

The Beginning of Good and Evil

Since a knowledge of good and evil is primarily a human evaluative and conceptual activity, it must have had a beginning in human history. Only with the emergence relatively recently in geologic time of intelligent beings did conceptions of right and wrong begin to evolve. They evolved out of the remembered experience of people, who were able to trace connections between actions and consequences. Moral codes embody the experience of human beings.

To suggest how I believe standards of right and wrong developed, I turn to a record of human experience, the Bible. If I lived in a different culture, I could probably find similar illustrative material in the scriptures of that culture. Although there is evidence that the earliest societies of which we know anything profited by learning from other cultures, each culture developed its own peculiar pattern of moral norms out of its own experience. The moral standards are relevant to particular historical situations. Still, comparison shows that sensitive people in widely varying cultures have converged on about the same basic principles. Such social virtues as courage, honor, faithfulness, veracity, justice, temperance, magnanimity, and love are almost universally celebrated, no doubt because they were found to be of value to the survival of major societies everywhere. Therefore, I turn to the early records of our own Judeo-Christian tradition to trace the origin of some of our moral norms in Western culture.

For example, let us take the ninth of the Ten Commandments (Exodus 20:16), "You shall not bear false witness against your neighbor." The Book of Exodus (23:1) in following chapters goes on to admonish, "You shall not utter a false report. You shall not join hands with a wicked man, to be a malicious witness." How do you suppose the early Hebrew people came to evaluate slander as an evil? The record shows that they had experience with the consequences of slander. In the First Book of Kings (21:1-24) we find the account of the use of a malicious witness by Queen Jezebel to secure a neighboring vineyard for her husband, King Ahab. King Ahab wanted to buy Naboth's vineyard which adjoined the palace, but Naboth refused to sell. Ahab was so vexed he would not eat. Jezebel told him she would secure the vineyard for him. She arranged a dinner party at which she employed two men to accuse Naboth falsely, saying, "You have cursed God and the king." Naboth was immediately taken out and stoned to death, and King Ahab took possession of the coveted vineyard. This deed so outraged the sense of justice of the prophet Elijah that he warned Ahab that as a consequence "of the indignation which you have aroused," his own blood would flow where Naboth's had been spilled, as indeed it turned out. The beginnings of such an injunction as "You shall not bear false witness" are found in the bitter experience of people with the chain of consequences which follow malicious slander.

The sixth commandment (Exodus 20:17), "You shall not kill," or "murder" as some translators believe is the more faithful rendition, evolved slowly and did not reach its highest form until New Testament times. In the period of the Book of Judges (15:8)—about 1300 to 1000 B.C.—Samson could avenge an injustice he had suffered "with great slaughter." It was an improvement when, instead of unbridled vengeance, the Book of Exodus (21:23-25) defined a code of strict retributive justice, "Life for life, eye for eye, tooth for tooth, hand for hand, foot for foot, burn for burn, wound for wound, stripe for stripe." But, as the Chinese sage Lao-tse observed, a strict justice does not end resentment. Only a loving forgiveness can terminate the chain of retributions by ending hatred. So the continuing experience of the Jews led them to a higher ethical norm: the Book of Proverbs (24:17; 25:21) enjoins, "Do not rejoice when your enemy falls"; "If your enemy is hungry, give him bread to eat"; and, "Do not say, 'I will repay evil'; wait for the Lord and He will help you." By the time of Jesus (Matt. 5:43), he could say, "You have heard that it was said, 'You shall love your neighbor and hate your enemy,' But I say unto you, love your enemies, and pray for those who persecute you."

Similarly, the Commandments against stealing, adultery, and coveting could be provided with antecedents in experience. Norms of good and evil, of right and wrong, did not spring full-blown from somebody's head; they developed slowly over generations of trial and error. It is part of the mark of being human that we benefit from the experience of others. "There are values which men have tested for centuries and found to work," says Hudson Hoagland (1966, p. 143).

Now that we have learned to control the process of experimentation we have greatly speeded up the process of arriving at what is right and wrong in a course of action. Through "simulation procedures," astronauts learned to anticipate most contingencies they might meet in space flight, and the right way to cope with them, before they left the launching pad. Consequently, they were able to venture into the unfamiliar environments of space and the moon and return successfully.

To recognize that concepts of good and evil are derived from human experience is to give them a timeless validity, insofar as conditions have remained constant. The realization that morals are empirically grounded does not invalidate traditional norms, it greatly reinforces them. When we penetrate the primitive claims of divine authority for the early catalogs of moral laws, we find that their experiential origins give them contemporary relevance. In a classification of behavioral norms, the traditional customs of societies, the "mores" governing such things as food and dress or status in the social organization vary with cultures and times, but the closer we come to values related to human nature or the nature of being, the more timeless the moral norms become. But even such a basic value as care for the elderly can change with the situation: the Eskimos living in the Hudson Bay region of Canada as a hunting culture necessarily left behind to die their parents who had become too feeble to travel, but when they became sedentary cannery workers, they took care of their elders until death.

Obscured Wisdom

A hindrance to taking seriously the virtues grounded in human experience is that, as Lippmann (1960, p. 226) says, "The wisdom deposited in our moral ideals is heavily obscured at the present time." The wisdom of traditional morality is partly obscured by a confusion between "natural law" and enacted law. Knowledge of the values of courage, honor, temperance, veracity, faithfulness, and love originated in the realization that these qualities were necessary to survival and the attainment of happiness. They were *descriptions*, generalized and simplified, of types of successful behavior. But they were converted into *prescriptions* to be enforced by the fear of punishment by some human agency with a sanction to use force. Generalizations about successful and unsuccessful behavior emerged as observations of the consequences of choices but, to insure compliance, were assigned supernatural origins and backed up with enforcement procedures. In reaction, the modern mind is prone to identify all moral laws with *enacted laws*, whether they be canon laws or civil legislation, and to repudiate the right of any such authorities to define good and evil. What is overlooked is that the Christian tradition has had a concept of "natural law" which is not arbitrary but which states an observed uniformity of succession of events. It is declarative in mood, describing what will probably happen if a certain activity is engaged in. In my view, all valid moral laws have been natural laws. On this basis were built the sciences, which use the term "natural law" to mean a statement of predictable relationships among phenomena.

The great difference between enacted law and natural law is in their respective imperatives to compliance. *Enacted law* entails *arbitrary* punishments not necessarily related to the proscribed act—a term in jail, for instance, as punishment for embezzlement. *Natural law*, on the other hand, also entails undesirable experience, but it is simply *a consequence* of the evil act—embezzlement, for instance, betrays a confidence so that the perpetrator is no longer entrusted with the privilege of managing someone else's property. In a violation of natural law, no judge decides that a person has done wrong; the act simply sets in motion a train of events which do not produce desired results. Moral laws are like natural laws; the imperative to voluntary compliance is not fear of detection and arbitrary punishment, but unwillingness to suffer the physical or psychic pain which experience has shown generally follows certain kinds of acts. Moral laws are *descriptive*, not *proscriptive;* they describe what will probably happen under certain conditions if you engage in certain acts, they do not simply announce what is legally prohibited. Moral laws are "if . . . then" propositions which predict what the situation will be like in the future if we respond to the present situation in a particular way. Moral laws are like rules in art, which are intended to "preserve the fruits of experience more reliably," says Rudolph Arnheim. He points out that the same shift in understanding the rules of painting has occurred as is now occurring in our understanding of the rules of ethics:

Traditionally the rules of the trade were intended to tell the artist what was prescribed and what was forbidden. This is no longer so. We now think of rules as "if-so" propositions. They do not tell us what we have to do but rather predict what will happen as a result of a certain procedure. They also say: "If you wish to obtain a particular effect this is what you can do!"

The imperative of natural moral law is the feed-back from the environment in response to human actions which results in contributing to or in diminishing the viability of a being in a particular ecosystem—natural selection. In natural selection there is no punitive judgment, there is only the chain of events initiated by an action. Acts have unavoidable consequences since they are choices in time which inevitably exclude alternatives in that particular constellation of possibilities. It matters what we do as we have to live through the consequences, whether intended or unintended. We can correct our course, but we have to go on from where we are. It is not just an aphorism but a law of being that "you can't have your cake and eat it too." The usefulness of any law, whether physical or moral, is to provide grounds for sound expectations. Self-control is predicated upon reliable prediction as to the consequence of one's actions. Given the dynamic integration and unity of the world, moral laws are just as reliable, if not so precise, as laws of physics.

The penalties of violating legislated law can be avoided; you may not be *caught* parking illegally or shoplifting. We tend to generalize from this that all laws, including moral laws, can be violated with impunity if we just don't get caught. In fact, our system of jurisprudence requires that one be proven guilty. Under the moral law, there is no avoiding consequences; it makes no difference whether or not someone else has noticed your misbehavior, your act is recorded in the events. St. Paul (Galatians 6:7) recognized the inevitability of retribution, though expressed in a different context, when he wrote, "Do not be deceived; God is not mocked, for whatever a man sows, that he will also reap." The inevitability of the operation of natural laws was illustrated by James Luther Adams in a lecture on ethics at Meadville Theological School, by saying, "If a man steps off the edge of a roof, he does not violate the law of gravity, he illustrates it." The pain and frustration which many people experience, aside from tragedy and great catastrophe, only illustrate the error of their earlier judgment.

As we shall see when we discuss the reasons, some good and some bad, that people take risks in violating moral laws, the *voluntary compliance* with the knowledge of good and evil is far from totally effective. In order to reinforce those moral norms vital to social organization, civilizations convert moral laws into enacted laws. Since the working of the natural process is slow and indirect, governments impose *immediate penalties* for infractions of legislated morality. Persons may destroy themselves with relative impunity, but when they threaten to destroy society as a collective life-support system, other members of the society understandably seek to impose direct restraint. A breach of contract becomes not only immoral but illegal. The legal definition of right and wrong is more than punitive, however, it is normative; it defines what kind of behavior a particular society believes to be necessary for maintaining its integrity, and is effective only if a majority of the citizens voluntarily accept the definition and *internalize* it so it serves as a selective principle. It is physically impossible for a state to use force to impose a particular behavior pattern upon all of its citizens, except for brief reigns of terror and violence under authoritarian dictatorships; even enacted laws function to guide human behavior only if they are *accepted* as meaningful because they give "an unforced unity to experience," in Bronowski's phrase. Exacting penalties for misbehavior is only a social strategy for more directly making people wish they hadn't. B.F. Skinner says that "should" or "ought" simply means "You will wish you had." Though the unified process in which we live will ultimately make people wish they had, the interposition of arbitrary penalties tends to speed up the process and minimize the infractions of interaction patterns which structure a particular society.

We have learned that *morality* can't be legislated, in the sense that a person's internal values are not necessarily changed by the enactment of a law, but that *behavior* can be legislated—for instance, by civil rights legislation restraining racial discrimination. The victims of evil action rightfully expect society to protect them from those whose morality is deficient, whether it be repression based upon racial prejudice, or theft based upon moral myopia. Legislation is one way that societies give concrete form to the accumulated wisdom of the past, and is a precious product of culture by which we have improved our condition.

However, legislated morality runs counter to one of the basic laws of survival among human beings, namely the flexibility of culture. Cultural adaptation to a changing environment is the exceptional coping procedure of human beings. Legal codification crystallizes a moral value in time and tends to make behavior patterns rigid and inflexible. Morality evolves, but enacted laws of church or state, once they are "on the books," tend to be fixed and immutable. When we practice a lenient interpretation of outmoded law, or ignore it altogether, we introduce confusion into respect for law. Or if we insist upon a slavish adherence to legislation which has lost its foundation in morals, we tend to become legalistic. Jesus (Matthew 23:23-24) long ago realized the perils of legalism, saying, "Woe unto you, scribes and Pharisees, hypocrites! for ye pay tithe of mint and anise and cummin and have neglected the weightier matters of the law, justice, mercy and faith; these ought ye to have done without neglecting the others. Ye blind guides, straining out a gnat and swallowing a camel."

To be true to its genius, a viable society will keep its legalized definitions of good and evil to a minimum consistent with protecting all its citizens from the depredations of a few. Societies such as ours try to restrict punishment only to evil acts, not sinful thoughts, and this distinction should be jealously guarded. We have learned that in disciplining children, we should make "the punishment fit the crime" in that any penalty exacted should be obviously related to the misdeed. Penalties exacted by legislation should likewise be as clearly as possible correlated with the probable harm that would result from a wrong act. But, instead of seeking to pass a law to remedy evil behavior, in order to produce orderly behavior citizens should rely on clarifying and disseminating knowledge of the natural imperatives to good and evil.

Physicist Lawrence Cranberg (1967, p. 265) suggests that "An acceptable definition of 'good' social laws surely requires that they be 'liberating,' freeing men from fear, confusion, and arbitrary power, in significant analogy with the effects of the laws or hypotheses of science." The law of the conservation of energy in science is a statement about the probable course of future events, he (1967, p. 263) explains:

> . . . namely, that history has not yet recorded an authenticated set of experiences whose interpretation contradicts the hypothesis; and that anyone planning a future course of action would be well advised to assume its continued relevance. The situation seems not different in kind from that in law, private morality, or politics, where to guide us in the ordinary affairs of life we turn to history, to custom, the precedents of the past for the guidance they offer to a perpetually uncertain future. We can recognize differences of degree of assurance with respect to future expectations without being obliged to assert that they are dealing with fundamental differences in the quality of those expectations.

In order to avoid confusion between inevitable moral law and inflexible enacted law, perhaps we should adopt the terminology used by philosopher May Leavenworth (1969, pp. 38, 41). Instead of moral laws, she uses the word "principles," and says that "principles are empirical generalizations that have resulted from many instances of evaluating in conflict situations and observing the effectiveness of actions chosen in fulfilling human needs, interests, or desires." Principles become institutionalized and "provide implicit or explicit major premises from which particular judgments of value may be derived"; they are "the basis for normative judgments." Institutionalized values, she adds, will always be subject to re-evaluation, including re-evaluation of the situation, principles, and information.

We might be helped in getting past our semantic block about the validity of moral laws if we thought of them more realistically as principles we may employ as normative in making our decisions and choices. Their usefulness in helping us benefit by the wisdom of other people's experience would be enhanced if we conceived of the symbolic repository of human learning as principles, not laws with the implication that other human beings are imposing their particular behavior patterns upon us.

We might be less judgmental in our relations with other people if we recognized that the principles we serve operate just as inevitably for the evil as for the good. In practice, Christians have often belied their belief in a just and omnipotent God by arrogating to themselves the responsibility for punishing wrongdoers, as though, if Christians did not exact retribution, the wrongdoer would not be judged. A more compassionate attitude toward the suffering of error is contained in the Judeo-Christian tradition. St. Paul (12:19) wrote in his letter to the Romans, "Beloved, never avenge yourselves, but leave it to the wrath of God: for it is written, 'Vengeance is mine, I will repay,' says the Lord." If the Puritans in Nathaniel Hawthorne's novel, *The Scarlet Letter,* had really believed that, they would not have required Hester Prynne, unwed mother, to wear a scarlet "A" for adulteress stitched to the bosom of her dress. They would have left the retribution to God. Today, people who believe in the unity of the total environment will leave retribution for moral infractions to the working of the evolutionary process, devoting themselves to compassion and redeeming works of love. At best, the knowledge of good and evil is a faltering guide and we human beings are often in error. Besides, moral principles, like physical laws, are but probability predictions which do not describe precisely what must be done to achieve prospective ends.

Moreover, in the field of human behavior, the variables are more complex than in the physical sciences because of the indeterminacy introduced by the range of mental purposes which motivate people. Since we are already jeopardized by the operation of the feedback in the great living system, we are placed in double jeopardy if our fellows ostracize and punish us. Retribution is a function of the system; it is the function of people to redeem each other from the needless secondary effects of errors in judgment. In the interaction of the living system, deeds are registered as consequences for good or evil, but then the process goes on making the best it can of the new configuration; only people can become "impaled on a brain's agony," in play- wright Maxwell Anderson's phrase, and have their development arrested by symbolically recycling past mistakes in the form of guilt. Christianity has perceptively stressed the importance of forgiveness and acceptance toward wrongdoers as a means of minimizing the corrosive effects of evil. In the Gospel of John story of the woman (not the man?) taken in adultery, Jesus' only judgment was on the accusers who wished to stone her to death. "Let him who is without sin cast the first stone"; to the woman he simply said, "Go, and sin no more." The pathos of the human situation as people struggle to direct the course of their lives with the uncertain guidance of empirical concepts undergirds the traditional virtues of compassion and forgiveness.

Since the knowledge of good and evil is a form of knowledge, it is subject to the indeterminacy characteristic of all knowledge, as I indicated in chapter 4 on "The Search for Hidden Reality." Moral principles are not precise definitions of what must be done at every juncture calling for decision; they are probability projections that still require the exercise of discrimination. Even with the help of moral principles, we have to assess the situation in order to determine which act will really further our intentions. As in the laws of particle physics, the principles of morality become more indeterminate when we are dealing with decisions of small immediate consequence. It is only when such acts are considered in large quantity that their good or evil consequences become apparent. This is an additional reason that we should be chary of legislating private morality, and that we should be charitable in our attitude toward our fellow human beings.

Order—A Unifying Principle

We human beings constantly search for unifying principles that can integrate our experiences and simplify our responses to the environment. In ethics, various unifying principles have been suggested, such as love, or maintaining homeostasis, or doing no harm to others, or observing the Golden Rule, or surviving the process of natural selection. It seems to me that if we consider the nature of life itself, we will recognize a unifying principle which can guide us in living and which provides an incentive to compliance.

Life, according to the hypotheses I outlined in chapter 2, is the mutual attraction of matter into bounded organization within which interaction can take place for the transformation of energy. Life is the process that counters entropy, the natural tendency of matter toward disorder and chaos where energy is dissipated. Only out of such a process has an organism evolved which is aware of its environment and can express how it feels about it: our-selves. Since the alternative to life is sheer unappreciated chaos, I can see no alternative but to cherish life. People who are bitterly disillusioned or depressed can despise life intellectually, but the whole spontaneous bent of an organism is to preserve life—more, to enhance life. The will to live is more than a premise, it is a given. We can't go behind the will to live; it is identical with life itself. Ralph Burhoe (1967, p. 78) is of the opinion that "we cannot help ourselves in adopting 'life' as the primary, or, as the philosophers would say, the 'intrinsic' value relative to which other values are 'instrumental.'"

Then, it seems to me, that *good is what preserves and enhances life* while *evil is what destroys life or diminishes the capacity to live.* The preservation of life is intrinsic to the living.

Therefore, since order is the condition of life, at every level of life *good is what increases order* and *evil is what decreases order*—the order of relationships and interactions, or organiza-tion. Righteousness is whatever transforms disorder into order, whether it be repairing a broken stove or improving personal relationships. A city councilor who betrays public confidence by accepting bribes to influence a judgment is disorderly no less than the husband who deceives his wife. Since entropy, the tendency toward a state of disorder, is one of the basic laws of existence—the second law of thermodynamics—the amazing phenomenon is that there is order. Death is the ultimate state of entropy for an organism. Therefore, the generic evil is entropy and the ultimate good is negating entropy. A house-cleaning home-maker or a corporation-managing executive are negentropic.

Evil is easy since the tendency toward disorder, toward the lower energy level of randomness, says chemist Frank L. Lambert (1968, pp. 126-28),

> . . . is a normal, spontaneous event in inanimate nature. It is only kept from occurring in the patterns of man's brain and behavior by a continuous forcing together of order and disorder, by his appli-cation of unifying patterns to a disorderly world of motions and emotions, of matter and energy.

Evil, he says, "is a clear and simple concomitant of the physical world in which we live, a world which does not favor an unstable equilibrium of order and randomness in general."

Good, or order, is not the natural state of existence; it is an achievement, first of evolution and then of humans. Lambert (1968, p. 118) comments:

> Life in any form is a thermodynamically improbable arrangement of matter in that it consists of matter at a high energy level and maintained at a metastable, always imminently changeable, tension point between the two opposing tendencies of order and randomness.

If we human beings are to exercise our freedom of choice, it has to be on the side of order. Disorder needs no help—it's all downhill. Maybe that is why evil is so attractive, until it disintegrates life in disorder. That act is good which maintains or increases orderly relations within which energy can be transformed at a high level. However, the tendency toward disorder cannot be exorcised from the world, since it is a natural tendency of all arrangements of matter, nor can it be controlled by a rigid structure. Lambert (1968, pp. 121-22) says:

> Both complex order and the great possibility of randomness are combined in living creatures . . . it is this elegant interrelation of substances and cells, this physiological homeostasis, which is

essential to maintenance of the metastable equilibrium. . . . Death can be caused by either thermodynamic tendency becoming dominant: by excessive ordering ("crystallization") so that there is limited adaptability toward stress, or by excessive disorder in any part so that the whole interrelated organism fails to function as a unit. And the death of the organism is the ultimate evil to the individual's physical being.

A "metastable" equilibrium means an equilibrium "marked by only a slight margin of stability." Matter which has been attracted to organize itself into a centered being has the continuing impulse to preserve its slender margin of stability in its interaction pattern; when symbolic thought emerges as a factor in maintaining and enhancing that metastable equilibrium, it has an intrinsic incentive to choose on the side of order.

"All order matters," says philosopher of science Peter Caws (1967, p. 100):

What we sometimes call the order of nature—relative densities of different substances, the alternations of night and day, the balance of hormones—consists just in those arrangements which if changed would affect our interests most profoundly. When in fact there are serious lapses in this order we call them disasters.

Physicist R.B. Lindsay (1959, p. 381) proposes that "the thermodynamic imperative" is an ethical principle which

. . . urges all men to fight always as vigorously as possible to increase the degree of order in their environment so as to combat the natural tendency for order in the universe to be transformed into disorder, the so called second law or principle of thermodynamics.

"Thermodynamics," says Lindsay (1959, p. 378), "is a physical theory of great generality impinging on practically every phase of human experience. It may be called the description of the behavior of matter in equilibrium and of its changes from one equilibrium state to another." Two hypotheses describe changes in the state of equilibrium: the first law of thermodynamics states that the amount of energy remains constant, though transformed, in all changes; and the second law of thermodynamics states that within any closed system the amount of available energy tends to dissipate, so that no system remains stable without the incursion of new energy. This state of dissipated energy is entropy, and is countered only by order. "Increase in entropy means a transition from a more orderly state to a less orderly state," says Lindsay (1959, p. 382). Energy is a constant, while the variable in the process is order, which requires deliberate intention to maintain. The conservation of energy is possible only through orderly interactions. Lindsay (1959, p. 382) says:

> . . . local decreases in entropy are possible, provided one is willing to pay the price. The most striking is that manifested by the living organism. The production of a living creature, on no matter how humble a level, is a vivid example of the transformation of disorder into order.

"Life, then," adds Lindsay (1959, pp. 383, 379), "may fairly be said to consume entropy, since, with the transition from disorder to order, the entropy of the universe decreases." Because of the law of the conservation of energy (first law of thermodynamics), "you can't get something for nothing," which is also a fundamental moral principle. The conservation of energy, he (1959, p. 378) says,

> . . . is exemplified in practically every aspect of man's life, from the purely personal biological functions of his metabolism to the associated necessary activities of food raising and provision for shelter, warmth and light. . . . But, through it all, we are faced with the apparently inexorable situation: in no way can we create energy; we may merely transform it . . . as long as we can find the wherewithal to transform.

He (1959, pp. 383-84) adds that "The development of civilization itself may be, in a certain sense, looked upon as the result of the attempt of man to introduce order into his environment." He suggests that the thermodynamic imperative is "another way of expressing that 'reverence for life' which has made Schweitzer's ethical point of view so satisfying. For all life is entropy consuming."

Mere survival is not enough for human beings. We are not satisfied with just any pattern of order that assures continued existence. We are so concerned with the quality of existence that we will risk our lives to improve our condition. Matter tends to occupy the lowest energy level available to it, while each form of life achieves a level of energy use possible to its ordering capacity. Driven by our imagination, we seek ever more complex forms of order with higher energy consumption which provide more stimulating and exciting experiences, more opportunity for appreciative awareness of beauty, and more comfort and security for the present. Systems analyst Anatol Rapoport (1966, pp. 473-74) points out that we would not be satisfied with certain very successful forms of order: "the ants have been around for 40 million years, and the cockroaches still longer," which indicates that "survival potential has no necessary relation to the quality of existence. After all, who wants to be a cockroach?" To the Roman-oppressed Jews Jesus (John 10:10) announced, "I came that they may have life, and have it more abundantly." It is the abundant life we strive for, not just enough order to survive. Nor can we abide a rigid order which stultifies our proclivity for exploration.

Anthropologist Anthony F.C. Wallace (Burhoe, 1967, p. 80), in summarizing the essence of an estimated one hundred thousand varieties of religions in human cultural evolution, concludes that "this dialectic, the 'struggle' (to use an easy metaphor) between entropy and organization, is what religion is all about." Ralph Burhoe (1967, pp. 80, 79) comments, "A wide scientific community seems to see this negentropic or order-building goal as the primary good or value of life, running as a common thread from the primitive organic chemicals to the highest religions." And he concludes:

> I would summarize this revelation of the sciences as saying that life is a system of order maintained in an environment that ordinarily decreases order and the primary direction, goal, or value of life, which was established by the natural selection that is an inherent characteristic of the general environment, is to continue that order or, in the history of evolutionary development, to increase that order. Here I think we have a definition of the

primary, intrinsic, or ultimate goal or value of any living system, a definition established by the nature of the cosmos itself in creating living systems. Any act of a living system that violates this primary value simply weeds out that living system.

Feedback—An Incentive to Morality

As a constituent of the great living system, we are a "selective system" locked into comprehensive selective systems. You recall that in chapter 2 on "The Great Living System," I outlined the hypothesis that all living systems are bounded organisms which respond to their environments selectively, from one-celled amoebas through animals such as ourselves to social organizations and to the world as an ecosystem. A characteristic of any living system is that it regulates internal and external interactions through a communications system or "feed-back loops."

We human beings tend to identify all communication with the use of language which may call for action, but the symbols are not themselves events impelling a response; the response is *voluntary*. Cybernetics has generalized communications theory to include other levels of communication which are more direct and imperative than language. In addition to *symbolic communication* there is *physical communication,* such as the electro-chemical signals in our brains, or the chemical signals transmitted in biological cells. Though such organisms may selectively accept the input from other parts of its system, the imperative to respond with the output required by the larger system as a whole is concrete. The ecological systems with which we interact communicate by events which are inescapable. Such physical communications systems were urgently regulating organizations before we human beings evolved the capacity to communicate with symbols. It is the imperative of physical communications which I emphasize by using the phrase "feed-back." Feed-back is the imperative which determines right and wrong behavior, and is the basis for human definitions of good and evil.

Stephen C. Pepper (1969, p. 264) writes, "The selective systems that produce the norms for human conduct are those natural feedback systems that apply directly to human individual and social behavior." Pepper describes the process by which norms are developed. Since we have few reflexive responses, when appetitive or aversion drives are blocked, we try other responses and are conditioned by the success of our trial and error — the successful acts are repeated. "The organism learns to discriminate between the incorrect and the correct trials and to reject the former and to retain the latter," says Pepper (1960, p. 22). When this information is converted into symbolic criteria for future behavior, they are "natural norms." "By becoming aware of them and observing their interrelations carefully," says Pepper (1960, Preface pp. v-vi), "men may find how their moral decisions are factually justified and ultimately reconciled."

Feedback operates at all levels of being, but it does not always work to the advantage of the individual. "The ultimate test," says geologist Kirtley F. Mather (1969, pp. 255–56), "in every case, is whether the behavior increases the chances, not of the individual, but of species survival." This is as true for social systems as it is for biological systems. Anatol Rapoport (1966, pp. 468–69) comments:

> We know . . . that neither the life of an individual nor, by exension, his well being are, as a rule, the overriding factors in large scale ethical imperatives; that is, those involving collective social action. Here the "viability" of other kinds of systems takes precedence in decisions, which become binding on all individuals subject to social constraints (and this means all of us).

This means that allegiance to ethical norms will not always preserve our personal identity, but may preserve the identity of our species, or of our culture or subculture. This is the essence of *tragedy,* that individual lives are lost or damaged in the intentional or inadvertent service of higher principles than those of personal survival. But it is also the avenue for insuring the survival of the life-support system on which the lives of the constituent individuals are dependent. It comes down to a matter of whether all shall be lost, or the survival of a few shall be sacrificed for the survival of not only many but also of the system which supports many. The trouble is that we do not always know what is required to save the next higher order of being from extinction; aspects of that more-inclusive system may have become outmoded. Kluckhohn and Murray (1948, p. 23) comment that "Often it is impossible to decide whether a particular [culture] pattern is an expression of the profound 'wisdom of the culture,' or merely, like a man's coccyx, a vestigial fixation." The moral question is, will the acts required by the system's feedback actually contribute to the viability of the system, or will it make the system increasingly discordant with still more inclusive systems. To be more than expedient, moral choices have to have in view not only the next higher system but also the feedback from more inclusive systems up to the ultimate system conceivable. This is the significance of the phrase "under God" in the Pledge of Allegiance; the order of the nation stands under judgment of a higher order. A citizen's preferred actions may be in tension with the current order of a state, and yet be motivated by a concern for the preservation of the state in a higher order.

Psychologist B.F. Skinner (1953, p. 430) suggests that the natural selection of evolutionary theory functions in much the same way as the more generalized feedback process which he calls "operant reinforcement." He says that "Just as genetic characteristics which arise as mutations are selected or discarded by their consequences, so novel forms of behavior are selected or discarded through reinforcement." Natural selection may be the ultimate test of the capacity of a species or of an individual to survive, but the same process also serves to mold behavior short of deselection.

Feedback exercises a reinforcing influence not only from the environment, but also internally in what we call *conscience*. Each person as a selective system, has his or her own value pattern dynamically imbedded in his or her system. Any violation of that pattern is felt as a vague uneasiness, while any reinforcement of it is felt as satisfying. Abraham Maslow (1962, pp. 4-5) comments:

> The serious thing for each person to recognize vividly and poignantly, each for himself, is that every falling away from species virtue, every crime against one's own nature, every evil act,

every one without exception records itself in our unconscious and makes us despise ourselves. Karen Horney had a good word to describe this unconscious perceiving and remembering; she said it "registers." If we do something we are ashamed of, it "registers" to our discredit, and if we do something honest or fine or good, it "registers" to our credit. The net results ultimately are either one or the other—either we respect and accept ourselves or we despise ourselves and feel contemptible, worthless, and unlovable.

Such is the source of remorse or guilt. Each of us is aware when we have violated our personal integrity. We can avoid the subjective negative feed-back from our conscience only by hardening our hearts, and the price of such callousness is *decreased sensitivity* to all experience.

Henry Margenau (1966, p. 275) says:

Conscience is the concentrated experience of the race, . . . it is the residue, itself both memory and prompter, within an individual mind, of mankind's (or a limited society's) past experience in ethical achievements and frustrations, a record of its slow movement from imperatives to goals.

Conscience is thus not an a priori source of moral norms; conscience is composed partly of self-awareness of what is good for one's own identity, partly of a sense of identity with other persons, and largely of social conditioning. The nature and home of conscience, says biologist Oscar Riddle (1967, p. 38),

. . . is well summarized in this single sentence of T.H. Green: "No man makes a conscience for himself; he needs society to make it for him." A human being reared in isolation, wholly apart from all mankind, would have no conscience. This valued human asset is among the magnificent evolutionary emergents at the family and social level—a product of suitable human association.

Conscience may be in conflict with the requirements of a society because it is capable of rearranging what it has learned from the society in such a way as to give priority to values not then being served by the society.

Earlier, I discussed the difference between spiritual and material values; material values being those which are consumed in their enjoyment, while spiritual values are those which can be shared, which can enrich others as well as the creator. The same distinction seems to hold for personal and social values. Stephen C. Pepper (1969, p. 11) comments:

> As I read the evidence for an empirical theory of value, there are two opposite dynamic poles for the generation of value—the maximization of individual satisfactions through prudence and intelligent social cooperation, and the continuous necessity of biological adaptation, whatever it may cost in the sacrifice of satisfactions in periods of emergency. Through social intelligence men may keep the impact of the sanctions for survival at a distance and so allow satisfactions a wide range of freedom to expand. But if this social intelligence lags and fails, the penalties of biological maladaptation to the life zone man himself has largely brought into being will inexorably take its toll.
>
> And the most dangerous way by which our social intelligence could fail today would be persistent blindness to, and denial of, the existence and sanctioning power of survival value and its polar opposition in periods of emergency to the values of satisfaction.

The point is that though both individual satisfaction and biological adaptation enter into the formation of human values, "the immediate purposive consummatory aesthetic satisfaction of pleasure for its own sake," says Pepper, must yield to "the ultimate biological selective system of the adaptive preservation of the species." The higher system prevails over the lower, and the constituent systems either become extinct or recede to a lower level of appreciative awareness if they fail to heed the feedback from the comprehensive system. However, the interaction of living systems is a mutual relation in which the output from constituents also modifies the interaction pattern of the total system; parts influence the development of the whole.

As early as 1898, pragmatic philosopher John Dewey (1898, pp. 321-41) wrote of the ethical advantage of a scientific understanding of the structure and dynamics of the cosmos:

> . . :. I question whether the spiritual life does not get its surest and most ample guarantees when it is learned that the laws and conditions of righteousness are implicated in the working process

of the universe; when it is found that man in his conscious struggles, in his doubts, temptations and defeats, in his aspirations and successes, is moved on and buoyed up by the forces which have developed nature, and that in this moral struggle he acts not as a mere individual but as an organ in maintaining and carrying forward the universal process.

Perennial Morality

To dismiss the moral principles preserved in our tradition as the arbitrary conventions of a naive people is to underestimate the intelligence of our ancestors. Unless we presume that human beings became intelligent only in the twentieth century, which is belied by the technological and cultural achievements of our ancestors back at least to the dawn of civilization about five thousand years ago, we will credit their ability to derive from their experience moral principles which are perennial. Mores change with the situation, but some of the basic moral principles have not been discredited by a better understanding of ourselves and our environment; they have been reinforced.

As illustrations of perennial moral principles which are validated by more knowledge, let us take the concepts of the values of cooperation, tolerance, honesty, and love.

Cooperation is not just an ideal which would be nice if more practiced by human beings; it is a principle whose survival value has been tested. Most animals cooperate to some degree, from the simple crowding together of buffaloes for mutual defense against an enemy to the highly organized division of labor of ants. In the struggle for survival, cooperation has been reinforced by natural selection—those who cooperated being more capable of surviving. Edmund W. Sinnott (1957, p. 170) says, ". . . some biologists conclude that natural selection often actually puts a premium on mutual aid and cooperation rather than on competition only." Alfred E. Emerson (1968, p. 147) writes that "Co-operation within the organism and within the intra-species population often increases efficiency and well-being and is therefore subject to positive selective pressure." And sociologist William G. Mather (1967, pp. 253-54) points out that for human beings,

Continuous oestrus, long pregnancy, extended infancy, overlapping progeny—these forced upon the members of the family
group (now of mixed sexes and ages and states of health and
conditions of dependency) the necessity of understanding, working
with, and "putting up with" people different from each other. . . .
family members had to live with each other or perish. . . . Those
who mastered the art of living in groups survived and propagated
their kind and passed their way of living on—the others
disappeared.

The cost to people of ignoring the moral principle of
cooperation is too high—extinction.

Tolerance as a moral principle has been emasculated by being
confused with indifference—the failure to be committed to any
moral principles. But tolerance also has solid grounding in
experience. Since human beings are not omniscient, we cannot be
sure that the course we have chosen is the only viable way. The
environment has many niches, there are many ways of relating to
reality that can be successful. Therefore, we should be accepting
of behavior patterns differing from our own, even though we are
committed to our own way. This principle has come to be valued
in our society as "cultural pluralism," the recognition that the
various subcultures really strengthen a culture by keeping the
options for the future open. Robert S. Morison (Hoagland and Burhoe,
1962, p. 41) sees validation of cultural pluralism in biological
"polymorphism" — many forms:

It may indeed turn out that modern biology, by giving us the
concept of balanced polymorphism, has laid a sound scientific
foundation for a system of morals and ethics. . . . Western man
seems to have arrived at his concept of a pluralistic society, in
which no one way of life is considered absolutely better than
several others, largely because he recoiled in horror at the number
of heretics who would have to be killed if he persisted in his search
for the single "best" way of reaching salvation. The concept of
polymorphism gives him a much better reason for cherishing
pluralism, for it makes it part of the demonstrable order of nature.
It would be a pity if, just at the moment when genetics has given us
this highly sophisticated notion, we should turn aside to use that
science to pursue a single-minded, idealized vision of what man

might become. For, in the very act of divining the good, we may limit the possibilities of goodness.

The related concept of active cooperation between people of differing races and ethnic traditions "rests upon firm biological principles," says Alfred E. Emerson. St. Paul's insight that God "made from one every nation of men to live on all the face of the earth" (Acts 17:26) is confirmed by Alfred Emerson's (1968, p. 160) observation that the human exploitation or killing of members of different races will be deselected, while cooperation, integration, and compromise will be positively selected. "Ethics," he says, "leading to firmer integration and mutual benefit between races of man is in conformity to biological trends."

When people speak of the "new morality," they really don't mean that honesty has gone out of style. The most impassioned advocate of the new morality still believes in telling the truth. And for good reason. *Honesty* is demonstrably essential to the most precious of human experiences, cooperation. Alfred E. Emerson (1968, p. 163) writes:

> . . . honesty enhances confidence between the cooperating individuals, whether the social unit be the sex pair, the family, or the social system. Honesty is thus ethical because it tends to establish firmer co-operation between individuals, between business firms, or between nations. Dishonesty tends to be destructive of group homeostasis and is consequently unethical. Lying and cheating in international diplomacy, in business transactions, or in games tend to destroy the mutual trust necessary for the attainment of mutual welfare.

Let's take a generic example of dishonesty, infidelity. Infidelity is basically a deception of partner and of self. A betrayed wife feels the separation when her husband tries to keep his infidelity a secret; she is being hurt without understanding the reason. It is a case of the excluded alternative. The confidences, the time and money, as well as the physical and emotional energy, a husband devotes to the pursuit of the other woman are not available for his wife. "Whatever he gives her in effect he must take away from his

wife," says psychiatrist Alexander Lowen. The worst consequence is not the deception of his wife, but of himself. "He is also
concealing from himself the truth about the effect of his infidelity
on his marriage." Lowen (1969, p. 116) explains:

> It is when we feel we must lie to someone who trusts us and whom
> we like or love that we are trapped in what psychologists call a
> double bind. Whatever we do, we lose. This is what an unfaithful
> husband faces when he returns home to a wife he genuinely loves.
> He wants to restore his sense of closeness to her, but he knows
> that of course he cannot tell her where he has been and what he
> has done. So he lies. But the lie divides, just as the truth unites, and
> so his lie has a boomerang effect. Instead of bringing him closer to
> his wife, it leaves him feeling further away from her. The lie that
> spared him from her anger and rejection brought with it a pain of its
> own. In such situations, the stronger a person's desire to be close
> to the one he is deceiving, the greater the pain over the lie that
> divides them.

Deception disorders a marriage. Worse, it disorders the self. The
deepest deception is self-deceit when the unfaithful partner
deceives himself that he is keeping his affair secret. Says Lowen
(1969, p. 116),

> . . . self-deception requires the suspension of self-awareness. . . . he
> is out of touch with his true feelings and dominated by his
> rationalizations. . . . The liar does not know the full price he pays
> for lying to himself . . . the biological price of self deceit. In the short
> run it means coping with pain. In the long run it means enduring the
> deadness that diminishes him as a person.

This is no idle consequence, it produces stress, which can
record itself in bodily discomfort. Lowen comments:

> The liar is gripped by acute discomfort not only because he feels
> separated from the one he loves, but also because he feels
> separated from himself. Having lied, he can no longer speak from
> his heart; he has lost his inner harmony. Instead he must monitor
> every thought before expressing it, fearful that a lapse of memory
> may betray him. He is indeed a divided man, constantly on guard—
> against himself. The result is still more discomfort.

This pain, says Lowen (1969, p. 116) is rooted in the body.

> Physical tension grips us when we lie, and nothing we can do will stop it. We do not have conscious control over our breathing, perspiration and heart-beat (lie detection instruments seek to measure these physiological changes), and so our bodies bear witness to our inner conflict.

The inner pain of deception and self-deception is attested to by a major student of the stress of life, Hans Selye (1956, p. 299), who has found that:

> Mental tensions, frustrations, the sense of insecurity, and aimlessness are among the important stressors. As psychosomatic studies have shown, they are also very common causes of physical disease. . . . How often are migraine headache, gastric and duodenal ulcer, coronary thrombosis, arthritis, hypertension, insanity, suicide, or just hopeless unhappiness actually caused by the failure to find a satisfactory guide for conduct?

Yes but, you may protest, some people get away with it. But do they? Lowen (1969, p. 116) observes that some people who apparently do not feel the pain of deceit "are in actuality coping with it in a self-destructive way."

> They generally do not care very strongly about anything or anyone. They are, in a contemporary phrase, turned off; they have diminished all emotional responsiveness. . . . He must accept himself as a person of limited emotional depth.

For instance, a study of unwed mothers shows that not only do the mothers suffer, but the fathers also suffer psychic damage in that they must deny the emotion aroused by repudiating their own child and by rejecting the woman with whom they have shared the intimate experience of making love; the callousness they develop to protect themselves from this experience diminishes their sensitivity to further experience.

The breakdown in orderly relations caused by deceit undermines one of the most important institutions for nurturing full humanness, the family. Lowen (1969, p. 114) comments:

No living creature, man or animal, will move forward if the ground under its feet cannot be trusted; it will freeze where it stands. This principle, as psychiatry has amply demonstrated, functions on the psychological level as it does on the physical. When a husband and wife cheat (which is the term used by many of those who engage in extramarital sex), when each knows or suspects that the other lies, neither is capable of healthy individual growth, much less of teaming up to create a good home.

Lowen (1969, p. 116) provides a final word on the value of honesty: "We cannot move away from the pain of inner conflict until we feel it; then we will start reaching for the restored pleasure of inner harmony. This is a biological principle as basic as the law of gravitation in physics."

Love is the central concept of the gospel of Jesus, and of New Testament Christianity. When Jesus was asked by a scribe, "Which commandment is the first of all?" (by which he meant which of the moral principles recorded in the Old Testament was most important), Jesus responded by quoting passages about love from Deuteronomy (6:4) and Leviticus (19:18): "Hear, O Israel: The Lord our God, the Lord is one; and you shall love the Lord your God with all your heart, and with all your soul, and with all your mind, and with all your strength.' The second is this, 'You shall love your neighbor as yourself.' There is no other commandment greater than these." (Mark 12:29-31). Paul in his First Letter to the Corinthians writes a paean to love: ". . . If I have prophetic powers, and understand all mysteries and all knowledge, and if I have all faith, so as to remove mountains, but have not love, I am nothing. . . . Love is patient and kind; love is not jealous or boastful; it is not arrogant or rude. Love does not insist on its own way; it is not irritable or resentful; it does not rejoice at wrong, but rejoices in the right. Love bears all things, believes all things, hopes all things, endures all things. . . . So faith, hope, love abide, these three; but the greatest of these is love. " (I Cor. 13:1-13). John writes in his First Letter, "God is love, and he who abides in love abides in God, and God abides in him. . . . If one says, 'I love God,' and hates his brother, he is a liar; for he who does not love his brother whom he has seen, cannot love

God whom he has not seen." (I John 4:16 and 10).

When as a youth I realized that "love" was the key word in Christianity, I asked a minister what it meant. His answer was so vague that I concluded that Christianity had nothing to offer but pious sentimentality. Not until I was deep in the study of psychology did I realize what a powerful and basic concept love was. For instance, psychiatrist Karl Menninger (1942, p. 5) writes that, in addition to the instinct to hate, ". . . Freud showed us that the impulse to live and love is likewise an instinctual endowment of human beings and a source of strength in opposition to the self destructiveness. Die we must, ultimately, but in the meantime we can live, if we can love." He (1942, p. 272) defines love:

> Love is experienced as a pleasure in proximity, a desire for fuller knowledge of one another, a yearning for mutual identification and personality fusion. This we show to one another by our efforts to be understood, and by indulging the less imperious longing to understand. To be understood means, of course, that some of our *worst* impulses as well as our best ones are recognized by our friend, who knows all about us and likes us, anyway.

And psychoanalyst Erich Fromm (1960, pp. 97-98) tries to clear up some of the confusion about love by qualifying it as "productive love":

> There is hardly any word which is more ambiguous and confusing than the word "love." It is used to denote almost every feeling short of hate and disgust. It comprises everything from the love for ice cream to the love of a symphony, from mild sympathy to the most intense feeling of closeness. People feel they love if they have "fallen for" somebody. They call their dependence love, and their possessiveness too. They believe, in fact, that nothing is easier than love, that the difficulty lies only in finding the right object, and that their failure to find happiness in love is due to their bad luck in not finding the right partner. But contrary to all this confused and wishful thinking, love is a very specific feeling; and while every human being has a capacity for love, its realization is one of the most difficult achievements. Genuine love is rooted in productive- ness and may properly be called, therefore, "productive love." Its essence is the same whether it is the mother's love for the child,

our love for man, or the erotic love between two individuals. . . . Although the objects of love differ and consequently the intensity and quality of love itself differ, certain basic elements may be said to be characteristic of all forms of productive love. These are *care, responsibility, respect,* and *knowledge.*

Paleontologist Teilhard de Chardin (1961, p. 264) defines love as an "affinity of being with being," and adds, "Driven by the forces of love, the fragments of the world seek each other so that the world may come into being." This I take to mean that what functions at the human level as the dynamics of attraction, love as a sense of affinity of person for person or of acceptance of each other simply as human beings quite aside from whether we find each other pleasing, a "yearning for mutual identification and personality fusion," functions at all levels of being as a cohesive power. An "internal propensity to unite," as Teilhard de Chardin calls it, is not peculiar to us; it is a natural dynamism general to all life. All cohesive powers, all community-forming impulses, from molecular affinities to cosmic gravity, from sexuality to shared goals, including the human capacity for diffused love, are essential to creativity and negentropy. For they bond the relations within which interaction takes place and energy is transformed. Love at the human level performs the same function of unification as does the "strong tendency to combine with other chemicals" of acetylene, which stretches "out into longer chemical chains, in particular to form benzene, which is a building block of pyridine, and other amino acids essential to life." (Thomas O'Toole, Oct. 4, 1970, Sec. B-1). Love is as essential to the formation of human groups as molecular attraction is to the formation of the simplest, one-celled forms of life. Without love, human beings would be alienated from each other by their cultural differences and competition for food; with love, human beings can accept each other in spite of differences and form organizations within which cooperation mutually provides life support. Love is a nexus or bonding agent that integrates social systems. Far from being a mere sentiment to be indulged as a luxury after the necessities of life have been provided, love is a necessity to the social complexity which enriches life.

Sex As Nexus

The propensity for love is stronger in us not only because we can symbolically identify with others of our species, but also because of unique human sexuality. Among human beings, *sex is a nexus.* Sex is the biological dynamic for love, out of which grows the diffused capacity for loving. Our pervasive interest in sex is not prurient; it is an awareness that sexuality is vital to humanity. Perhaps if we understand the role of sexuality in human survival, we will recognize the validity of moral norms or values which have emerged from human experience regarding sexual behavior, such as monogamy and fidelity, whether in a "legal marriage" or a "committed relationship." Human sexuality is the dynamic of community and cooperation that makes possible civilization.

Human sexuality is a unique phenomenon among the creatures of the earth. Its peculiarly human function is distinguished by its relatively constant availability as an experience to the same partners. Among other mammals, the female is receptive to the advances of the male only when she is biologically prepared to conceive; women are more perennially attractive and receptive to male attention. Is this unique evolutionary development just so we human beings can have more fun, or does it serve some fundamental survival need of humanity? Surely, the process of natural selection, which tests the coping ability of specific characteristics to contribute to species survival in a given environment, did not permit the evolution of the special refinements of human sexuality solely for the pleasure of human beings. Sexuality has a more generalized and vital function among us than propagation or mere self-indulgence.

A limitation of traditional sexual morals is that they have been too much influenced by observation of the sexual behavior of animals. The stricture of Pope Paul on conception control is based upon a "natural-law" definition of the function of sex as procreation, with only a passing reference to its "unitive" function. If sex were exclusively for procreation, women would still share the periodic sexually receptive rhythms of other mammals. A sound moral principle regarding sexual behavior will take into account the distinctively human function of sexuality.

As I suggested in chapter 3 on "The Unfinished Animal," human sexuality serves the additional function, besides procreation, of being a constantly available source of mutual gratification which is a bonding energy in creating a social unity, the family, within which the human infant can receive the extensive nurture it requires to become human. In addition, sexuality provides the stability of intimate relationships which the adult personality requires. Human sexuality is a cohesive power of mutual attraction that makes the human race viable. It is not a periodic procreative impulse such as is manifested by birds in the spring, but is a nexus or pervasive unifying urge that stabilizes a small community within which adult emotional needs can be secure and the young can be nurtured. Sexuality institutes what Eiseley called "prolonged bonds of affection" necessary to human fulfillment.

Biologist Herman B. Chase (1966, pp. 8-9) makes the best exposition of the integrative function of human sexuality in his book, *Sex: The Universal Fact*. He writes that sex has been an essential factor in the evolution of most living organisms by shuffling the chemistry of genetic material to obtain new combinations, and by allowing the division of labor of male and female while ensuring the reproduction of the species. He says

> In human society, however, while sex is still important as a shuffling agent and an agent for reproduction, it has attained a new and transcendent usefulness, that of integrating and preserving the family group and thereby our social organization and civilization itself. Sex for pleasure becomes not only permissible, but evolutionarily desirable.

He points out that the "biological oddity" whereby human sexual intercourse often occurs when no pregnancy could result, instead of just when the female is in "heat," makes possible frequent sexual intercourse and the consequent integration of the family unit; that is, the male can be enticed to stay around. This is the basis of monogamy, and he suggests that monogamy may well have been a decisive factor in the survival of the human race.

Zoologist Desmond Morris (1967, p. 63) calls us "the naked

ape," and says that we are "the sexiest primate alive." The reason human beings evolved heightened sexuality, according to Morris. was the need of the helpless human infant with a large brain to have extended care in order to furnish the brains with the information it needed to survive; the need of the mother bearing a series of infants, and thus confined by care of them, to secure constant help from the father to supply food and protection; and the need of the father to be freed from sexual competitiveness so he could cooperate with other males in the hunt.

Moreover, during the long period of infant nurture, humanity became dependent for its sense of well-being upon sustained intimate relationships. Prolonged childhood bred in adults a need for security in warm and accepting relationships. Morris (1967, pp. 64–65) explains:

> During the long, growing years he will have had the chance to develop a deep personal relationship with his parents, a relation-ship much more powerful and lasting than anything a young monkey could experience. The loss of this parental bond with maturation and independence would create a "relationship void" — a gap that had to be filled. He would therefore already by primed for the development of a new, equally powerful bond to replace it.

Evidence for the uniqueness of a sexual development in humans mentioned by Morris are such specialized erogenous organs as lips, earlobes, breasts, and genitals. Other primates do not possess erogenous fleshy earlobes. All primates have lips, but not enlarged and rolled outward as are ours. The evolution of enlarged, rounded breasts in the human female, which is not necessary to milk producing capacity, is an example of "sexual signaling," suggests Morris; female breasts have developed to replace the visual stimulation of the buttocks lost when man generally adopted a frontal approach for sexual intercourse. "Face-to-face sex is 'personalized sex,' " says Morris. The human male has the longest and thickest penis of any primate, and the female clitoris has developed a particular susceptibility to stimulation that makes her capable of orgasm, which is unique among female primates. But, suggests Morris (1967, pp. 66–82), the unique hymen serves as a deterrent to a maiden's becoming sexually involved without pair-formation so she is less likely to find herself a parent without a partner. These highly developed erogenous features of men and women are happily given an opportunity for maximum exercise due to continuous estrus, a biological difference which is an advantage to humans.

In contrast, says Morris (1967, pp. 62-63):

> The period of sexual receptivity of the female monkey or ape is more restricted. It usually lasts for about a week, or a little more, of their monthly cycle. Even this is an advance on the lower mammals, where it is limited more severely to the actual time of ovulation, but in our own species the primate trend towards longer receptivity has been pushed to the very limit, so that the female is receptive virtually at all times. Once a female monkey or ape becomes pregnant, or is nursing a baby, she ceases to be sexually active. Again, our species has spread its sexual activities into these periods, so that there is only a brief time just before and just after parturition when mating is seriously limited.

Morris (1967, p. 80) sums up by saying "that with both appetitive and consummatory behavior, everything possible has been done to increase the sexuality of the naked ape and to ensure the successful evolution of a pattern as basic as pair-formation, in a mammalian group where it is virtually unknown." The significance of pair-formation is that it is the basis of the family and of society. Biologist Oscar Riddle (1967, p. 38) says,

> . . . the very possibility of "family life" arose when our primate ancestors added a non-seasonal sexuality to the ancient mammalian concern of a mother for her young—in other words, when a female could be interested in a husband and children at the same time. Only in a permanent group like this could children be taken care of through a longer infancy; only where all this was true was it possible for *language* to be developed. With language came the possibility of abstract thought and for truly human society.

Not only is sexuality the basis of the family, it is a condition for extended cooperation which is the basis of civilization. Because the human male could be satisfied with one female, once a pair-bond had been established the male was relieved of the compulsion to compete for other females, or to protect a harem of females from young and aggressive males. He could cooperate with other males, which issued in a more important role in the economy for the human male than for the male of any other species. Since he is not just a stud, each man is more indispensable to society than are the males of any other species. Geneticist Theodosius Dobzhansky (1962, p. 199) writes:

> Continuous sexual receptivity of the female made monogamous family life possible and thus freed the male from the constant necessity of warding off interlopers. He could now specialize in hunting and food gathering away from home, while the female could remain more nearly stationary, tending her offspring, gathering food in the near vicinity of her abode, and doing the domestic chores that accumulated with the growth of technology and, particularly, with the use of fire. As the male was now able to relax his aggressiveness and dominance, particularly over his mate, domination could change to cooperation and in the long run even to chivalry. If man is "pre-eminently a sexual animal," he has at least managed to make his sexual urges less acutely competitive than they were in his remote ancestors. Cooperation between mates made possible the extended family (individuals of several generations with their respective mates living together) and eventually clans, tribes and nations. Different males now could cooperate to provide for the families and this permitted stalking, cornering, and killing big game that was inaccessible to the lone hunter until he was equipped with powerful weapons. Cooperation in turn made communication a necessity, and stimulated the development of language.

In circular causation, the enlarged brain may have facilitated the development of the enlarged penis in man. Sexuality is no longer simply a biological impulse in human beings, but has become a generalized interest. This is why I have been speaking of "sexuality" rather than the more universal reproductive act of "sex." Human sexuality is correlated with symbolic thinking; we seek repetition of sexual gratification not only from immediate stimuli, such as a suggestive shape or scent, but also in response to imagery of delightful experiences we are capable of evoking in our minds through memory and imagination. A capacity for symbolic thinking is thus a further condition for the heightened sexual activity which makes human sex a nexus. The emergence of the non-biological—we may say "spiritual"—dimension of sexuality is peculiarly human. Sexuality issued in love, eros flowered into agape, and the scope of this creative dynamic for bringing people together was extended.

The peculiar habits of human beings is another manifestation of our unique sexuality. Among other species, it is the male who wears the brighter colors and who struts and preens to attract the favor of a female in a mating mood. Among us, it is the woman who enhances her natural endowments by using aesthetic arts to make herself more, and more constantly, attractive to the always ready male. She doesn't do this because she has an urge to conceive a child, but because she desires the constant companionship of a male.

That men and women are sexually attracted to each other long after the women are of childbearing age is additional evidence that sexuality has evolved a function beyond procreation. Stable relationships are mutually beneficial in avoiding a sense of alienation and loneliness long after the last child has gone out on his/her own, or even where no child has issued from the union.

As we well know, the impetus of sexuality toward stable pair-bonds is not inevitable. The very powers of attraction that make a continued relation with one partner satisfactory also make the possibility of relationships with other people exciting and inviting. What Morris (1967, p. 95) calls "sexual imprinting" or falling in love, is not exclusive. To reinforce love, culture has developed the *commitment* of marriage vows. A public declaration of intent or purpose is a peculiarly human way of orienting behavior; it works to raise human interaction to levels of stability not achievable on an instinctual basis. As Erich Fromm (1956, p. 57) has written,

> To love somebody is not just a strong feeling—it is a decision, it is a judgment, it is a promise. If love were only feeling, there would be no basis for the promise to love each other forever. A feeling comes and it may go. How can I judge that it will stay forever, when my act

does not involve my judgment and decision?

And after extensive study of the factors that make for successful marriage, sociologist Ernest W. Burgess (1953, p. 300) concludes, "A strong force stabilizing and reinforcing marriage is the expectation that 'for better for worse' it will be a continuing relationship." Thus, marriage tends to be more stable and supportive than a relationship based upon affection alone. Alexander Lowen (1969, p. 112) says, "A marriage exists when a man and a woman live together, fortified by the feeling of total commitment that extends from the present into the future. Each considers the happiness of the other an end in itself." And psychologist Seymour L. Halleck (1969, p. 23) says on the basis of his experience of many students who have experimented with the new morality:

> A major goal of marriage is the achievement of intimacy with another person. Intimacy depends upon trust and shared experience. It is unlikely to develop between a couple who have serious reservations as to how long they will stay together. This is because in those situations where there is no deep sense of commitment, people are unwilling to risk vulnerability or to strive for that kind of openness which allows intimacy to develop. The rewards are simply not high enough to justify the risk.

What it comes down to is that a person would be reluctant to invest capital in a business whose fiscal soundness was uncertain — how much more risk investing one's self in a relationship whose stability is in doubt. The existential commitment of marriage adds a further life-giving dimension to love.

Human sexuality does not issue in uniform patterns of relationships in all cultures. In Margaret Mead's study of New Guinea societies, she showed that in three societies, sex drives brought the men and women together, but the manner of their coming together and the meaning of their roles as spouses and parents were defined and regulated by their cultures. This would seem to indicate that it doesn't make much difference what form sexual bonds take. However, Morris (1967, p. 83) points out that monogamy is normative in all major societies, while polygamy obtains in a few minor cultures, and then only by a minority of males, and raises the question about polygamy: "It is intriguing to speculate as to whether its omission from almost all the larger cultures has, in fact, been a major factor in the attainment of their present successful status." It is at least significant, if not conclusive, to note that in countries which have practiced polygamy, as soon as women are liberated, they attack the institution of polygamy. Apparently, monogamy has not only species survival value, but also value in the personal dignity of women. Monogamy, far from being just an arbitrary custom of the Puritan ethic, seems to be grounded in the biological and spiritual needs of human beings. In a universe which tends toward entropy in human relationships as well as in everything else, marriage seems to be one of the heroic attempts of human beings to enhance orderly relations and to provide a stable community for the nurture of children, as well as for the security of emotional investment in each other.

To protect the integrity of the pair-bond or marriage, incest and adultery have been almost universally disapproved. Desmond Morris (1967, p. 81) points out that pair-bonding involves possessiveness towards each other among all animals, which is threatened when progeny become sexual rivals at puberty. "In most pair-forming species the family splits up and spreads out when the young grow up. Because of its cooperative social behavior the naked ape cannot afford to behave in this way," says Morris. For this reason, exogamy, or incest taboos, evolved to make it possible for the generations to live together. Of adultery, Alexander Lowen (1969, p. 70) reports:

> Infidelity is as old as recorded history. Four thousand years ago the Babylonians decreed that "if a man be found lying with another man's wife, they shall both of them die." Over the centuries different societies exacted different and generally less drastic penalties, but their codes consistently denounced adultery. This is true in the present as it was in the past. A recent study of 148 cultures notes that "premarital sexual relations are allowed in a clear majority of human societies, but extra-marital relations are almost universally condemned."

Since sex is what the "new morality" is all about, I have looked deeper into the function and dynamics of human sexuality to see what grounds are provided for sexual morality. It seems to me that the scene has not changed as much as the introduction of improved methods of conception control has led us to believe, since conception is by no means the only, or even the most important, function of human sexuality. Though particular cultures and subcultures may implement morals of sexuality in different ways, the basic morals regarding sex which have sprung from its unitive function are perennial and universal conditions of human fulfillment.

The Pill and a declining emphasis upon large families may modify the family pattern in several generations. Perhaps alternate arrangements for nurturing children, and for filling the adult need for reliable intimate relationships, will evolve. Subculture experiments in the patterns of relationships motivated by sexuality will doubtless continue. Not only the viability of the species, but also the sense of well-being of individuals, depends upon the success of such experiments; meanwhile, the personal problem is not to become casualties of change. The philosopher Descartes, when he set out to reformulate his philosophy of life, first resolved to be guided by traditional morals until he had defined reliable alternatives.

The Law In My Members

Moral people are disturbed by their failure consistently to do good. Paul wrote, "I do not understand my own actions. For I do not do what I want, but I do the very thing I hate. . . . For I delight in the law of God, in my inmost self, but I see in my members another law at war with the law of my mind and making me captive to the law of sin which dwells in my members" (Rom. 7:15 and 22). Apparently influenced by Greek Platonic thought, Paul attributed this law in his members to lust of the flesh—". . . with my flesh I serve the law of sin." Through Augustine and Calvin, "carnal desire" became the basic motive for sin in Christian orthodoxy. No doubt, sexual desire does sometimes move us to disrupt orderly social relations, but on the whole sex has been more unitive than evil. I think we have to look further for the sources of our failure to behave according to the moral principles we have accepted.

Order is monotonous and dull. Human moral principles do not serve as strictly to determine behavior as do animal instincts. Humans are not only more flexible, but are more exploratory and adventurous than instinctive creatures. Order and security do not content us; we need behavioral outlets which are stimulating and exciting. Well-established order becomes boring and we seek new outlets for our curious nature. We will jeopardize the routinized system which supports us in quest of new possibilities. We will take risks, and this is a source of our creative genius. Human civilization has not remained at a static level, as has the order of the ants, because we conceive of new possibilities and enjoy trying them. Frank L. Lambert (1968, p. 126) writes:

> . . . we find pleasure in seeking new unstable situations—and this includes code breaking—because of a basic emotional feedback which was once (and still may be) an evolutionary necessity, a requirement for survival. Only those protohuman individuals in the past of the race who had the reward of a pleasurable psychological and advantageous physiological feedback ventured consistently beyond the established boundaries of primitive learning—circumscribed as it was by a hostile environment and by the earliest taboos. Those singular creatures in whom play and rudimentary experimentation were emotionally rewarded were best able to survive new environmental conditions and to mate. We carry their genetic inheritance in the primal chemical and electrical programming of our brains: the search for new untested patterns, and thence for new metastable equilibria is the basis of creative human activity. We should not be surprised (or develop a theory of original sin) when this fundamental pleasure in code breaking conflicts with our culturally acquired programs of ethical codes.

The dislocations of established order by exploratory humans in experimenting with new forms of order do not include such code-breaking as lying, cheating and violence; such behavior only causes a social system to break down, but does not develop new forms of social order.

Even though moral laws are empirically based, the violation of them in specific instances entails only a risk, not a certainty, since moral laws are no more absolute than physical laws. There are too many variables in the environment, and too much indeterminacy in human behavior, to be precise in predicting the consequences of a specific act. Moral laws are derived from a large number of cases and describe a probable sequence, not what is bound to happen in every instance. Some kinds of behavior seem to be worth the risk, or the experience is so attractive that a person will ignore the signals of pain. Charles Fried (1970, p. 178) calls this a person's "risk budget." He says:

> The notion of the risk budget is a probabilistic one. A person in making a life plan and establishing a risk budget does not choose the moment at which he will die. He chooses the levels of risk. . . . It is to choose a life plan and risk budget by which one stands an unusually high risk of not living past, say, twenty-five. But one does not thereby—except in rare instances—choose to die at twenty-five.

The worst kind of evil is self-deception, the taking of self-destructive risks without recognizing the danger. If people choose to risk violating moral principles, they should do so knowingly and with a whole heart; "Sin bravely," said Martin Luther. A noble sinner was the moth in Don Marquis' memorable little poem, "The Lesson of the Moth," who knew that the risk it was taking in fluttering around a flame was real, and why it chose to do it anyway:

> fire is beautiful
> and we know that if we get
> too close it will kill us
> but what does that matter
> it is better to be happy
> for a moment
> and be burned up with beauty

than to live for a long time
and be bored all the while

The moth at least knew what it was doing when "he went and immolated himself on a patent cigar lighter." We may sin the more bravely if that is our choice, but we should not delude ourselves that what we do makes no difference. We are free agents, but we should be aware of what the risks are.

Youth, who have not yet learned the inexorable inner logic of existence, are beguiled by the moral confusion of the society into believing that it makes no difference what they do, and when their expectations are not fulfilled, youth feels betrayed and resentful. Adults have a responsibility to youth to warn them of the perils of evil, of the risks of self-destruction entailed in certain behavior. While youth accumulate experience and wisdom by which they can be self-determinative in making responsible choices, adults have a responsibility to define limits within which it is safe for youth to experiment, limits which have to be expanded with maturation, to be sure. Abraham Maslow (1962, p. 47), who has made a particular study of successful people, says of the child's need for safety in exploring the dangerous environment:

> Assured safety permits higher needs and impulses to emerge and to grow toward mastery. To endanger safety, means regression backward to the more basic foundation. What this means is that in the choice between giving up safety and giving up growth, safety will ordinarily win out. Safety needs are prepotent over growth needs. . . . In general, only a child who feels safe dares to grow forward healthily.

Until youth reach the age of discretion, they need to be protected from taking too great risks, or to be informed of the risks involved. Otherwise, ignorance leads them to close doors to further development — the youth who prematurely drops out of school to earn money to buy a car, only later to discover that it is not prepared more fully to take advantage of the opportunities in the culture; or the young wife, bemused by the "new morality," who warmly shares herself with a fellow worker, only later to discover that she has bankrupted the intimate confidence of her husband; or the youth, beguiled by reports of instant creativity through "mind expanding" drugs, who takes drugs repeatedly, only later to realize that he or she has been out of touch with reality while on psychedelic trips.

If youth are to exercise control over the direction of their own development, they need to understand what people have learned by experience about high-risk activities. They need to realize that it is not only the condemnation of their elders which they risk, but also deselection by the environment because they have not suited themselves to survive in it. Otherwise, to youth the world does not make sense, choices become meaningless, and rebellion can lead only to anarchy. Young people who later discover that they have been misled tend to become cynically alienated from society, which in turn berates their rejection of it. Youth need to be informed about where the dangers are. Then, at least, they can make deliberate choices, opt for meaningful risks, and accept the reasonable consequences. There is nothing so demoralizing as to be caught in circumstances that seem meaningless.

Order is boring. We have developed safe compensations in play and games for the ennui of regularized order. Play and games provide diversion from responsibility and routine and are carefully isolated from the rest of life. The domain of play and games is a "restricted, closed, protected universe," according to French sociologist Roger Caillois (1961, p. 7). Games, an artificial microcosm defined by arbitrary rules and having a definite limit in time and space, are a civilizing influence in teaching respect for order, as well as a source of legitimate excitement. Festivals, parties, dances, and carnivals reinforce the coherence of routine life by giving a limited and safe release from the moral order. People get into trouble when they fail to realize that the party is over. Gambling, except for the compulsive gambler, Caillois (1961, p. 117) says, is merely "a parenthesis" in the ordinary lives of people who pass through; "The basic pattern of the culture has not been appreciably affected." Masked carnivals, and our equivalent office parties, are conducted "like a game; i.e., conforming to pre-established conventions, in an atmosphere and within limits that separate it from and do not entail any consequences for ordinary life," writes Caillois (1961, p. 131). "Masks are a brief compensation for the decency and prudence that must be observed the rest of the year."

We are often confronted by choices which are ambiguous. Even with the most careful calculation, we suffer undesirable consequences. The situation does not always offer a clear choice of good. In such a dilemma, any choice, or no decision, does not turn out the way we would prefer. Some failures and frustrations seem to be inevitable. "The essence of tragedy is the conflict of one good or right with another," comments Joseph Fletcher (1966, p. 113). And Alfred North Whitehead (1929, p. 517) writes:

> The nature of evil is that the character of things is mutually obstructive. Thus the depths of life require a process of selection. But the selection is elimination as the first step towards another temporal order seeking to minimize obstructive modes. Selection is at once the measure of evil, and the process of its evasion.

Albert Schweitzer expresses the same view, but in another way:

> The World . . . offers us the horrible drama of Will-to-Live divided against itself. One existence holds its own at the cost of another: one destroys another. Only in thinking man has the Will-to-Live become conscious of other Will-to-Live, and desirous of solidarity with it. This solidarity, however, he cannot completely bring about, because man is subject to the puzzling and horrible law of being obliged to live at the cost of other life, and to incur again and again the guilt of destroying and injuring life.

The problem of our too frequent failure to implement the moral values we know cannot be dismissed as the original sin of a corrupted will; we can seek to minimize the inefficiency of choosing between competing goods by guiding our choices with a fuller knowledge of their consequences.

A New Ethic

A new ethic is required for our age, an ethic consistent with the new ethos which has emerged from the new epistemology, and which deals not just with inter-personal relations, but with our interaction with the whole environment. A wholistic ethic is needed to help us relate constructively and successfully to a wholistic environment. When the planet seemed inexhaustible, we human beings could be primarily concerned with the problem of our relations to each other; now we realize that we have also to be concerned with moral judgments about our relations with all other living systems, including the great living system. Since we no longer conceive of ourselves as passive witnesses to the drama of life but as active participants in directing the plot, to avoid increasing the entropy of our living system we need an ethic of the possible, as well as the probably inevitable, consequences of human behavior, of the "live options" as well as the risks.

"New occasions teach new duties; Time makes ancient good uncouth," wrote James Russell Lowell in one of his poems now set to a hymn tune. For instance, during the formative period of Christianity, James could write, "Religion that is pure and undefiled before God and the Father is this: to visit orphans and widows in their affliction, and to keep oneself unstained from the world" (The Letter of James 1:27). In our complex society where thousands of employees in a single industry can suddenly be afflicted by layoffs, a more inclusive ethic is required than ministering to the needs of orphans and widows, though they still need help.

Moral codes accruing from the limited recollected experience and information of early societies may well be augmented by laws-of-being discovered by the physical, biological and social sciences in their reconstruction of the evolutionary processes of life in the past two billion years and more. Not that all we have known as good and evil is displaced. The sciences have taught us that the discovery of new principles does not necessarily obviate all of the old. Physicist Charles H. Townes (1966, p. 304) notes that many physical laws are still valid in the spheres in which they were discovered:

> In spite of all the changes in our views, it is reassuring to note that the laws of Nineteenth-Century science were not so wrong in the realm in which they were initially applied—that of ordinary velocities and of objects larger than the point of a pin. In this realm they were essentially right, and we still teach the laws of Newton and Maxwell, because in their own important sphere they are valid and useful.

For instance, he says we still navigate ships with the assumption of the Ptolemaic cosmology that this is a stable world, though if we chart the course of a spaceship, we work in the Copernican model. Likewise, many of the features of the Judeo-Christian ethic are still valid in the primary relationships in which we live.

However, they are inapplicable in frames of reference other than those in which they were conceived. They are no more universals relevant to all conditions than are Newton's physical laws. Henry Margenau (1966, p. 268) points out that the laws postulated by science do not pretend to universal applicability:

> Every textbook which teaches them is careful to state the accessory conditions under which they hold. The principle of universal gravitation is effectively suspended in favor of Coulomb's law when we calculate the force between two electrons. We regard this as normal and do not speak of conflict between scientific principles. Why should the situation be different in ethics?

Morality is "system-sensitive," according to biologist Garrett Hardin (1968, p. 1245). He points out a "not generally recognized principle of morality, namely: *the morality of an act is a function of the state of the system at the time it is performed.*" For instance, it did not make much difference how a lonely American frontiersman disposed of his waste, but in Miami Beach it is now becoming a critical problem as the septic tanks and sewerage outfalls into canals are seriously polluting Miami's only source of water, ground water. Episcopal priest Joseph Fletcher (1966, p. 124) calls a *functional* approach to morality "situation ethics." All the actual implications or consequences of a choice must be taken into account in the decision. The *situation ethic*, says Fletcher, acknowledges and uses ethical principles, but does not make absolutes of them. It relates them to the actual situation and tries to see how love (agape) can best be fulfilled. Situationism uses moral norms for illumination, for guidance, but not as ready-made conclusions. Situation ethics recognizes that ethical principles are derived from cumulative experience, and thus serve as guides and warnings, but does not employ them as absolute laws to be implemented in every case; they are maxims, not rules. "The new morality, situation ethics," says Fletcher, "declares that anything and everything is right or wrong according to the situation."

Two circumstances have created a *new situation* requiring an augmented ethic— an *augmented morality,* not simply the abandonment of the entire old morality, but an ethic adequate to the situation in which we find ourselves today. The two circumstances are the new problems and the new cosmology.

The *new problems* are such phenomena as the invention of weapons of mass destruction, the population explosion, the deterioration of our environment through pollution, the rapid exhaustion of natural resources, and the degeneration of the human gene pool. For instance, regarding weapons of mass destruction, biologist Hudson Hoagland (1967, pp. 57-58) comments:

> Since the Hiroshima bombing, a new factor has been introduced by man into the human environment, a factor to which he must adapt or perish. So far we have shown little realization that this is so. Men still talk and act in terms of concepts of lawless national sovereignty and unilateral international relations as if nuclear weapons did not exist.

Less well known because its effects are less immediately threatening is genetic degeneration. Concerning this problem, Hoagland (1966, p. 141) says:

> In relation to our inherited endowments there is a slowly accumulating crisis, a sort of time bomb, concerned with the deterioration of our irreplaceable genetic material. This genetic

material is in the form of the chemical code of DNA molecules located in the nuclei of our sperm and egg cells. All of the material of the DNA in all the germ cells in all of the people in the world if added together would weigh only a small fraction of an ounce. It has taken three billion years to produce this coded material to pass on information to the next generation to tell it how to make a person. We are facilitating the occurrence of mutations, 99 per cent of which are deleterious, of this code by a number of practices. For example, a more serious assault on our genes than that of present levels of radioactive fallout is humane medical practice, which is saving lives of persons with genetic defects that would have been lethal under conditions of natural selection. These people, many of whom are valued citizens, are passing accumulated genetic deficits along to their offspring, and, over generations, deterioration of our genetic code is increasing slowly.

In the past few generations we have become accustomed to finding technological solutions to our problems. We have been so successful that we have precipitated a situation of overcrowding in which our problems no longer admit of technological solutions, according to biologist Garrett Hardin (1968, p. 1234):

. . . most people who anguish over the population problem are trying to find a way to avoid the evils of over-population without relinquishing any of the privileges they now enjoy. They think that farming the seas or developing new strains of wheat will solve the problem—technologically.

The population problem cannot be solved in a technical way, he says, because "a finite world can support only a finite population." Paul Ehrlich has pointed out the inner dynamics of this limitation: increased wheat crops require increased nitrogen fertilizers, and the run-off into the seas threatens to kill the seas, as it has already killed some lakes. Instead of being a solution, technology has become part of the problem in a crowded world.

The second circumstance is the *new cosmology* which has given us a radically different view of our environment and of our relation to it. If the model of the structure, dynamics, and evolutionary origin of the environment as a whole, which I presented in the previous chapters, impresses you as satisfying because it unifies experience, then a different notion of our ethical responsibilities follows. If we are not the darling of the universe but a product of the evolutionary process, then our ethic must guide us to cooperate with that process. Our strategy for survival must be congruent with the system which transcends us, else we will weaken or destroy our life support system.

The first consequence of the new cosmology is the realization that, since this planet was not created from some infinite source but evolved from the matter existent in space, *our planet is finite*—a realization reinforced by photographs of our beautiful blue and white planet from outer space. Our planet is limited in what we can take from it and what we can do to it. We are already aware that there are limits to the store of energy in fossil fuels and limits to how much we can manipulate the surface of the earth to raise food. There may be limits to the amount of energy we can convert from any source, since we have not yet minimized the risks of the development of atomic energy nor have we developed ways of economically transforming the direct rays of the sun into usable power. Since energy conversion is the *sine qua non* of industrialized society as a living system, there are limits to growth. Up to the present, civilizations have flourished by exploiting and manipulating the environment; the imperative of the new ethic may be to adapt to the limitations of this planet as a life support system, and of our technological skill in manipulating it. An anticipation of this ethical change may be seen in the new "life styles" which are replacing the emphasis on child bearing with an emphasis on inter-personal relations as the fulfillment of personal life (though families will probably remain the optimum situation for raising the next generation), and by the choice of a less energy-consuming standard of living rather than the conspicuous consumption of consumer goods as a measure of success.

The second consequence that follows from viewing the environment as a wholistic living system is a new realization of what is considered to be of worth, of what is to be revered, of what is sacred. Instead of designating certain phenomena as sacred and the rest as secular, all being is revered as sacred. Astronomer

Harlow Shapley (1966, p. 285) thinks that "reverence for life" should include the whole natural world:

> Life arises out of the inanimate world; why not revere also the amino acids and the simple proteins from which life emerged? Or, why not go all the way and avow reverence for all things which exist, all that is inanimate as well as that which is animate, all that is touched by Cosmic Evolution, and reserve the greatest reverence for Existence itself?

Because all existence constitutes one great living system, "the Body of God," *all the constituents are sacred.* However, in the hierarchy of being, some subsystems have a priority over others because of their immediacy and relevancy to our interest. Moreover, it is not the matter which is sacred, it is the organization of matter, the configuration of interaction, which is to be approached with reverence. It is not the rocks in the Grand Canyon, but their formation into a system which is to be respected in our efforts to exploit its water and power; the more remote consequences as well as the immediate advantages of building dams have to be taken into account. It is especially as living systems that *all being is to be revered.* The Judeo-Christian tradition has properly emphasized loving our neighbors, as human beings are the most important part of our environment, but it is now becoming clear that our love should be extended to all degrees of order, including flora and fauna and ecological systems. Of course, when any particular political system ceases to function constructively, it is not an idol beyond criticism and reorganization. The genius of culture is that it is flexible, and when a social system becomes ossified, it has lost its survival value in a dynamic environment. A society, as a living system, is to be revered, but when it begins to lose its capacity to preserve order and creatively transform energy, it must yield to the requirements of the higher order.

The second proposition which emerges from an evolutionary conception of reality is a different understanding of the process of reform and of a strategy for change. *Evolution, not revolution,* is the consciously chosen tactic for change. If you believe in "original creation," the model for creativity is a superior, absolute power imposing order; if you believe in the evolutionary process, the model for creativity is self-organization, communication, and interaction. Which of these models you believe in determines what kind of social and political tactics you pursue. Contemporary revolutionaries act on the implicit notion that the only way to induce change is by coercion and terror. On the other hand, those who believe in the evolutionary process will recognize that change is a collective enterprise, and that there is no instantaneous change but that all mutations are the result of an accumulation of small changes in a constructive direction. To preserve order, those who implicitly assume original creation will think in terms of police or military power, while those who assume evolution will think in terms of communications and feedback. Those who believe in original creation will tend towards establishing an autocratic or authoritarian government, while those who believe in evolution will tend toward organizing a democratic form of government.

Democracy as a form of political organization turns out to be not just one of several theories which we can try, but the most desirable form just because it is unspecialized and flexible. Democracy does not begin with a blueprint which is imposed on a people; it organizes relations to facilitate interaction. In chapter 2 on "The Great Living System," I proposed that living forms are a product of a democracy of influences which become centered but have no autocratic director. Living systems are self-organized and self-directed by the pattern emerging from the multiplicity of influences interacting. If this be a cosmic law of organization, then we will recognize that it is the model for social organization. Political strategy will then facilitate mutual interchange and influence, rather than depend upon coercion. "In their ultimate individuality things can only be influenced, they cannot be sheerly coerced," says Charles Hartshorne (1941, Preface p. xvi). Democracy is to be revered as a manifestation in political organization of the cosmic order.

"Man masters nature not by force but by understanding," says

J. Bronowski (1965, p. 10). For instance, a scientist discovered that the way to control a corn-destroying virus was not with chemical sprays but by planting it later in the season when the temperature was higher. In Israel and some European countries hybrid corn was being dwarfed or destroyed by a virus carried by a tiny plant hopper. Isaac Harpaz discovered that the virus was heat sensitive and ceased reproductive activity when the temperature reached 76 degrees. By suggesting that the corn be planted late in May, instead of early in April, he solved the problem. When the seedlings emerged early in June, the few viruses left in the plant hopper were too sluggish to infect the corn. Adjusted for local temperature variations, later plantings were successful also in Czechoslovakia, Bulgaria, and Italy.

Or take the discovery that mating mismatched mosquitoes could control elephantiasis. In Burma, German geneticist Hannes Laven released thousands of laboratory-raised male mosquitoes of the same strain as the local mosquitoes but with a lethal genetic trait, "cytoplasmic incompatibility." When the more virile but genetically incompatible intruders preempted the indigenous females, the females remained unfertilized and thus the mosquitoes became extinct, and no longer carried the filaria which caused elephantiasis from one host to another.

Microbiologist Rene Dubos (1970, p. 2) says:

> Man can use many different aspects of reality to make his life, not by imposing himself as a conqueror on nature, but by participating in the continuous act of creation in which all living things are engaged. Otherwise, man may be doomed to survive as something less than human.

The strategy for survival indicated by knowledge of the structure and dynamics of the system is like the principles of jujitsu, that Japanese art of self-defense which maneuvers an opponent into using his own strength and weight against himself. Or it is like the procedure for burying a rock; it is much easier to dig sand from under the rock and let it slide into the hole of its own weight than to try to force it into the sand with sledgehammer blows on top of the rock. We use this principle in designing space flights; in planning the trajectory of a spacecraft we do not blast it on a straight line toward a distant planet, we plan the route so as to take advantage of the impetus and guidance given the spacecraft by swinging around the gravity field of intermediate planets. In our self-direction of the evolution of culture, the efficiency of such procedures as this should be kept in mind.

In an ethic for meaningful living, humans accept responsibility for what happens to them individually and collectively. Our culture pattern of adaptations to our environment is accessible to our control. As Robert S. Morison (1965, p. 351) points out:

> The evolution of culture is many orders of magnitude faster than conventional biological evolution, and its course and direction are at least partially under conscious human control. It is this that places the burden of *responsibility* on man's shoulders.

But to accept responsibilities, we have to be aware of what is happening to us.

Our culture has made such strides that it is overtaxing the environment, both by draining its irreplaceable resources and by polluting its air and water systems faster than they can recycle the wastes. The quality of the environment is being degraded, and we can become used to it, we can adjust to it. It is said that a frog dropped into a kettle of boiling water will immediately jump out, but if a frog is dropped into a kettle of cold water which is gradually heated to a boiling point, the frog will sit there and boil to death, unalerted by the gradual change in water temperature; he *adjusts* to his changing environment. Rene Dubos (1970, p. 2) warns:

> The dangers inherent in adaptability were dramatically shown by the illustrious French bacteriologist Louis Pasteur in a lecture to students of the Ecole des Beaux Arts in Paris in 1864. Pasteur pointed out that most human beings crowded in a poorly ventilated room usually fail to notice that the quality of the air they breathe deteriorates progressively; they are unaware of this deterioration because the change takes place by imperceptible steps.
>
> Then, to illustrate the danger of such adaptation to an objectionable environment, Pasteur placed a bird in a closed

container and allowed it to remain in the confined atmosphere for several hours. The bird became rather inactive but survived. In contrast, when a new bird of the same species was introduced into the same cage where the first bird remained alive, it immediately died.

And Dubos (1968, p. 167) summarizes the dangers of adjusting to overpopulation:

> Congested environments, even though polluted, ugly, and heartless, are compatible with economic growth and with political power. Similarly, social indifference, aggressive behavior, or the rat race of overcompetitive societies will not necessarily destroy mankind. Crowding, however, can damage the physical and spiritual qualities of human life through many mechanisms, such as the narrowing of horizons as classes and ethnic groups become more segregated, with the attendant heightening of racial conflicts; the restrictions on personal freedom caused by the constantly increasing need for social controls; the deterioration in professional and social services; the destruction of beaches, parks, and other recreational facilities; the spreading of urban and suburban blight; the traffic jams, water shortages, and all forms of environmental pollution.

Traditional ethics hardly prepare us to cope with such creeping blights on living as over-population, pollution and the energy shortage. Growth in population, consumer goods, and energy consumption is proving to be counter productive as we confront the finiteness of land, water, mineral resources, and energy supply, about which traditional ethics has little to say. We continue to negotiate peace under the old ethical assumption of a victor after a limited war, while weapons of mass destruction proliferate. Biological science has presented us with a new understanding of the emergence of life, and medical technology has raised new problems about death.

Though reverence for life is a traditional ethical value, the new understanding of the life process has altered what is good and evil in regard to life. An organism is "living" only when it is capable of functioning as a whole in maintaining its own autonomous existence. When we realize that a human being was not created at conception, that in the first three months as an embryo it recapitulates pre-human evolution, and that as a fetus it is not viable until after at least six months gestation, it is clear that abortion is not "murder." Reverence for the life of the actualized woman takes precedence over the potential life of the not-yet living embryo. The potential for life exists in the sperm and egg, but it is not fully realized until the fetus grows capable of living apart from the woman's nourishing body. Meanwhile, the fetus is dependent upon the body which the woman controls. Women knew this intuitively and claimed the right to abortion long before the Supreme Court found biological justification for authorizing abortion in the first six months.

At the other end of human life, medical technology has inadvertently produced a new moral problem of "death with dignity." Since medical technology has discovered how to keep some organs of the body functioning long after the body is capable of functioning as a self-actuating whole, instead of prolonging life medical technology is *prolonging the agony of dying.* The medical profession is redefining the vital signs, including the presence of brain waves over a period of time, the absence of which indicates death, as a criterion for knowing when the body will not again be able to exist on its own. Heart pacers prolong the valuable life of many human beings, but "heroic measures" do not square with the physicians' Hippocratic oath to prolong life. *Passive euthanasia,* "mercy death" by withdrawal of artificial measures, is becoming increasingly acceptable, especially with the numbers of people whose "living wills" provide such instructions. *Active euthanasia,* the rational determination by others that a life should be terminated for whatever reason, arrogates a power over life and death which is inimical to the autonomous nature of life; death should be left to the "wisdom of the body," not to some panel of experts however well intentioned.

The authority of a state to take a human life by the legal *penalty of death* is a mark of desperation, and should be resorted to only when it can restrain destructive behavior in no other way. We still legalize the death penalty as a *punishment,* not as a final *restraint* upon violence which threatens the integrity of the higher social order. One of Thomas Jefferson's proposals in 1779 for "the Bill proportioning crime and punishment" in Virginia was an attempt to restrict the penalty of death to a few limited cases for it was, he (Gilbert Chinard, 1939, p. 94) said, "the last melancholy resource against those whose existence is become inconsistent with the safety of their fellow citizens."

A by-product of the advance of medical science is the problem of *aging*. It used to be that those who lived past the age of retirement were generally taken care of, often in "extended family" homes where they could live in dignity. Now, with a larger proportion of people living in retirement, many of the elderly live in poverty and neglect or are "warehoused" in nursing homes, where I have heard a very old lady cry, "Why don't they let us die?" We have practically eliminated "the old man's friend"—pneumonia— yet we let the elderly live in indignity through a prolonged old age, a state which most of us will eventually share; and we have not accepted the moral responsibility as much as we should for this universal problem.

Social problems require social solutions. When the problem is inequity or inadequacy of the whole, it is not enough to be per- sonally righteous; each person must also be socially responsible. The solution to social problems requires "the power of organiza- tion and the organization of power," says James Luther Adams (1976, p. 18). An adequate ethic to respond to the collective prob- lems of our times requires participation in voluntary or political associations which work for solutions to social and ecological problems. The solution is not found in a call for increased personal morality but in the creation of a higher social or political order within which conflicting interests are integrated and can interact.

New problems pile upon us which are so urgent that by the time experience shows us what we ought to have done, it may be too late. For moral guidance in such problems, we cannot rely simply upon the wisdom of the past; a smug compliance with established moral principles while ignoring the problems for which there are not yet moral norms issues in what James Luther Adams calls "the evil that good men do." People may be faithful to their spouse, good to their children, friendly to their neighbors regardless of race or color, reliable on their job, good in their credit rating, and honest in paying their taxes, but if their ethic says nothing to them about entropic disorders in their environment, such as mass unemployment, poverty, war, pollution, and overpopulation, they are still "sinners." Those things they ought to have done, and not leave the other undone. They are "sinners" in the sense that they are not negating entropy, they are not enlarging the field of creative interaction, and the consequences to them and the species will not be what they intended, nor will they find them good.

Therefore, a new ethic will seek to provide guidance as to what is right and wrong in choices for which there is no precedent by employing all available skills to *project future consequences*. Where we have no past experience to help us make a right choice, we have to seek to understand the situation in its full complexity by gathering information, conducting experiments, running through simulation procedures, and using our imagination. If we recognize that everything we do affects a system for good or for ill, in lieu of experience we will try to employ *foresight* as to the consequences of our act. With our technological ability to introduce vast changes into the environment, it becomes mandatory that we project consequences before we act lest we inadvertently smother ourselves, as well as other forms of life.

One aspect of our creative genius is that we can design machines and structures, laying out the whole construction in blueprints and then building it according to these specifications. This works fine for non-living structures. But if by analogy we seek to pursue the same process in guiding the development of living systems, we run into trouble. Plans and social blueprints ignore the fact that living systems, such as social systems, evolve by interaction. A plan cannot take into account all the variables and contingencies, and generally ends up being restrictive rather than creative. From his understanding of biological evolution, Robert S. Morison (1962, pp. 41-42) warns:

The real point is to recognize that all such visions are in the long run inadequate. To cite a biological analogy, all known visions of man and his future suffer from the evolutionary defect of overspecialization.

This was the fatal flaw in Marx's scheme for a revolutionary society; conditioned by the age of industrialization in which he lived to think in terms of machine analogies, he did not anticipate that the free enterprise economic system would develop increased benefits for labor, so his blueprint for the inevitable revolt of labor has proven to be false.

War in defense of our culture—whether by aggression or by resistance—has become too dangerous to the survival of the human race for it to be considered a viable alternative to politics. However, just being "against war" will not suffice to obviate this peril to human survival; we have to identify the dynamics of international conflicts and devise a political alternative in the form of an inclusive organization with adequate feedback processes. If we take as a premise the human nature outlined in chapter 3 on "The Unfinished Animal" and recall that the major differences between people are not biological, but cultural, we can organize a higher order political system which will integrate cultural differences without war, not by eliminating the cultural differences but by integrating them. Zoologist Alfred E. Emerson (1968, p. 161) reminds us:

> Viewing national warfare from the point of view of biological trends over millions of years, one might predict an ultimate social evolution beyond this stage of national conflict toward a world order of mutually co-operative relations among nations. . . . There is no trend toward uniformity of function within organized biological systems, and there seems to be no reason to fear that all provincial customs and artistic accomplishments will be lost in the future world order.

The epistemology outlined in chapter 4 on "The Search for Hidden Reality" can provide us with a common basis, not for uniformity, but for communication. The sciences have already bridged the cultural gaps by developing generally agreed upon methods for arriving at truth. And it is to the sciences we turn for projections as to the consequences of proposed acts and policies. Lest we think the sciences are a fragile reed to lean upon, let us recall that this way of knowing has been accepted for only a few centuries and has still to penetrate some cultures. The saving grace is that as societies develop devastating technologies, they also have previously developed a scientific discipline shared with the other potent societies of the world. Science has a universal epistemology which facilitates cross-cultural communication. We can preserve a cultural pluralism while developing a political system "coextensive with the gene pool." All we have to do to believe this is possible is to look at the variety of life styles existent in a "climax forest"; such an ecological system achieves duration not by uniformity but precisely because of the variety of mutually contributing elements.

So far in the evolution of the earth, the quality of life has been enhanced by the organization of ever more complex systems. The time has come to recognize that *nationalism* is no more an ultimate than was the tribe or the city-state. ". . . the true security of modern man lies in the largest possible group he can create," says William G. Mather (1967, p. 259). The United Nations must be respected by the participating nations as more than a platform for dialogue, but as a system within which the nations respond to feedback from each other and from the U.N. itself. For instance, this means specifically that in the interests of a more effective federal organization of nations, the United States (not to mention other nations) needs to repeal the "Connally reservation" which limits the jurisdiction of the International Court of Justice to those cases that do not affect the vital interests of the United States, in the unilateral judgment of the United States. The ethics of sandlot baseball cannot hold for nations; "If you don't let me pitch, I'll take my bat and ball and go home." Relinquishing national sovereignty does not destroy the autonomy and integrity of a nation, which is a necessary cultural and political unit, any more than a city or a state loses its identity by integration into the higher order of a nation. Anatol Rapoport (1966, p. 473) comments:

The United Nations was to perform an anti-carcinogenic function in the community of nations. . . . What has been forgotten is that any nation can become a cancerous threat to the human race by taking the law into its own fists and by declaring itself to be the guardian of virtue.

Nothing so quickly unites a feuding family as a common enemy. I have wondered what could unite the world in principle as it is united in fact until I read Pogo in the comic strip saying, "We have met the enemy and they are us." We human beings may have created just the ecological crisis which will unite us. Pollution knows no national boundaries. Wind and water, and the human pollutants they carry, are not restricted by lines drawn on maps. To save ourselves from smothering to death in our own offal we may have to establish the communications and organization that also will save us from mutual atomic annihilation. Global transportation and communication systems, as well as multi-national corporations, already provide the framework for a higher political order. The new ethic includes imperatives to moral responsibility for implementing a global political order commensurate with the existing economic and ecological interdependency.

Chapter 6

Morale For Meaningful Living

IN a popular song Alfie's girlfriend plaintively asks, "What's it all about, Alfie. . . . Is it just for the moment we live?" That is a basic human question which most of us ask at one time or another. We are asking, *What is the meaning of living? What makes sense of my experience? What makes life worthwhile?*

The meaning of life is an intellectual not an existential question which can occur only to human beings who evaluate present experiences in terms of mental images of the remembered past or hoped-for future. My dog seems to experience life, enjoying the experiences he finds satisfying and accepting unpleasant or painful experiences without questioning whether it could be otherwise; human beings compare and evaluate the present with the past and the future represented symbolically in their minds.

Moreover, the question of meaning occurs most sharply when we are frustrated by a gap between our *expectations* and our *experiences*. We have no problem when things are going well, when our expectations are being fulfilled. We ask about the meaning of life when what we anticipated is not coming true for us. Almost everyone has occasion to ask this question at one time or another, no matter what his circumstances in life, since sickness, failures, and separations—including the ultimate separation of death—are universal experiences; and we try to make sense out of our experiences. *How we respond* to painful experiences depends upon *how we interpret* them, upon whether the events make sense to us or whether they outrage our confidence in the order and reliability of the universe. The meaning of life becomes a problem when our *mythos is not justified by existential realities.*

243

The religious traditions of various cultures have proposed *different answers* to the question of the meaning of life. Our culture has been largely conditioned by the answers given by the Judeo-Christian tradition. The myth of the ancient Jews was that they had a covenanted relation with Yahweh and that if they observed the Mosaic laws contained in the Torah, they would be blessed with a good life. Experience taught them that life was not like that, and that there was no correlation between being good and being free from suffering.

The Old Testament Book of Job deals with the problem of *suffering under the sovereignty of a just and benevolent God.* Job, you may recall, was a righteous man, blameless and upright, fearing God and doing no evil. Life went along well for him until a series of reverses struck him: his servants were slain, his sheep were killed, his camels were stolen, and all of his children were killed in one disaster. Finally, he was afflicted with "loathsome sores from the sole of his foot to the crown of his head." Job cursed the day of his birth and complained in the bitterness of his soul that there was no justice. His friends admonished him that since he was suffering, he must have sinned. Job demands to know of God what he has done wrong: "Let me know why thou dost contend against me." "Then the Lord answered Job out of the whirlwind: 'Who is this that darkens counsel by words without knowledge? . . . Where were you when I laid the foundation of the earth? Tell me, if you have understanding. Who determined its measurements—surely you know! . . . Do you know the ordinances of the heavens? Can you establish their rule on the earth?'" (Chapter 38). "Then Job answered the Lord: 'I know that thou canst do all things, and that no purpose of thine can be thwarted. . . . Therefore have I uttered what I did not understand, things too wonderful for me, which I did not know. . . . I had heard of thee by the hearing of the ear, but now my eye sees thee.'" (Chapter 42). It seems to me that what Job realized was that he did *not stand in a bargaining relationship with God,* that he did not have a contract with the Almighty that if he were good he would be happy. What Job learned was that he was part of a vast creation *he did not make or understand* and that he could not demand an explanation for what seemed to him unjustified suffering; he was in no position to pass judgment on creation.

Through the centuries another myth evolved among the Jews to help them become reconciled to suffering. Israel was a small nation on a corridor between the great powers of Egypt and Babylonia and was repeatedly invaded and almost continuously dominated by a foreign power, which did not square with its developing concept that Yahweh was sovereign over all nations. The myth developed of the coming *Messiah* who would liberate Israel from its oppressors and establish peace and justice on earth. To include the Jews who died before the coming of the Messiah, the day of judgment was to be accompanied by a resurrection of the dead.

The Jewish disciples of Jesus identified him with the expected Messiah, calling him the "Christos" or anointed one. After the crucifixion of Jesus, the myth was promulgated that he would return to establish the Kingdom of God upon earth, and that his disciples should prepare for the event by living as if the divine kingdom were already established. As years passed and the Messiah did not return, the myth was modified to assure the believers that on their death they would enter upon an eternal life with Jesus in a celestial heaven for which they were preparing in life.

You can see that the myths of both the Jews and the Christians identified the meaning of life with events which were to take place *later*, either at the culmination of history with the establishment of God's sovereignty on earth, or at the end of life in personal immortality.

The *myth of personal immortality* has been broken for many contemporary people by the biological evidence that life is not transmitted by a pre- and post-existent immortal soul. Without hope of future fulfillment, many people have focused upon self-fulfillment, a form of personal salvation by self-realization. But the meaning of life cannot be found in solitude. I recall a woman who bitterly mourned the meaninglessness of the death of her son in the Korean War: "I've always been a good Christian Scientist and have done nothing to deserve this," she said. The *contingencies of*

life which she had ignored had invaded her private mental preserve. As important as personal growth and renewal are, the
cultivation of the self does not give meaning to life. Meaning is
found in relation to what *transcends* the self, in the transcendent
process of life itself.

In preceding chapters I have outlined the process by which
living beings emerge from non-being, order from disorder, through
the *love* or attraction (including atomic or electro-magnetic) which
establishes relationships in mutually beneficial organizations
bounded by a semi-permeable membrane within which creative
interaction can take place. The meaning of life is realized by participation in this life-creating process at our level of being by
entering into organized creative relationships at levels from the
family, through voluntary associations, business and industrial
organizations, and nations to a world order. An individual life is
not self-justified; it is justified by integration in the hierarchy of
ordered relationships.

Professor of religion J. Edward Barrett (1968, p. 172) says of the
word "meaning" in the present context that it *"describes relationships, asking if they are mutually supportive and if they collectively compose a purpose which transcends while uniting the
purpose of each component part."* Jonas Salk, Director of the
Salk Institute for Biological Studies, says (1972, p. 68), "If it were
not for 'relationships,' societies would not exist, nor would organisms or cells, or the molecules of which cells and organisms are
comprised. It would follow that if it were not for 'relationships,'
man would not exist. Thus, 'relationships' are inextricably a
characteristic of living substances." *The meaning of life is found in
fulfilling life as relationships.*

In the first chapter of this book I suggested that what is required
of us today is a *shift in consciousness.* Robert E. Ornstein (1972,
p. 139), research psychologist at the University of California
Medical Center, San Francisco, says:

> The survival problems we are now facing are collective, rather than
> individual. . . . A shift toward a consciousness of the intercon-
> nectedness of life, toward a relinquishing of the "everyman-for-

himself" attitude inherent in our ordinary construction of consciousness, might enable us to take those "selfless" steps that
would begin to solve our collective problems.

This shift is toward "awareness of the earth as one system that is
part of ecology," and Ornstein (1972, p. 140) continues:

> It is the shift from an individual and analytic consciousness to the
> attainment of an over-all perspective of "unity," of "Humanity as
> one organism," which is the purpose of the esoteric traditions and
> the aim of . . . meditation exercises.

Some people arrive at a perception of the natural unity of all
being by an almost mystical insight. Naturalist Joseph Wood
Krutch (1956, p. 215) finds that "acute awareness of a natural
phenomenon, especially of a phenomenon of the living world" is
an experience from which he draws joy and courage:

> And whether you call the experience infrarational or superrational,
> it involves the momentary acceptance of values not definable in
> terms of that common sense to which we ordinarily accord our first
> loyalty. And to all such experiences one thing is common. There is
> a sense of satisfaction which is not personal but impersonal. One
> no longer asks, "What's in it for me?" because one is no longer a
> separate selfish individual but part of the welfare and joy of the
> whole.

Krutch (1956, p. 216) further says that his happiness is com-
pounded of the following realizations:

> First of all, perhaps, there is the vivid assurance that these things,
> that the universe, really do exist, that life is not a dream; second,
> that the reality is pervasive and, it seems, unconquerable. The
> future of mankind is dubious. Perhaps the future of the whole earth
> is only somewhat less dubious. But one knows that all does not
> depend upon man, that possibly, even, it does not depend upon
> this earth. Should man disappear, rabbits may well still run and
> flowers may still open. If this globe itself should perish, then it
> seems not unreasonable to suppose that what inspires the stem
> and the flower may exist somewhere else. And I, it seems, am at
> least part of all this.

In 1958 when our concern was intense about the total destruc
tion of human life on this planet by a general atomic war, I tried to
reassure a friend that in that event life would still not be meaning
less since the self-creating life process would probably again
evolve intelligent, self-conscious beings on this earth, and prob
ably had already done so on other planets. He exclaimed, "But
these are my people, and this is my earth!" Most of us cannot help
but share a *humanistic* concern for the welfare of our own species
and of our own life-support system—in response to which this
book is written.

Morale for Meaningful Living

Whether the mythos by which we order our lives is arrived at by
reasoned understanding or by direct intuition, it is *not effective*
unless it affects our lives, unless we live by it. To live by our
mythos, our conceptual vision of the human situation, we have to
believe in it, we have to bet our lives on it. Then our mythos
becomes *determinative of our behavior.* So long as our vision of
reality remains a "head trip," it does not give meaning and pur
pose to our lives. A conceptual understanding of the environment
as a whole is an abstraction. An intellectual construct does not
necessarily affect behavior until it is adopted as a working model
until it becomes a religion which is reinforced by rituals and sym
bols. The difference between a *philosophy of life* and a *religion is*
that a philosophy of life is an intellectual exercise; a philosophy of
life becomes an operative religion when a person accepts it and
becomes committed to it. A religion is a model of existence with
which people identify, whether by accepting the religious tradition
in which they are raised or by a decision for a new model, a transfor
mation by the renewing of the mind.

Morale for meaningful living is motivated by implicit acceptance
of a mythos or a theology, each of which provides a meaningful
frame of reference for living. "Morale" in my Webster's dictionary
means: "Prevailing mood and spirit conducive to willing and
dependable performance, steady self-control, and courageous
determined conduct, despite danger and privations, based upon a

onviction of being in the right and on the way to success." In rimitive cultures, myths explain the human situation and provide ounds for moral choices. In more developed cultures, the *myths* *re rationalized in a theology.* The religion of the ancient Jews as based upon myths, legends, and historical events with very tle intellectual justification. After Christianity had spread rough the Hellenic world, the influence of Greek philosophy enerated a theology to rationalize Christian beliefs and values. forale to live by a mythos or a theology comes from *believing it is* ue and from ritual reinforcement in community celebrations. Ritual that maintains the organism in some sort of shape to cope ith reality by keeping anxiety low and confidence high certainly as survival value," says anthropologist Anthony F.C. Wallace 966, p. 63).

An example of the failure of morale, or loss of nerve, was the oral collapse of the intellectuals in Germany with the rise of azism. When Hitler rose to power in Germany in the 1930's, the tellectuals—the professors, the politicians, the journalists, the hilosophers, the psychologists, the clergy of the established urch—for the most part offered little or no resistance. Nazism ecame a national religion winning or enforcing fanatical loyalty. he groups which had the morale to stand up to the violence, xcesses and depravities of Nazism were the groups who had a eligion of their own, such as the Jehovah's Witnesses and the ommunist Party. (Marxism has many of the earmarks of a reli- on.) And when devoted members of such groups were put in oncentration camps, their will-to-live was sustained by their faith the meaning of life as they defined it. One conceptual frame- ork may be truer than another, may be more *related to the* ature of reality, but it is not effective until it is converted into a ersonal religion to live by. Morale for meaningful living results om *internalization* and commitment to a belief system.

An effective religion is reinforced by *emotive* symbols, rituals, nd ceremonies. The truths of a religion become accepted and ternalized through repetitive celebrations which touch the emo- ons. We need not only to know the truth but also to reaffirm it in shared experiences. The repeated celebration of myths and values in a religious community makes a belief system vivid and motivating. A *ritual* is the dramatization of a mythos which creates an image of a familiar and orderly world; it transmits the wisdom of a culture and gives its adherents the morale to live by their convictions. Ideas alone are not provocative until they reach our *subconscious*. Until the decision-making center of our being, our soul, is affected, concepts do not serve to determine behavior. That is the function of religion.

Do We Need a New Religion?

All through this book I have pointed out that some of the ancient and traditional theological interpretations of the human situation and the meaning of life are inadequate and that a new, more reliable theology whose intuitions are supported by empirical evidence is emerging from the sciences. Does this mean that we need a new religion? If we are going to internalize the contemporary mythos based upon an understanding of the nature of life itself as living systems culminating in a great living system, if we are going to convert such concepts into convictions, do we need to invent a whole new cult of rituals, ceremonies, and symbols?

I do not think so. Religion precedes theology. The mythos and cult of a religion evolve out of human experience living in nature, and theology later develops to explain and justify the beliefs and practices. *Religion* is a spontaneous expression of the human spirit which has become routinized, while *theology* reflects the level of information and understanding of a culture. Religion is existential, while theology is intellectual. Theology may invalidate certain religious customs and practices, but it cannot establish a new cult; a cult of myths and rituals *evolves*. A theology as an exposition of a religion is a personal affair, while a religion is a shared experience.

When people say, "I'm not very religious, but . . ." they go on to explain their personal philosophy of life or theology. What they mean is that they do *not identify with a cult, a way of celebrating and reaffirming their beliefs*. Religion is a system of beliefs and practices in which people participate, the rites and ceremonies by which people reaffirm their confidence in certain values and purposes. In religion, communication is not so much verbal as ritualstic, the repetition of a familiar formula or the contemplation of a significant symbol. Behavior is influenced by sharing in a celebration of meaning and value in a *group experience.*

A study was done a number of years ago of what moves people to make radical changes in their lives. The study was of factors which prompted people in this country to sell their homes, quit their jobs, cash in their bonds, take their kids out of school and move to Israel. How did the Zionist movement prompt people to make such a drastic change in their lives? Of the couples who made this decision, the typical pattern was that they were invited to a Zionist benefit bridge party, then to parties with Zionist friends, then to a lecture on Zionism, and then to participate in Zionist discussion groups. They became more involved until they *joined* the Zionist organization. This act of *commitment to a group* who shared the same basic convictions was what gave them the courage to make a radical life change; by *joining* the group they adopted the ideas of the group.

It is joining a group which gives people the courage of their convictions. Even the lonely prophet receives moral support from those who accept the prophet's vision. The tighter the group is knit, the more effective it is in maintaining its witness and in giving its members morale to persist in its value system. This is the strength of orthodoxy, on which evangelical religious movements capitalize. Being "true believers" in their way of salvation, evangelicals have a high compulsion to save others. This concern comes across to potential converts as an act of personal caring. To the true believers, converts bolster confidence in the believer's position. However, success in winning converts has little to do with the truth of the belief system; in fact, often the contrary. I think that *evangelical zeal is inversely proportional to the credibility of the theology*; the less credible it is, the more vigorously it must seek converts. Doctrines which more truly describe nature and human nature will not prevail unless people are committed to them and receive group support to live by them.

As a chaplain with the Marines during World War II I learned several important things about religion. You may think war is a strange place to learn about religion, but with all of its horrors of casualties, death, and destruction, it reduces existence to fundamentals, not only in the physical necessities of living but also in the survival margin, especially if you are assigned to a combat outfit, as I was. Before I volunteered for the Navy and was assigned to the Marine Corps for duty, I had been assistant minister for two years of a Unitarian church in Rockford, Illinois. In a relatively homogenous congregation with its own traditions, shared assumptions and rituals, my role was unchallenged. But when I joined the 7th Regiment of the 1st Marine Division on Pavuvu in the Solomon Islands, I found myself serving a constituency of some 3,000 men, 90 percent of whom did not share my theology, and without the normal routines of parish life. I was confronted with the question, "What am I doing here?" What is the function of religion and of a minister with men who are preparing for the perils of active warfare?

In the training area, the traditional preaching "Divine Service" in a canvas-topped chapel seemed to fulfill expectations. After our landing on Okinawa, however, I found that men meeting in the open under combat conditions were in no mood for sermons on the meaning of life. As I moved around to meet with Marines just off the lines of combat, I found that the ritual of the communion service seemed most meaningful. We had previously shared in the communion service I had adapted to serve the needs of the varieties of Protestants in the regiment, and it meant something to the men to join in the familiar ritual of gospel songs and hymns and the communion, especially when I repeated the phrase, "present your bodies a living sacrifice."

Another time I learned that at the death of a buddy, only a ritual could serve to express our sense of loss. I was attached to the sick bay and one day I was notified that some dead had been brought in. It was my practice to identify the dead and try to learn the circumstances of their death so I could write the next-of-kin with information as to what had happened to their son or husband. The first poncho I drew back from a form on a stretcher uncovered the face of a Marine I had known well. Others standing there also knew and loved him. *He was dead, and some special notice needed to be taken,* but no discourse about the meaning of death was appropriate and I had no ritual. As I put the poncho back over his face, I turned away with a heavy feeling because I had not sufficiently acknowledged that a man we loved was dead; I did not have a way to express for the little group our shared feeling of grief. I noticed that the Catholic chaplain at the other end of the row of dead was methodically fingering the dog-tags of the bodies and when he identified an "R.C." he gave the body "extreme unction." Whether or not I believed he was gaining the soul's access to heaven, it was a meaningful act to the Catholics standing by, and to all of us signified that *profound attention was being paid.* There are times when no homilies are appropriate and when ritual acts are meaningful—especially if the ritual has a shared meaning. Meaningful rituals cannot be spur-of-the-moment innovations; the participants must have *shared* in them previously, *understood their intention,* and *believed in them.*

When I joined the 7th Regiment, it was obvious that everyone was preparing for his role in combat and reducing his gear to the essential minimum. For guidance as to what was a chaplain's role in combat, I called on the chaplain of a neighboring regiment who had been through the previous landing at Peliliu. He was a high Episcopal priest, and when I asked him what he did in combat, he replied that he gave the wounded extreme unction. "Extreme unction" is a sacrament in which the priest anoints the dying on their foreheads, eyes, lips, and toes with consecrated oil. The intention is to mediate forgiveness for any sin they may have committed so that, if they die, their souls can go directly to heaven, and to give the wounded courage to get well. I jokingly commented that I guessed I would have to get a vial of holy oil. He sharply retorted, "But you have to believe in it or it won't work!" Since I did not believe in that, or any sacrament, this was no help to me.

A *sacrament* is a channel to mediate the Grace of God, a super-natural power with magical efficacy. And it doesn't work, even psychologically, if you don't believe in it. On the other hand, the function of *ritual* is to bring the assurances of a previous experi-ence or myth to bear upon a present situation. It reaffirms what was once learned as true or of value. It strengthens morale by vivi-fying feelings associated with a peak experience or a moment of insight; it preserves tradition. Rituals are not esoteric; most of us engage in them. Most families have rituals for celebrating birth-days and other anniversaries, or for special holidays. Most people who live together intimately share little rituals, reaffirming some shared values or recalling memorable experiences. Baseball games, courts, and parliaments open with rituals.

Rituals are not necessarily outmoded by the replacement of a supporting myth by a supporting theology. The myth of a personal god who listened and responded was the ground for *prayers* of petition and thanksgiving. Even when the psychology of religion explained that the function of prayer was to change the mind, not of god but of the people praying, by relating their concerns to a larger frame of reference and by heightening their consciousness of interdependence, the prayer ritual remained effective.

In my family, we found that saying "grace" before dinner, which was in the form of holding hands and singing a ritual song of thanksgiving, served to center and quiet our family for the pleasure of a shared meal. Instead of *bed-time prayers*, my wife and I took turns sitting on the edge of the beds of each of our two daughters and asking them what made them happy and what made them sad that day. This ritual of "happy and sad" functioned like prayer in that it gave them an opportunity to talk about what was most important in their minds, to finish the day, and to go to sleep at peace with the world. Even *praying for other people* has the value not of directly affecting their lives, but of bringing them vividly to *our consciousness* so we are more apt to express our concern for their welfare, as I found in my daily meditations when separated from my family by war or professional responsibilities. Even with the mythos of traditional prayer, the centering and the reaffirmation of relationship with the "not-me" in prayer serves to reinforce morale for meaningful living. The popularity of the meditation disciplines of the many para-religious groups in our society attest the pragmatic value of such a ritual.

Broken Myths

Rituals sometimes become obsolete, however, when the supporting myths or theology become *broken* by new insights and understanding. When people become disenchanted with the justifications of a ritual, repetition of the ritual signifies nothing and becomes an empty performance. Religions, being essentially conservative movements, tend to continue reenacting rituals long after they have lost their power to move people or affect their morale. In the course of human history, thousands of religions have sprung up and died when they lost their effectiveness.

Myths are broken by increasing knowledge and understanding, and people can no longer credit the explanation given for a particular ritual. The Lord's Supper or *Communion* began as a ritual commemorating the last supper of Jesus with his disciples, and was theologically transformed into the sacrament of the Mass, interpreting the bread and wine as the real body and blood of Christ with magical powers to infuse grace, forgive sins, and strengthen charity. Since many of us cannot believe in the vicarious atonement of Christ's death, taking communion can mean nothing to us. It is interesting, however, how often the bread and wine turn up as elements in experimental worship services; these symbols of the staff and joy of life seem to be generic, natural, and universal.

Another source of *disenchantment* with religion is the *history of violence* spawned by the rigidity and bigotry of Christian orthodoxy—the persecutions, inquisitions, slaughter of heretics, and the religious wars such as in Northern Ireland, and between Christians and Moslem orthodoxies in Lebanon. Many of us will have nothing to do with an expression of religion which causes so much bloodshed. The root of these evils, however, is not the religion, but that the religion has become *orthodox,* its system of beliefs has been authoritatively declared to be true and undebatable. Its doctrines have been converted into dogmas. A *doctrine* is a statement of faith; everyone who has a belief system that can be articulated as a position-statement has a doctrine. A doctrine is debatable and open to change. A *dogma* is a statement of faith which some authority has ruled may not be questioned or challenged, on pain of punishment or death. When a theological position is made inflexible and beyond question, its dogmatic partisans have often sought to *defend* it by physical *force*. Since one of the basic laws of living is adaptability to change, a religion must evolve like any other culture system.

The myths and rituals of a society are also broken by radical *acculturation,* the modification of a primitive culture by contact with an advanced culture, such as happened to the ancient Hawaiians. After 500 years of isolation on their mid-Pacific islands, the Hawaiians were brought into contact with other cultures by the arrival in 1778 of Captain Cook and the first "tour group." The Hawaiians had developed a high stone-age culture with a religion of tabus which was rigid and especially restrictive upon women. *Doubts* were raised about the validity of their myths and practices by the immunity with which the foreigners violated local tabus, and by the obvious advantages of the new culture with its woven cloth, metal tools and weapons, ceramic utensils, and writing. Disenchantment with their own religion set in and by 1819 they deliberately violated their own tabus, under the leadership of women, burned their effigies and destroyed their sacred places. Being in a religious and moral void, the Hawaiians were receptive to the Christian religion brought to the islands by the arrival of the first Congregational missionaries in 1820.

The acculturation going on in our society is internal and not so radical as that encountered by the Hawaiians. The stress in our culture is induced by the *disparity between two epistemologies,* the traditional way of knowing by *special revelation* and the contemporary way of knowing by the *scientific method.* The latter has the obvious advantage of a record of creative achievements. The incongruity between the two ways of knowing has induced wide disenchantment with traditional Christian orthodoxy and increased confusion in the society, which threatens its stability.

Revitalization

In any non-authoritarian society, the regularity of patterned behavior depends upon the ability of the members to *perceive the pattern of the system as a whole* and act in accordance with requirements to maintain the integrity of the system. As anthropologist Anthony F.C. Wallace (1965, p. 505) points out, the present conflicting models are unsatisfactory and are inaugurating a *revitalization movement*. "A revitalization movement," says Wallace (1965, p. 504), "is defined as a deliberate, organized, conscious effort by members of a society to construct a more satisfying culture." This revitalization may be a rather abrupt shift to a new gestalt, a new theology which enjoins new relationships and traits, *implemented by human intention* rather than by the slower change of natural cultural evolution.

However, the new gestalt does not necessarily require such a radical change in religion, in symbols and rituals, as the Hawaiians experienced. In fact, the *emergence* of the *great religions* was not by radical innovation, but *by revitalization* or reformation. All the great religions of the contemporary world have come into being through consciously-directed human revitalization of ancient traditions: Buddha revitalized Hinduism; Jesus revitalized Judaism; Mohammed revitalized the religion of the Old Testament books in a more radical direction; Lao-tse revitalized "the wisdom of the ancients" in China in one way and Confucius in another; Luther, Calvin, Zwingli, Smyth, and David reformed Catholicism with varying Protestant emphases; and even Joseph Smith and Mary Baker Eddy incorporated the Bible in their religions. A religion strengthening morale to meet the challenges of our time will not be original but a *recycling* of the still meaningful rituals and symbols of our culture.

Ralph Waldo Emerson in his *Divinity School Address* of 1838, which caused such a furor among Unitarians as well as orthodox Christians, warned that the church was dying because "men have come to speak of the revelation as somewhat long ago given and done, as if God were dead," and suggested that "it is the office of a true teacher to show that God is, not was; that He speaketh, not spake." He challenged the members of the Harvard graduating class about to enter the ministry: "Yourself a newborn bard of the Holy Ghost—cast behind you all conformity and acquaint men at first hand with Deity." After rejecting theology based upon ancient revelation and proposing a new theology of transcendentalism, Emerson (1961, p. 111) says:

> And now let us do what we can to rekindle the smouldering, nigh quenched fire on the altar. The evils of the church that now is are manifest. The question returns, What shall we do? I confess all attempts to project and establish a Cultus with new rites and forms, seem to me vain. Faith make us, and not we it, and faith makes its own forms. All attempts to contrive a system are as cold as the new worship introduced by the French to the goddess of Reason—today, pasteboard and fillagree, and ending tomorrow in madness and murder. Rather let the breath of new life be breathed by you through the forms already existing. For if once you are alive, you shall find they shall become plastic and new.

I agree with Emerson because I believe that *creativity is by evolution,* that all significant novelty in biology, culture, and religion is the consequence of the *cumulation of small changes* in continuity with the past, and not by some creation in discontinuity with previous forms. I also believe that new rituals and symbols cannot be created by definition but that they acquire meaning beyond themselves by emerging from shared historical experiences. *Theology may undergo sudden transformation, but symbols and rituals take time to evolve and emerge by evolution, not revolution.*

The new religions I experienced in Japan in 1971 are revitalizations of Buddhism and Shintoism which, except as national shrines and conventions for marrying and burying, are in their traditional forms as moribund as orthodox Christianity in this country. At Tsubaki Grand Shrine, the hereditary priest Yukitaka Yamamoto has revitalized his historic shrine by emphasizing its roots in the laws and order of the "Great Nature" of Shintoism, by

reinterpreting the meaning of its purification rituals as a commitment to live in unity with Great Nature, and by instructing lay
devotees in the meaning of Shinto rituals. At Rissho Kosei-kai,
Nikkyo Niwano, a milkman, in 1938 revitalized Buddhism by
implementing the "Bodhisattva principle" in the Lotus Sutra of
helpfulness to those who are suffering, by organizing lay-led
"Hoza" ("truth sitting" or group counseling). Rissho Kosei-kai has
grown into a non-monastic Buddhist movement with millions of
members and many service institutions. At Konkoyo, founded by
a farmer named Konko in 1859, Shintoism has been revitalized by
instituting "Toritsugi," or mediation of the "way of the Kami" to
suffering human beings. The supreme Kami (of many human or
natural sacred or revered beings) is the parent of all humanity and
cannot exist without people, nor people without the Kami; human
sorrow is the Kami's sorrow, and human redemption is the Kami's
redemption. For people whose relationship with the Kami has
broken down, a mediator (a minister who meditates in a Konko
church about 12 hours a day) is available not only to counsel but
also to *share the burden of insoluble suffering* with the Kami.
Konkoyo has millions of adherents. In different ways, both Rissho
Kosei-kai and Konkoyo have devised rituals from their respective
traditions to provide people concrete support in realizing the Old
Testament assurance, "Cast your burden on the Lord, and he will
sustain you." (Psalm 55:22)

The history of the emergence of the great religions of the world
and of the new religions in Japan indicates the nature of the *revitalized religion which will emerge in this country* out of the convergence of the Judeo-Christian tradition and the new theology
emerging from the sciences. Some of the traditional rituals have
lost theological justification and become vestigial and will be abandoned. Some of the moral norms were culture-specific and no
longer apply. But *most of the cultus and ethic are generic and will
be revitalized.* Once we become alive with the new theology, we
will breathe new life into many of the old forms.

Spiritual Habits

Any religion supportive of human morale will meet basic human needs. *Religions which endure have some pragmatic value transcending the individual in time and space.* One of the basic human needs is for rhythm in the pattern of living which reflects the *rhythms of the body and of nature.* Any organism needs periods of rest and relaxation interspersing periods of work and stress. Inorganic forms, such as a cement pillar or steel girder, can bear continued stress, though they too become "tired." Living systems endure longer by alternating action and rest, stress and relaxation; the heart beats and rests, the whole body works and sleeps. Although the pattern varies, everybody has a *circadian rhythm* synchronized by the diurnal rotation of the earth. The larger rhythms of the seasons are established by the revolution of the earth about the sun. *Since human beings have evolved in harmony with those rhythms, persistent violation of them violates the nature of our own being.* My experience is not unusual in that when I press my body to function beyond its normal rhythms, it takes its own holiday in reduced efficiency, if nothing else.

Religious rituals reinforce these rhythms. In earlier hunting-and-gathering societies, the activity rhythm was probably dictated by the seasonal food supplies: when there were berries to pick or fish to catch, there was work to do; when food was scarce or an adequate supply was on hand, there was time for rest and play. After the development of agrarian societies about 8,000 years ago, there was *no end to the work that could be done* to increase production; when crops were not in season, land had to be worked and domesticated animals tended. With the development of technology, the compulsion was greater to work longer to produce more goods and thus more wealth. Primitive societies work only by sunlight; one of the characteristics of a developing society is the invention of oil lamps and candles so that manufacture can continue after sundown. Now we can turn on the light and work round the clock. To regulate their activities in keeping with their biological needs, human beings evolved *cultural rhythms,* holidays and festivals, ceremonies and rituals—spiritual habits.

The ritual of the *7th day of rest* may be based upon a biological rhythm and not a solar rhythm. The Sabbath, which means "rest," is a significant contribution of the Judeo-Christian tradition to Western culture and ultimately to the world. Since the 7th day of rest did not emerge in all agrarian societies, I don't know why it did among the Jews, nor why the 7th day was settled on; but I have no doubt it met a basic human need in an agrarian society for a day of rest from cumulative fatigue. The myth justifying the Sabbath was the model of God in the work of creation as told in the Old Testament book of Genesis (2:1-2): "Thus the heavens and the earth were finished, and all the host of them. And on the seventh day God finished his work which he had done, and he rested on the seventh day from all the work which he had done." The Jews codified this practice in the Fourth Commandment: "Remember the sabbath day, to keep it holy. Six days shall you labor, and do all your work; but the seventh day is a sabbath to the Lord your God; in it you shall not do any work, you, or your son, or your daughter, your manservant, or your maidservant, or your cattle, or the sojourner who is within your gates." (Exodus 20:8-10). The Jews did not even go to their place of instruction and worship, the synagogue, on the Sabbath, which fell on what we now call Saturday. A significant consequence of sabbath observance was that abstaining from the routine daily tasks allowed time for the *cultivation of intellectual and spiritual interests.* In addition it punctuated life, arbitrarily finishing tasks which were interminable and thus relieving monotony and boredom, much as periods and paragraphs break a steady stream of thought into comprehensible units. When through the centuries the restrictions on sabbath activities had become rigid and restrictive, Jesus said, "The sabbath was made for man and not man for the sabbath." (Mark 2:27)

The Christians changed the day of rest to the *first* day of the week, Sunday, probably partly to distinguish themselves from the Jews, and ascribed it to a *different myth*—the resurrection of Christ on the 1st day. The Roman Emperor Constantine, who by adopting Christianity raised it from being a subversive religion, decreed in 321 AD regulations against Sunday labor. The Catholic church observed Sunday not only as a day of rest and attendance at Mass, but also as a day of *enjoyable recreation*.

My Puritan ancestors confined Sunday observances to going to church, which was the social and communications center of the community, and pious study. As children visiting my Presbyterian grandfather's home, we could not even swim on a Sunday afternoon, let alone go to the movies. Such strictures, and the reputation of the earlier Puritan "blue laws" restricting Sunday activities, caused many people of my generation to abandon any ritual of Sunday observance, though we retained the value of an alternation of activity.

I would like to see a scientific study done of the biological value of the *7th day of rest* in contributing to human survival and creativity, in *contrast* to cultures whose *periodicity* is marked only by *seasonal festivals*. My hypothesis would be that the 7th day of rest and recreation contributed to making cultures dynamic and creative, and spread beyond Jewish and Christian cultures as a consequence of its empirical value.

It is clear, I hope, that the ritual of the 7th day of rest is still valid, even though the myths by which it has been justified have changed from a supernatural Creator's day of rest, or the resurrection of a Messiah, to the universal function of providing for the physical and spiritual needs of human beings based upon a biological rhythm. Even though most of us no longer work six days on a farm or at other hard labor, the interlude of a day of rest and recreation is valuable—even more valuable if it is devoted to spiritual or intellectual development, by which I mean the pursuit of interests we ordinarily don't have time for, not sitting in a stupor before the TV. Sunday is a ritual we all observe in some fashion, though many of us would not think of the 7th day of rest as part of our religion.

A ritual associated with Sunday in Christian cultures is going to church for a worship service. "Worship" means "worth-ship" or revering things of worth. *People gather to celebrate the concepts that give meaning and value to their lives, to proclaim, transmit, and transform those ideals, and to apply them to their personal and social lives.* There are various forms of worship, and the alternative forms have been thoroughly explored and practiced. Worship is a group experience, so opportunity is provided for *congregational participation* in the responses, hymns, group meditations, and even the sermon—which is a group experience, even though the hearers are not vocal, as there is a dialogue going on in each head. *The content may be changed to express a new theology, but the form of the ritual can remain the same.*

The *rhythm of the seasons* is marked with festivals associated with significant natural events which vivify the sequence of happenings we experience as time. Seasonal rituals also give meaning to living by raising to consciousness the rhythms of change and renewal. Various myths are given to justify them, although they are basically natural and universal. Seasonal rituals occur at different times in different places on the planet, and may be transported to climes where they no longer fit the season, such as Christmas in Southern California.

Christmas in northern climes is a mid-winter festival associated with the mid-winter solstice, the shortest day of the year. Although the festival is at least 4,000 years old, Christians have tried to preempt it by "putting Christ into Christmas" and justifying the festivities with the myth that it celebrates the birthday of Jesus of Nazareth. As a matter of fact, first century Christians were not much interested in the birthday of Jesus; they expected him to return soon. Then the birthday of Jesus was celebrated on dates from early in November until late in April until a pope in the 4th century decided it should be celebrated on December 25, the time of the Roman festival of Saturn. The Saturnalia, beginning December 17, was a period of singing in the streets, exchange of greetings and gifts, and also of general license and excess. There are still some Saturnalia elements in Christmas, but the *Christian myth refined* the mid-winter festival by adding the beautiful story of a babe born in a manger accompanied by a star in the east and wisemen bringing gifts and shepherds hearing "a multitude of the heavenly host praising God, and saying, Glory to God in the highest, and on earth peace, good will toward men." (Luke 2:13-14,

King James Version) This myth, along with the "Santa Claus" and "Rudolph, The Red-Nosed Reindeer" myths, *focused this joyous festival on and for children and families* instead of the orgiastic aspects of the Saturnalia.

The rich cluster of symbols and rituals associated with this winter-solstice festival reveals its *essence as a universal folk festival,* especially in the northern temperate zone where it marks a turn toward longer and warmer days and the return of spring. In Mesopotamia some 4,000 years ago the season was celebrated by the lighting of bonfires on hilltops to dispel the mid-winter darkness and to hasten the return of the sun. In northern Europe, Teutonic tribes went to the forest and decorated evergreen trees, which remained green during the winter and were taken as a symbol of the perseverance of life and which in later years were cut down and placed and decorated in their houses—the Christmas tree. Mistletoe also remains green through the winter and was taken by the Druids of Briton as a symbol of the persistence of life. We can see that if we understand the universals of the Christmas ritual, we can celebrate it with a whole heart as the *triumph of the human spirit over the adversities* of winter; just when winter stores are running low and living is most difficult and when other animals and plants are at their lowest annual ebb, the human spirit breaks forth with its brightest and most joyous celebration, filling the air with music—more beautiful music for this festival than for any other.

Easter is another annual ritual, a Spring festival associated with the renewing of the face of the earth at a time of the vernal equinox. The very name of the festival indicates its pre-Christian origin: "Eastre" was a Teutonic goddess of Spring, whose antecedents run back through various fertility goddesses with similar names to Ishtar (known to the Old Testament Hebrews as Ashtoreth) who stepped out of an egg which fell from the sky into the Tigris River in Babylonia. The basic meaning of the festival as a celebration of the annual renewal of life and of fertility is still symbolized in such associated traditions as the Easter egg and bunny, both symbols of fertility, and the display of flowers. Since the death of Jesus occurred at the time of the Passover Feast, the Spring festival of Judaism, the early Christians transmuted their despair over the death of the Messiah into a version of the ancient myth of the dying and rising god, and characterized the Spring festival as a celebration of the resurrection of Christ and an assurance of personal immortality. The ancient myths of the fertility goddess or of the risen god are obsolete and no longer serve to assure us of the triumph of the life process over individual deaths. Instead, we take the *recurring event of the springtide as symbolic of the significance of life in spite of defeat and death,* and rejoice in the Spring festival of Easter as a celebration of the continuing renewal of life. Instead of the cross, the more ancient and *generic symbol of the egg* carries the meaning that life transcends death, not by personal immortality, but by the *continuity of life.*

Another seasonal ritual is the *Fall harvest festival,* celebrated by the Jews for the ingathering of the crops and by praising God for the bounties of nature in the Feast of Tabernacles, based upon the myth of God's care for them during the Exodus. Americans celebrate it as *Thanksgiving,* based upon the Pilgrim's 1621 thanksgiving feast to express gratitude for plentiful food stores to supply a second winter in New England. Regardless of any justification, Thanksgiving is a ritual which *increases appreciative awareness.*

The *4th of July* celebrates our political roots in the Declaration of Independence and reaffirms the spiritual grounds of our nation—as John Adams said, ". . . the revolution was in the minds of the people." *United Nations Sunday* reaffirms the idea of a united world community which will obviate war. The annual celebrations of the *birthdays* of Washington, Jefferson, and Lincoln present us with the reminders of great lives and serve as an inspiration (a value which is obscured when the anniversary dates are moved to a Monday to provide a three-day holiday). We can think of other national holidays which ritualistically reinforce values.

A *world-wide event was the first glimpse of this planet from outer space* in the photographs brought back by the astronauts.

Archibald MacLeish (*N.Y. Times*, Dec. 25, 1968) wrote, "To see the earth as it truly is, small and blue and beautiful in that eternal silence where it floats, is to see ourselves as riders on the earth together, brothers on that bright loveliness in the eternal cold— brothers who know now they are truly brothers." That event *changed the human perspective* and raised the consciousness of unity of the whole human species. I propose that we *recognize the representations of our beautiful blue and white planet as a symbol of the great living system,* of the vital life-support system as a shared, revered value, of the sacred earth as a whole; and that as an annual ritual we celebrate *Whole Earth Day,* beginning in this country and intending that it become a world-wide event as a step toward cooperation in preserving our shared life-support system. Celebrations could be in keeping with the various cultural traditions. A natural time for a Whole Earth Day does not occur to me, but it might well be agreed upon by the United Nations agency of UNESCO.

Rites of Passage

Other rituals called "rites of passage" define and celebrate *significant stages in human life.* With an undifferentiated passage of years, children are sometimes expected to behave like adults; and adults sometimes do not realize that they have reached an age of moral responsibility: children come into an indifferent society; married people do not notice that they have changed their relationship; and the dead are unnoticed. With increasing longevity, we may even need a new rite of passage.

A *birth ceremony,* baptism, Christening, or Naming Celebration is a universal ritual celebrated in similar forms for many centuries in many lands and given various mythical or theological interpretations. In all forms of infant baptism there are *common elements:* the celebration of the marvel of a new life as one of the continuing miracles; the giving of a personal name which recognizes the individuality and personal dignity of the child; the formal reception of the child into the community with all its rights and privileges, including the opportunity to gain a living in the community's economy; the acceptance of community responsibility for providing a healthy, wholesome environment for the child's nurture and education; the use of water for actual cleansing or symbolic purification of the child; and the dedication of the parents to raising the child in the faith and values of the community. Without this kind of community commitment to the newborn, a society tends to feel no responsibility for its own members; we do not notice who is born or who is unemployed—that's their problem. But with responsibility goes control over who is admitted to the society.

Baptism in the early Christian community was an adult act of washing away old sins by immersion and was a commitment to the Christian way of life based upon the myth of the baptism of Jesus by John the Baptist in the river Jordan. But Christianity did not long adhere to the ritual of adult baptism, until the Baptists reintroduced believer's baptism during the Protestant Reformation. When early Christian missionaries moved into northern Europe they found to their consternation that Teutonic tribesmen claimed they had already been baptised as infants with water in the name of their god Wodin. Encounter with infant baptism elsewhere as well led the Catholic church to gradually adopt the practice of infant baptism, reinterpreting it theologically as a sacrament which removed the taint of "original sin." Whatever the explanation given, *infant baptism has functioned to celebrate the birth of a new human being, to give the infant the identity of a personal name, and to accept the newcomer into the community.*

In the gradual transition from puberty to adulthood, it is difficult for people to know where they are. *Puberty rites* are celebrated in many societies both as a period of instruction in the wisdom of the culture and as a mark of the adolescent's attainment of the privileges and responsibilities of adulthood. For instance, in the Jewish "Bar Mitzvah," which means "one to whom the commandment applies," a 13-year-old boy, after an extended course of instruction in the Jewish language and lore, reads from the Torah in a temple service, signifying that he has reached the age of moral responsibility for his own acts. Although some Christian communions have similar puberty rites in the preparation for and celebration of "Confirmation," our society in general notes too little this important passage; and then we wonder why so many young people are "irresponsible." The nearest thing our society has to puberty rites is driver's training and the issuance of a driver's license, unless it be high school graduation exercises.

Marriage is a ritual marking a passage from the family in which a person was raised to a family of one's own, supplying the human need for an accepting intimate relationship and recreating the supportive condition a person loses when leaving the home in which he or she was raised. Marriage is a ceremony in which a man and a woman confirm their love for each other by publicly exchanging vows of commitment to each other. *Commitments* are a peculiarly human way of ordering and organizing experience to make life meaningful, from making a business appointment to signing a contract to pay for a house over the next 30 years. The vows establish a covenant relationship in which the husband and wife accept *unconditional moral responsibility* for each other's welfare and for the welfare of any children they may have, all of which forms a *family* as a stable and basic social unity. It is a verbal commitment, no more effective than the integrity with which it is made, not a written legal contract with "whereas" and "in consideration of" clauses. The officiating minister or judge does not "marry" a couple; *the couple marry each other by the promises they make to each other,* after which the minister or judge *witnesses* that they have made such a pledge by signing the marriage license. *Love* brings the couple together and makes them feel they want to share their lives, and marriage *reinforces their implicit commitment to each other* with a public existential act of mutual affirmation; it stabilizes the relationship by augmenting love with an act of decision and will. Though various cultures have different customs for celebrating a marriage, the act of commitment is the basic and common element, and *all the major cultures of the world have converged* on the celebration of monogamous marriage as a basic ritual.

The final traditional rite of passage is a *funeral or memorial service.* All human societies have some kind of ritual for taking notice of the death of another human being with whom we symbolically and emotionally identify, and for dealing with grief over the final and absolute separation by death from a closely beloved person. In our society, the final care of the dead has been developed into an elaborate and expensive funeral service focusing on the body by making the body look as life-like as possible through embalming and cosmetology for the funeral service, followed by earth burial in an "hermetically sealed casket" enclosed in a concrete grave liner in a grave guaranteed "perpetual care," which is a luxury of a relatively young culture; older cultures such as China have learned that perpetual care is a physical impossibility as, in time, the preemption of land for burial exhausts land available for the living. Earlier cultures, such as Egypt, provided embalming and perpetual care only for kings, while most cultures relied upon cremation or other less pretentious means of reverently disposing of the body while focusing on the spirit of the deceased.

The continental association of some 150 non-profit, consumer-oriented *memorial societies* in the United States and Canada provides an alternative to the post-Civil War funeral-industry tradition for care of the dead. By arrangement with licensed morticians, memorial societies make available direct cremation or direct burial without embalming and other materialistic extras at a corresponding low cost, followed by a *memorial service* celebrating the memory of the spirit of the deceased. A memorial service without the corpse present, like a funeral service, helps grief-stricken people experience and accept the full enormity of their loss, and provides other mourners an opportunity to share in the experience by being there. A memorial service is for the benefit of the living, not of the dead, to help the grieved living continue their lives without the dead.

With the statistical increase in longevity, we now encounter the need for *another rite of passage, that of retirement.* The nearest ritual we seem to have is a visit to the Social Security Office. With increasing numbers of people living past retirement, perhaps we need a ritual to make this transition more meaningful and to *define the new status.*

By reinterpretation, old and new rituals such as these can give structure, meaning, and purpose to our lives without inventing a new religious cult. Nor do we find it necessary to organize new religious institutions; many of the present religious institutions in our society can be revitalized to provide morale for creative living.

Transformed by the Renewal of Your Mind

Religions are in the business of offering a means of transformation of personal and social life, of preservation or deliverance from difficulty, anxiety, or what is regarded as evil. In Christianity, the process is called "redemption" or "salvation." The question is, salvation from what? Paul (Romans 12:2) said, "Do not be conformed to this world but be transformed by the renewal of your mind, that you may prove what is the will of God, what is good and acceptable and perfect." Fundamentalist Christians have interpreted Paul's injunction, "Do not be conformed to this world," to mean non-involvement in social and political organizations and abstaining from evil, narrowly-defined as dancing, drinking, smoking, profanity, and going to movies. Liberal Christians have interpreted Paul's injunction to mean involvement in the affairs of the world to deliver us from injustice, discrimination, poverty, and war. There have been many definitions of evil and of salvation.

The differences in definition of salvation were demonstrated to me at an Alabama revival meeting. I was in Selma in August of 1958 as part of the Unitarian-Universalist continuing presence following the great civil rights march led by Martin Luther King from Selma to Montgomery. On Friday the 13th I went to adjoining Lounds County with members of the Student Non-violent Coordinating Committee including Stokely Carmichael, Reverend Richard Morrisroe, a Catholic priest, and Reverend Jonathan Daniels, an Episcopal priest. They were young men who the next day participated in a civil rights demonstration in Ft. Defiance and were arrested with 21 young blacks and thrown in jail in Hayneville. When released a week later, Daniels was shot and killed and Morrisroe seriously wounded by a deputy sheriff in the streets of Hayneville. Yet, on that Friday Morrisroe and I were invited to a black bricklayer's home for supper and then to a revival meeting in the pine woods of Alabama. It was a beautiful summer night and as we entered the small wooden church, Father Morrisroe was picked up by young people and taken to sit with the choir, while I was ushered to a seat in the front row with the deacons. The singing was enthusiastic and beautiful; there were scripture readings, prayers, and an elaborate ceremony of receiving the offering. Then the visiting evangelist launched into his sermon, working up to the point where he invited the people in the congregation to raise their hands if they had been saved. Along with everyone else in the church, I raised my hand and, looking across at the choir, I noted that the young priest also had raised his hand. Neither of us was letting the evangelist define "salvation" for us, though I doubt if he thought either Morrisroe or I were saved. Neither Morrisroe nor I thought the evangelist was saved, let alone each other. There were several definitions of salvation at work in the church that night, and many more in the society at large. The difference is what we are being saved from—or for.

All of us have problems, stresses, dangers, and anxieties from which we wish to be delivered, redeemed, or saved—if not personally, then collectively. If we can get over our reaction to the definitions of salvation from our childhood or radio evangelists, we can revitalize the question, "What must I do to be saved?"

For the Baptist evangelist, being saved was from the personal sins of the flesh such as drinking, gambling, adultery, lying, cheating, stealing—all worthy moral purposes as far as they went. Salvation meant being "born again" by accepting Jesus Christ as your personal savior, being forgiven for your sins ("Christ died for your sins"), and being redeemed so you could renew your life without guilt. You feel acceptable because you have been accepted. Your reward will be eternal life in heaven.

The Catholic priest had a different definition of salvation in his mind. Catholic salvation is mediated through participation in such sacraments as baptism, confession, and the mass. Salvation is from "original sin"—a corrupted will inherited from the first sin of Adam and Eve by eating the fruit of the tree of knowledge in the

Garden of Eden; or from such sins as conception control, divorce, or abortion. Those who fulfill their religious obligations and merit the grace dispensed by the Church are also assured of eternal life in heaven.

Whatever the definition of salvation, insofar as it gives morale to face life's problems and reinforces personal integrity, the family, and tender loving care for children, it works to benefit humanity— "These ought you to have done, without neglecting the others," said Jesus (Luke 11:42). It's the neglected others which are an important part of salvation to me. To me, salvation is also from the evils which confront the human species and the great living system which created and sustains us. Salvation is not *from* the world, but *in* the world; not in an *after life*, but *now*; not by creeds, but by deeds; not by faith, but by works—as James (2:18) said, "Show me your faith apart from your works, and I by my works will show you my faith." Salvation is not just personal but social.

There really is no *personal* salvation; natural selection controls the survival of *species*, not individuals. If the species *Homo sapiens* is not creative enough to survive, no individual human being will be saved. Salvation is inevitably social. We can make our lives less complicated and more efficient by observing the laws of being, especially the principles of being human. But there is no salvation apart from the salvation of all. A classic Christian debate has been whether salvation began in the hearts of people by "accepting Christ" or in society through social action. Salvation will not come about simply by people being "good" in their little econiches. As James Luther Adams has said, "The evil that good men do" can take this country down the road to hell. We can lose our morale in a morass of personal disorder and not engage the overwhelming problems for which we humans are largely responsible. Or we can lead good personal lives; but if our definition of salvation is so limited that it does not include organizing ourselves to play a constructive role in the continuing process of evolution, we are also doomed. If our lives do not include working for a higher and more inclusive social order, if we are not creative of new solutions, the old problems will overcome us.

English physicist Launcelot Law Whyte says there is a basic formative tendency toward unification which he calls the "morphic process." "Morph" is a combining word indicating a specified form, shape, or structure. In evolution there has been a basic tendency toward new, more inclusive, more complex forms. Hence, says Whyte (1974, p. 83), ". . . the total processes in organisms are not merely life-preserving, but life-enhancing, not merely adaptive but formative and sometimes creative." Salvation is not a static event, it is a continuing, dynamic process of *creativity*—it is life-enhancing. I can't say, "I've been saved." I can say only that I am participating in the process of redeeming the human situation. As Whyte said, the evolution of living forms has been a creative process, the tendency to form new orders, the emergence of novelty. Even human beings tend to spend their time planning to solve yesterday's problems, protecting themselves from last year's perils, while the solution to present problems has always been the emergence of new types of order. In coping with contemporary problems, the flexibility with which we are endowed by intelligence means that by renewing our minds we can be as creative, and more quickly, than the natural evolutionary process.

However, to save the species and the whole earth requires a *conversion experience*—a conversion to a new vision of the nature of reality and of human nature, a conversion to seeing the world not as a static creation but as a dynamic process and to seeing human nature as an especially creative part of the process, a conversion which can release us to experience the joy of living in spite of stress and sorrow and which can give us hope for the future. To be effective, the conversion requires commitment to living in harmony with the new vision, participation in the ritual reinforcement of its values, and creative activity.

My hope for the future does not mean that I have a blueprint of what the future will be like. Predictions about the future are too often flawed because they cannot take into account the novelty introduced by the process. On one hand, I am old enough to recall some projections which have not yet come about: beautiful plans for multi-level inner cities which have actually degenerated into slums; instead of the "progress onward and upward forever" mood of the 20's, we ran into the great depression of the 30's; and "peace in our time" turned into World War II of the 40's. Even the Club of Rome's projection of "Limits to Growth" predicted an imminent oil shortage but did not predict that the Arabs would turn off the spigot. On the other hand, there have been unanticipated creative developments: in my youth no one predicted the swiftness of jet plane travel, the development of space satellite relay stations which facilitate world-wide communication, the practical elimination of smallpox and polio, or the decline of colonialism so that, under the aegis of the United Nations, the number of autonomous states in the world has increased from 51 in 1945 to 144 in 1976. At present, the proliferation of small nations increases the potential for disorder; but after the flush of nationalism has waned, perhaps the advantages will be realized of the creation of a new world order of nations within which present tensions can be worked out.

Many of the events of the living system of which we are a part are unpredictable. Since the future is shaped by the relations and sequence of operations of multiple autonomous variables, we cannot anticipate all contingencies; and we cannot pin our hopes for the future upon knowing exactly what it will be like. But we can count on *serendipity*—the occurrence of the unexpected, the unanticipated creative events which do not so much provide solutions as *obviate problems*. The New Mexican posse a century ago, trying to think of a way to eliminate horse stealing, probably thought of the traditional solution to crime—lynching. I doubt if it occurred to them to invent a horseless carriage. Yet, the invention of the automobile practically eliminated horse stealing, though it did bring the problem of car theft. That's the way it goes: we solve one problem only to encounter another. But that is life. Death is when we don't find a creative solution to problems, either because we are stuck in traditional responses or because we have given up hope and are not contributing to creative responses. After all, the princes of Serendip were looking for something when they experienced an unexpected good; we can't just sit and wait for something to happen.

And things are happening. Within one week I noticed that Bell Telephone Solid State Research Laboratories have significantly improved communications by transmitting infrared radiation through glass filaments. And I noticed that two University of Wisconsin scientists have made a breakthrough toward a more natural method of producing nitrogen which uses less energy and therefore can more economically provide fertilizer for agriculture. The solutions to our problems may be emerging quietly around us, even though we don't know how they will draw together to make a new pattern. If we have the morale to look for solutions, they will emerge in unexpected ways.

There are limiting conditions within which we may successfully contribute to creative solutions to our problems. The first is that we live on a finite earth with limited resources, which means recycling limited minerals, conserving fossil fuels, developing inexhaustible sources of energy and renewable resources, and limiting population growth—in short, becoming more organic. The second is that we live in the midst of a great living system with its own supervening laws with which we must live in harmony. Human intelligence is effective for understanding and cooperating with that system, not for controlling and dominating it.

Within these limitations, it is the essence of human beings to be creative by adding cultural evolution to biological evolution. Creativity is the survival process evolved in human beings during the stressful period of the last Ice Age. *Homo sapiens* emerged from that challenge with symbol-using intelligence as an adaptive skill. Human beings have flourished and spread over the planet through our ability to make innovative responses to new and various environmental conditions; surely we can now respond creatively to self-induced culture crises. If we generally are converted to confidence that we have this creative capacity, we can trust ourselves to participate in evolving a culture in harmony with the great living system. If we renew our minds with a new vision of the earth as a dynamic whole and of our role in it, we will be saved as a human species. We will inherit the future.

References

Adams, James Luther. 1976. *On Being Human Religiously*. Edited by Max L. Stackhouse. Boston: Beacon Press.

Barnett, Lincoln. 1962. *The Universe and Dr. Einstein*. New York: Mentor.

Barrett, J. Edward. 1968. "A Theology of the Meaning of Life." *Zygon* 3.

Benedict, Ruth. 1946. *Patterns of Culture*. New York: Penguin Books.

Blackburn, Thomas R. 1971. "Sensuous-Intellectual Complementarity in Science." *Science*, 4 June.

Botnariuc, N. 1966. "The Wholeness of Living Systems and Some Basic Biological Problems." In *General Systems, Yearbook of the Society for General Systems Research*, no. 11.

Bronowski, J. 1965. *Science and Human Values*. New York: Harper & Row.

―――. 1966. "The Logic of the Mind." *American Scientist*, March.

―――. 1970. "New Concepts in the Evolution of Complexity: Stratified Stability and Unbounded Plans." *Zygon* 5.

Brown, Sanborn C. 1966a. "The Nature of God and Man." Massachusetts Institute of Technology. Unpublished manuscript.

―――. 1966b. "Can Physics Contribute to Theology?" *Zygon* 1.

Brown, Warren S. 1975. "Left Brain, Right Brain." *Harper's Magazine*, December.

Buber, Martin. 1958. *I And Thou*. New York: Charles Scribner's Sons.

Burgess, Ernest W., and Wallin, Paul. 1953. *Courtship, Engagement and Marriage*. Philadelphia: J.B. Lippincott Co.

Burhoe, Ralph Wendell. 1966. "Sketches of a Theological Structure in the Light of the Sciences." The Meadville/Lombard Theological School. Unpublished manuscript.

―――. 1967. "Five Steps in the Evolution of Man's Knowledge of Good and Evil." *Zygon* 2.

Caillois, Roger. 1961. *Man, Play and Games*. New York: The Free Press of Glencoe, Inc.

Callahan, Daniel. 1972. "Search for an Ethic, Living With The New Biology." *The Center Magazine*, July-August.

277

Campbell, Donald T. 1975. "On the Conflicts Between Biological and Social Evolution and Between Psychology and Moral Tradition." *American Psychologist,* December.

Canady, John. 1958. *What is Painting?* Metropolitan Seminars in Art, portfolio 1. New York: The Metropolitan Museum of Art.

Caws, Peter. 1967. *Science and the Theory of Values.* New York: Random House.

Chase, Herman B. 1966. *Sex: The Universal Fact.* New York: Dell Publishing Co.

Chinard, Gilbert. 1939. *Thomas Jefferson.* Boston: Little Brown and Co.

Cox, Harvey. 1965. *The Secular City.* New York: The Macmillan Company.

Cranberg, Lawrence. 1967. "Science, Ethics, and Law." *Zygon* 2.

de Chardin, Pierre Teilhard. 1961. *The Phenomenon of Man.* New York: Harper & Row.

———. 1966. *Man's Place in Nature.* London: William Collins Sons.

Dewey, John. 1898. "Evolution and Ethics." *The Monist* 8.

Dobzhansky, Theodosius. 1962. *Mankind Evolving.* New Haven: Yale University Press.

———. 1966. "An Essay on Religion, Death, and Evolutionary Adaptation." *Zygon* 1.

———. 1967. "Changing Man." *Science,* 27 January.

Drucker, Peter F. 1957. "The New Philosophy Comes to Life." *Harper's Magazine,* August.

Dubos, Rene. 1968. *So Human an Animal.* New York: Charles Scribner's Sons.

———. 1970. "Mere Survival Is Not Enough for Man." *Life,* 24 July.

Edel, Abraham. 1955. *Ethical Judgment.* Glencoe, Ill.: The Free Press.

———. 1959. "The Concept of Levels in Social Theory." In *Symposium On Sociological Theory,* edited by Llewellyn Gross. New York: Harper & Row.

Edel, May, and Edel, Abraham. 1959. *Anthropology and Ethics.* Springfield, Ill.: Charles G. Thomas.

Eiseley, Loren. 1958. "An Evolutionist Looks at Modern Man." *The Saturday Evening Post,* 26 April.

———. 1961. *The Immense Journey.* New York: Vintage Books.

Emerson, Alfred E. 1966. "Commentary on Theological Resources from the Biological Sciences." *Zygon* 1.

———. 1968. "Dynamic Homeostasis—A Unifying Principle in Organic, Social and Ethical Evolution." Ibid. 3.

Emerson, Ralph Waldo. 1961. *Three Prophets of Religious Liberalism*. Introduction by Conrad Wright. Boston: Beacon Press.

Erikson, Erik H. 1950. *Childhood and Society*. New York: W.W. Norton & Co.

Feigl, Herbert. 1966. "Is Science Relevant to Theology?" *Zygon* 1.

Fenn, William Wallace. 1938. *The Theological Method of Jesus*. Boston: Beacon Press.

Fletcher, Joseph. 1966. *Situation Ethics*. Philadelphia: The Westminster Press.

Fosdick, Harry Emerson. 1938. *A Guide to Understanding the Bible*. New York: Harper & Bros.

Frank, Lawrence K. 1966. "Man's Changing Image of Himself." *Zygon* 1.

Frankl, Viktor E. 1962. *Man's Search for Meaning*. Boston: Beacon Press.

Fried, Charles. 1970. *An Anatomy of Values*. Cambridge, Mass.: Harvard University Press.

Fromm, Eric. 1941. *Escape From Freedom*. New York: Farrar & Rinehart, Inc.

– – –. 1956. *The Art of Loving*, New York: Harper & Bros.

–––. 1960. *Man For Himself*. New York: Holt, Rinehart & Winston.

Fuller, Robert W., and Putnam, Peter. 1966. "On the Origin of Order in Behavior." In *General Systems, Yearbook of the Society for General Systems Research*, no. 11. Edited by Ludwig von Bertalanffy and Anatol Rapoport.

Geertz, Clifford. 1965. *The Impact of the Concept of Culture on the Concept of Man*. Edited by John R. Platt. Chicago: The University of Chicago Press.

Gerard, R.W. 1962. In *Evolution and Man's Progress*, edited by Hudson Hoaglund and Ralph W. Burhoe. New York: Columbia University Press.

Goodenough, W.H. 1962. In *Evolution and Man's Progress*, edited by Hudson Hoaglund and Ralph W. Burhoe. New York: Columbia University Press.

–––. 1966. "Human Purposes in Life." *Zygon* 1.

–––. 1967. "Right and Wrong in Human Evolution." *Zygon* 2.

Gouldner, Alvin W. 1959. "Reciprocity and Autonomy in Functional Theory." In *Symposium on Sociological Theory*, edited by Llewellyn Gross. New York: Harper & Row.

Haftmann, Werner. 1965. *Painting in the Twentieth Century*. New York: Frederick A. Praeger.

Halleck, Seymour L. 1969. "The Toll Youth Pays for Freedom." *Think*, September-October.

Hardin, Garrett. 1968. "The Tragedy of the Commons." *Science*, 13 December.

Hartshorne, Charles. 1941. *Man's Vision of God*. New York: Harper & Bros.

–––. 1962. *The Logic of Perfection*. LaSalle, Ill.: Court Publishing Co.

Hoagland, Hudson. 1966. "The Brain and Crises in Human Values." *Zygon* 1.

———. 1967. "Ethology and Ethics—The Biology of Right and Wrong." Ibid. 2.

Hoagland, Hudson, and Burhoe, Ralph Wendell, eds. 1962. *In Evolution and Man's Progress.* New York: Columbia University Press.

Huxley, Sir Julian. 1959. "The Evolutionary Vision." In *Evolution After Darwin.* Chicago: The University of Chicago Press.

James, William. 1958. *The Varieties of Religious Experience.* The New American Library. New York: Mentor.

Katchalsky, A. 1971. "Thermodynamics of Flow and Biological Organization." *Zygon* 6.

Kluckhohn, Clyde. 1966. "The Scientific Study of Values in Contemporary Civilization. *Zygon* 1.

Kluckhohn, Clyde, and Murray, Henry A. 1948. *Personality in Nature, Society, and Culture.* New York: Alfred A. Knopf.

Krutch, Joseph Wood. 1956. *The Voice of the Desert.* New York: William Sloane Associates.

Lambert, Frank L. 1968. "The Ontology of Evil." *Zygon* 3.

Leavenworth, May. 1969. "On Integrating Fact and Value." *Zygon* 4.

Letvin, Jerome. 1965. "The Physiological Basis of Mental Activity." Paper read at meeting of American Association for the Advancement of Science, 29 December, University of California, Berkeley.

Libby, Willard F. 1965. "Man's Place in the Physical Universe." In *New Views of the Nature of Man,* edited by John R. Platt. Chicago: The University of Chicago Press.

Lillie, Ralph S. 1945. *General Biology and Philosophy of Organism.* Chicago: The University of Chicago Press.

Lindsay, R.B. 1959. "Entropy Consumption and Values in Science." *American Scientist,* September.

Lippmann, Walter. 1960. *A Preface to Morals.* Boston: Beacon Press.

Lowen, Alexander, and Levin, Robert J. 1969. "The Cast Against Cheating in Marriage." *Redbook Magazine,* June.

Malinowski, Bronislaw. 1931. "Culture." In *Encyclopedia of the Social Sciences,* vol. 4. London: The Macmillan Company.

Margenau, Henry. 1957. "The Modern Predicament and Its Possible Removal." *The Unitarian Register.*

———. 1966. *Ethics and Science.* New York: Dell Publishing Co.

Marquis, Don. 1933. *The Lives and Times of Archy and Mehitabel.* Garden City, N.Y.: Doubleday.

Maslow, Abraham. 1962. *Toward A Psychology Of Being.* Princeton, N.J.: D. Van Nostrand Co.

Mather, Kirtley F. 1969. "The Emergence of Values in Geologic Life Development." *Zygon* 4.

Mather, William G. 1967. "Man's Ability to Co-operate: A Contribution of Anthropology to the Christian Religion." *Zygon* 2.

Mayr, Ernst. 1972. "The Nature of the Darwinian Revolution." *Science*, 2 June.

Mendelsohn, K. 1961. "Probability Enters Physics." *American Scientist*, March.

Menninger, Karl. 1942. *Love Against Hate*. New York: Harcourt, Brace and Co.

Miller, James G. 1965. "The Organization of Life." In *Perspectives in Biology and Medicine*. Chicago: The University of Chicago Press.

Monod, Jacques. 1971. *Chance and Necessity*. New York: Alfred A. Knopf.

Morison, Robert S. 1962. "Comments on Genetic Evolution." In *Evolution and Man's Progress*, edited by Hudson Hoaglund and Ralph Burhoe. New York: Columbia University Press.

―――. 1966. "Darwinism: Foundation for an Ethical System?" *Zygon* 1.

Morris, Desmond. 1967. *The Naked Ape*. New York: Dell Publishing Co.

―――. 1968. "The Shame of the Naked Ape." *Life*, 8 November.

Murphy, Gardner. 1947. *Personality*. New York: Harper & Bros.

Oparin, A.I. 1953. *The Origin of Life*. New York: Dover Publications.

Ornstein, Robert E. 1972. *The Psychology of Consciousness*. San Francisco: W.H. Freeman & Co.

O'Toole, Thomas. 1970. "Life-Assisting Agents Found in Our Galaxy." *The Times of Los Angeles*, October 4.

Pepper, Stephen C. 1960. *Ethics*. New York: Appleton-Crofts, Inc.

―――. 1969a. "Survival Value." *Zygon* 4.

―――. 1969b. "On a Descriptive Theory of Value." Ibid.

Platt, John R. 1966. "Commentary of Theological Resources from the Physical Sciences." *Zygon* 1.

Polanyi, Michael. 1965. *The Study of Man*. Chicago: The University of Chicago Press.

―――. 1967. "Points of Tacit Dimension." Mimeographed. Chicago, Ill.: The University of Chicago, 9 May.

Pollard, William G. 1958. *Chance and Providence*. New York: Charles Scribner's Sons.

―――. 1966. "Indeterminacy, Mystery, and a Modern Epistemology." *Zygon* 1.

Pope, Alexander. 1901. *Essay on Man*. New York: Cassell and Co.

Rapoport, Anatol. 1966. "What Is A Viable System?" *ETC: A Review of General Semantics*, December.

Riddle, Oscar. 1967. "The Emergence of Good and Evil." *Zygon* 2.

Riesman, David. 1961. *The Lonely Crowd*. New Haven: Yale University Press.

Robertson, Howard Percy. 1967. "Cosmology." In *Encyclopaedia Britannica*, vol. 6. Chicago: Encyclopaedia Britannica, Inc.

Ross, Floyd H., and Hills, Tynette. 1956. *Questions That Matter Most Asked By The World's Religions*. Boston: The Beacon Press.

Salk, Jonas. 1972. *Man Unfolding*. New York: Harper & Row.

———. 1973. *The Survival of the Wisest*. New York: Harper & Row.

Schrodinger, Erwin. 1956. *What Is Life?* New York: Doubleday & Co., Anchor Books.

———. 1964. *My View Of The World*. Cambridge: The University Press.

Schweitzer, Albert. 1957. *Out Of My Life And Thought*. New York: The New American Library of World Literature.

Sears, Paul Bigelow. 1967. "Ecology." In *Encyclopaedia Britannica*, vol. 7. Chicago: Encyclopaedia Britannica, Inc.

Selye, Hans. 1956. *The Stress Of Life*. New York: McGraw-Hill Book Co.

Shapley, Harlow. 1966. "Life, Hope and Cosmic Evolution." *Zygon* 1.

Simpson, George Gaylord. 1958. *The Meaning of Evolution*. New York: The New American Library of World Literature.

———. 1966. "The Biological Nature of Man." *Science*, 22 April.

Sinnott, Edmund W. 1955. *The Biology Of The Spirit*. New York: The Viking Press.

———. 1957. *Matter, Mind and Man*. New York: Harper & Bros.

———. 1966. *The Bridge Of Life*. New York: Simon and Schuster.

Skinner, B.F. 1953. *Science And Human Behavior*. New York: The Macmillan Co.

Sperry, Roger W. 1965. "Mind, Brain, and Humanist Values." In *New Views of the Nature of Man*, edited by John R. Platt. Chicago: The University of Chicago Press.

Stiernotte, Alfred P. 1954. *God and Space Time*. New York: Philosophical Library.

Townes, Charles H. 1966. "The Convergence of Science and Religion." *Zygon* 1.

Von Bertalanffy, Ludwig. 1950. "An Outline of General System Theory." *British Journal for Philosophy of Science* 1.

———. 1968. *General System Theory*. New York: George Brasiller.

Van Peursen, C.A. 1966. *Body, Soul, Spirit*. London, New York: Oxford University Press.

Wald, George. 1965. "Determinacy, Individuality, and the Problem of Free Will." In *New Views of the Nature of Man*, edited by John R. Platt. Chicago: The University of Chicago Press.

———. 1966. "Theological Resources from the Biological Sciences." *Zygon* 1.

Wallace, Anthony F.C. 1965. "Revitalization Movements." In *Reader in Comparative Religion,* edited by William A. Lessa and Evon Z. Vogt. New York: Harper & Row.

———. 1966. "Rituals: Sacred and Profane." *Zygon* 1.

Watson, James D. 1968. *The Double Helix.* New York: Atheneum Publishers.

Whitehead, Alfred North. 1929. *Process and Reality.* New York: The Social Science Bookstore.

———. 1948. *Science and the Modern World.* New York: Pelican Mentor Books.

———. 1961. *Religion in the Making.* New York: The World Publishing Co.

Whyte, Lancelot Law. 1974. *The Universe of Experience.* New York: Harper & Row.

Wiener, Norbert. 1964. *God and Golem, Inc.* Cambridge, Mass.: The M.I.T. Press.

Williams, Gardner. 1968. "The Natural Causation of Free Will." *Zygon* 3.

Young, J.Z. 1966. In "The Scientific Study of Values and Contemporary Civilization," by Clyde Kluckhohn. *Zygon* 1.

Index

285